Blender
Studio Projects

Blender
Studio Projects

DIGITAL MOVIE-MAKING

TONY MULLEN

CLAUDIO ANDAUR

Wiley Publishing, Inc.

Acquisitions Editor: Mariann Barsolo
Development Editor: David Clark
Technical Editor: Carlos Ivan Hoffmann
Production Editor: Elizabeth Ginns Britten
Copy Editor: Sharon Wilkey
Editorial Manager: Pete Gaughan
Production Manager: Tim Tate
Vice President and Executive Group Publisher: Richard Swadley
Vice President and Publisher: Neil Edde
Media Associate Project Manager: Jenny Swisher
Media Associate Producer: Shawn Patrick
Media Quality Assurance: Doug Kuhn
Book Designers: Frank Baumhackl, Lori Barra
Compositor: Kate Kaminski, Happenstance Type-O-Rama
Proofreader: Nancy Bell
Indexer: Ted Laux
Project Coordinator, Cover: Lynsey Stanford
Cover Designer: Ryan Sneed

Dear Reader,

Thank you for choosing *Blender Studio Projects: Digital Movie-Making*. This book is part of a family of premium-quality Sybex books, all of which are written by outstanding authors who combine practical experience with a gift for teaching.

Sybex was founded in 1976. More than 30 years later, we're still committed to producing consistently exceptional books. With each of our titles, we're working hard to set a new standard for the industry. From the paper we print on, to the authors we work with, our goal is to bring you the best books available.

I hope you see all that reflected in these pages. I'd be very interested to hear your comments and get your feedback on how we're doing. Feel free to let me know what you think about this or any other Sybex book by sending me an email at nedde@wiley.com. If you think you've found a technical error in this book, please visit http://sybex.custhelp.com. Customer feedback is critical to our efforts at Sybex.

Best regards,

Neil Edde
Vice President and Publisher
Sybex, an Imprint of Wiley

To all the tenacious dreamers

Acknowledgments

More than any of the other books I've worked on, creating the content for this book was a highly collaborative affair. I'd like to thank my coauthor, Claudio "Malefico" Andaur; the book's technical editor, Ivan Hoffmann; and the rest of the team at Licuadora Studio: Manuel Perez, Diego Borghetti, and Juan Redondo. It's no exaggeration to say that this book couldn't have happened without them. I truly appreciate their involvement in making this book an enjoyable and educational experience for me. ▪ I'm very grateful to the editing and production teams at Sybex for bringing all of this to the printed page. Thank you to Mariann Barsolo, Pete Gaughan, David Clark, Liz Britten, and all involved in editing and producing this book. ▪ No Blender-related thank-you list is complete without a nod to Ton Roosendaal and the extraordinary team of developers, both paid and volunteer, who make the software what it is. Thank you very much for your wonderful work, all of you. ▪ Finally, I'd like to thank my wife, Yuka, and my daughter, Hana, for their love and patience.

—*Tony*

I'd like to thank Tony and Mariann for inviting us to be part of this book, for their interest in our little short movie, and for the trust they put in the project from the very beginning. ▪ My gratefulness and respect to my comrades at Licuadora Studio, Manuel, Diego, Ivan, and Juan, who were always there trying to get things done in time (for so many years now), and of course to Ton and the Blender developers, for giving me the tools I needed to change my life. ▪ Finally, I'd like to thank my wife, Laura, and my little girl, Rocío, for being so patient with me having long hours "playing" with the computer. :)

—*Claudio*

About the Authors

Tony Mullen, PhD, teaches computer graphics and programming at Tsuda College and Musashino Art University in Tokyo. His screen credits include writer, codirector, or lead animator on several short films, including the award-winning live-action/stop-motion film *Gustav Braustache and the Auto-Debilitator*. He is the author of *Mastering Blender, Introducing Character Animation with Blender*, and B*ounce, Tumble, and Splash!: Simulating the Physical World with Blender 3D*, all from Sybex.

Claudio "Malefico" Andaur was born in Buenos Aires, Argentina in 1970. After graduating as a chemical engineer from National Technological University in Buenos Aires, he worked in nuclear fuel research for several years. He always had an interest in art, so he became a self-taught 3D artist and eventually left engineering to dedicate 100 percent of his time to CG. Blender was his first 3D animation suite back in 1999 and still is the only 3D tool he uses regularly.

In 2005 he cofounded Manos Digitales Animation Studio and was involved in the production of the 3D animation feature film *Plumiferos* as script cowriter, character TD, and animation supervisor.

Always a free/libre/open source software (FLOSS) supporter, Claudio has given lectures and courses on the Blender and FLOSS pipeline in several countries throughout Latin America and Europe.

In 2008 he founded Licuadora Studio together with some of his former colleagues and continues to work there. In 2009 he was awarded the Blender Foundation Suzanne Award for Best Character Animation.

CONTENTS AT A GLANCE

Contents

Introduction

The past few years have been an incredible time for users and developers of Blender. Since 2006, with the release of the Blender Foundation's first open movie, *Elephants Dream*, each year has brought a bigger, more impressively ambitious open project, and with each project Blender's development has advanced by great leaps, focused on the needs of real artists in a fast-paced studio environment. The project currently underway, tentatively entitled *Sintel*, promises to result in the most impressive open movie yet, and the long-awaited Blender version 2.5 is set to make Blender accessible to a whole new audience of professional users.

Studio use of Blender hasn't been limited to the Blender Foundation's own open movie projects, either. CG creators around the world have been embracing Blender in ever-increasing numbers. Originally developed as an in-house 3D tool for a commercial animation studio, Blender has repeatedly demonstrated itself to be feature rich, stable, and fast enough for serious production use. Blender is fully cross-platform, working seamlessly and with an identical interface on Windows, Mac, and Linux. It boasts a wide variety of import and export tools and supports numerous formats for digital assets, making it easy to incorporate into just about any CG pipeline. It's open source, making it possible to modify and tailor the code to the specific needs of any studio. These factors come together to make Blender a very attractive option for many studios. As a generation of young Blender users grow up to be professionals, the increasing availability of a skilled workforce will only make Blender more appealing in the years to come.

As part of the *Studio Projects* series, this book focuses on Blender use in the context of a professional studio—specifically, Licuadora Studio of Buenos Aires, a commercial CG animation studio that, for reasons of economy and principle, chooses to rely entirely on open source tools for its CG work. The Licuadora team includes some of the world's most experienced Blender users; the studio's members were the original creative team for the Blender-made movie *Plumiferos*, which recently premiered as Argentina's first-ever all-3D CG animated feature and the only major full-length feature anywhere to be created with Blender as its primary 3D animation tool. In this book, you'll take a peek at the nitty-gritty details of how Licuadora's animation pipeline is set up and the steps involved in creating a CG animated short movie. Along the way, you'll learn many tricks and techniques for working with Blender that you could learn only from experienced, full-time pros.

Who Should Buy This Book

As the title indicates, this book is focused on using Blender for making movies in a studio environment. It's not intended for beginners who just want to learn how the software works. The techniques described in this book are techniques employed by professional users, and the descriptions of them assume that you generally already know which buttons to click and which windows to look in for the functionality. Although every effort has been made to give clear and thorough instructions, the book would be much longer if some Blender background wasn't assumed. If you're not sure what you're doing with Blender in the first place, please start with one (or several) of the numerous introductory and intermediate books on Blender that are currently available.

If you are thinking about adopting Blender for use in an actual studio or if you are an individual who wants to undertake a serious project with Blender, then this book will have a lot to offer. In this book, you'll learn about the many different roles that Blender can play in the animation pipeline, you'll see how file and asset management functionality can maximize your pipeline's efficiency, and you'll see how Blender can be supplemented by other open source tools. Along the way, there's a very good chance that you'll stumble across some killer Blender features that you had no idea existed, even if you're already an advanced user. In short, if you're a professional Blender user or just want to work like one, this book is for you.

Regarding Software Versions

Because Blender is open source, Blender users have unlimited access to stable and development versions, both new and old, at all times. This can sometimes be an embarrassment of riches, and version changes and upgrades are something that serious users need to be able to deal with intelligently. It's never wise to jump willy-nilly to the next available version on a single project without giving some thought to stability and continuity. This book focuses on a project being carried out using an in-house branch of Blender 2.49, which is the latest stable release at the time of this writing. However, the book also discusses considerations that need to go into an upgrade to the soon-to-be-released Blender 2.5.

Regardless, as mentioned previously, this is not a book about where the buttons are, so if you're reading it, you should already be knowledgeable enough to be able to abstract the techniques described and apply them in a newer version of Blender.

How to Use This Book

There's no right way to go through this book. Hand-holding is kept to a minimum, and a background in Blender is assumed, so you probably know all you need to know to dive in anywhere that takes your fancy. That said, the book is written in an order that roughly follows the process of content creation in a typical movie-making pipeline. Reading the book in order will preserve this, so if you want to get a sense of the big picture, I'd recommend reading the book from beginning to end.

What's Inside

Here's a glance at what you'll find in each chapter:

Chapter 1: Blender in the Studio gives an overview of Blender's use in commercial studios and describes the factors that might go into a studio's decision to incorporate Blender in its pipeline. This chapter also introduces Licuadora Studio, whose work will be the focus of the rest of the book, and describes the hardware and software that makes up the studio's animation pipeline.

Chapter 2: Planning and Preproduction covers the early stages of planning a narrative movie. Blender's sequence-editing functionality can play a significant role even in the 2D planning phase, and this is discussed in depth. This chapter also touches on other available open source software that can help you in conceptualization, writing, and storyboarding.

Chapter 3: Creating a 3D Animatic deals with the 3D planning and blocking stage of the preproduction. In this phase, Blender's 3D functionality becomes central, and you'll learn about managing 3D assets to work most efficiently, and how to time the 3D animatic to match the 2D animatic described in Chapter 2.

Chapter 4: Modeling describes the modeling stage of the animation pipeline, giving tips on how to optimize the topology of deformable meshes by using the Retopo tool. This chapter also encourages you to think outside the box in your modeling, giving pointers on how to use armatures, modifiers, and simulation as mesh modeling tools.

Chapter 5: Rigging Characters presents the tools available for rigging models for animation and discusses various alternatives to consider to optimize deformations. You'll learn tricks for using armatures and Mesh Deform modifiers in conjunction for the best possible effect. You'll also learn to use complex PyDrivers to create simple and intuitive controls for subtle combinations of morph shapes.

Chapter 6: Animating a Character Scene describes the process of creating a simple character-centered scene and bringing a rigged character to life. You'll read about how assets and timing are carried over from the 3D animatic, how animation curve types are used to support pose-to-pose animation, and how simulations work together with animated meshes to create a fully realized character animation shot.

Chapter 7: Descent into the Maelstrom guides you through a complete, moderately complex special-effects shot of a ship being pulled into an ocean whirlpool. The tour begins with the placement of 3D objects in the scene and continues through the final composited render. You'll see how to use models, textures, and modifiers together to create a breathtaking animated shot of high-seas peril, and learn even more about how assets can be split and organized for maximum workflow efficiency.

What's on the DVD

The DVD contains installations of Blender 2.49 for Mac OS X and Windows, and a source tarball for users of Linux or other Unix-like operating systems. In addition, Licuadora Studio's in-house branch of Blender, LicuaBlender, is included as a source tarball. In addition to the software, project files are included for exercises or further study, and the complete production tree is included for the relevant portions of the *Mercator* movie project.

CHAPTER 1

Blender in the Studio

This chapter introduces Blender as a professional tool for use by commercial animation studios. If you're not familiar with large-scale animation projects that have used Blender as their primary 3D software, you may be surprised by how powerful and versatile it can be in the context of a professional animation pipeline. This chapter will show you some projects that have made use of Blender. In particular, you'll be introduced to Licuadora Studio, a professional animation house in Buenos Aires that uses Blender as its primary animation tool. You'll learn why using Blender benefits the Licuadora team and how they deal with the challenges and idiosyncrasies of Blender in their professional pipeline.

CHAPTER CONTENTS

- The Professional Blender
- Welcome to Licuadora Studio
- The Blender-Based Animation Studio

The Professional Blender

Blender is unique as the only free, professional 3D animation and modeling application. It's not the only free software for 3D content creation, and it's far from the only professional application, but it is the only software around that can lay claim to being both. In the past, the *free* aspect of Blender has often tended to overshadow the *professional* aspect. This is hardly surprising; free is an awfully attractive price for software as powerful as Blender, and it makes Blender the obvious choice for students and hobbyists. But it's a mistake to think that Blender's appeal is limited to nonprofessional users. You don't judge an artist by the cost of her pencils, after all.

The truth is, Blender is widely used by commercial studios and in significant animation projects. Many of the studios and projects that have used Blender are widely known (sooner or later, mention of them is bound to crop up on the BlenderNation blog at www .blendernation.com). It is likely that many other professional uses of Blender fly below the radar. From a licensing perspective, using Blender is extremely convenient. No matter where you are or what computer you are using, it is a straightforward matter to download and install Blender. Even if your studio's primary software is a different application, this kind of easy, unrestricted access to Blender can come in handy. With Blender's powerful Python-based importing and exporting functionality, it's easy to take advantage of Blender without causing so much as a ripple in the studio's workflow, and have no one be the wiser.

This book is one of the first to focus on Blender as it plays a central role in the professional animation pipeline. In particular, this book will take a close look at Blender's role in the making of the animated short film *Mercator* currently in production by Licuadora Studio. Before that, however, it's worthwhile to get a bit more perspective on Blender as a tool for professionals.

Blender's Professional Beginnings

Blender was a professional tool before it was a free one. Blender originated as an in-house proprietary software application for the Dutch animation studio NeoGeo, founded in 1988. Blender's original target user audience, therefore, was a very small group of highly trained professional users. Broader use of Blender by the public was something of an afterthought.

This specific, professional targeting of Blender's early development can still be felt in Blender's design, for better or (according to some) for worse. The heavy reliance on keyboard shortcuts and the many nonstandard design choices resulted in a user interface that can be lightning fast for those who are accustomed to it. The downside is that it can present an intimidating cement wall for newbies accustomed to finding most of what they want from any software application on a conventionally organized menu bar.

The focus on professional users had many benefits for the development of Blender, but the focus on such a specific group of users also contributed to a perception of Blender as being somewhat impenetrable by outsiders. Much of the inflexibility has changed with the recent 2.5 code refactor, but the goals of Blender's interface remain focused on speed and efficiency for proficient users.

By the end of the 1990s, another company, Not a Number (NaN), was set up to market and develop Blender itself, with the goal of distributing the software to a broad user base. The main application was available for free, with additional functionality available to users who purchased a code called a C-key. This user base was crucial for the next phase of Blender's evolution, which occurred when NaN closed its doors as a commercial enterprise.

The Blender Foundation

Things didn't look good when NaN's investors halted operations in 2002. The company's assets, including Blender itself, were the property of the investors, and there were no plans to continue development on the software. In order to save Blender from oblivion,

Blender's lead developer, Ton Roosendaal, made an unusual proposal to the NaN investors: He would buy the code with money donated by Blender's worldwide users and release it as free software under the open source GNU General Public License (GPL). The investors went for it and the community rallied, donating the needed 100,000 euros in only seven weeks. On October 13, 2002, the Free Blender campaign was successful, and Blender was released as an open source project. The Blender Foundation was created as a nonprofit organization dedicated to supporting the continued development of Blender.

From the beginning, Roosendaal's focus was on supporting artists with the software. Software intended for artists could not be developed in a vacuum without focused, intensive input by dedicated power users. If it were, it would surely be doomed to become nothing more than a glorified programming exercise.

Now that NeoGeo was no more, it was important to find a way to promote the use of Blender by power users on serious projects. This was at least as important as the software development itself. The solution was for the Blender Foundation (and later, the commercial Blender Institute) to play the role of a studio. Whereas the software had supported the studio in the NaN days, the Blender Foundation studio came into existence to support and promote the software. The results have been impressive in several ways.

Elephants Dream

The first project initiated and coordinated by the Blender Foundation was the project code-named Orange, which resulted in the 10-minute short film *Elephants Dream*, the first *open movie*. The movie itself and all its production files are freely released under a Creative Commons license. The Orange project was very much an experimental effort. The project was coproduced by the Blender Foundation and the Netherlands Media Art Institute, Montevideo/Time Based Arts. The production was funded by a combination of grants and subsidies and DVD presales carried out by the Blender Foundation. For the production, six exceptional artists from the Blender community around the world were selected and invited to spend about eight months in Amsterdam working together full-time on a short animated movie. They were given complete creative control over their work. You can see a still from the movie in Figure 1.1.

The project was notable in that it not only used Blender as its primary 3D software, but attempted to use open source software exclusively for all stages of production. This was accomplished with the exception of the soundtrack (for which the Reaktor sound studio was used) and the supercomputing cluster on which processing time was donated by Bowie State University for rendering, which ran Mac OS X. The production of *Elephants Dream* resulted in great advances for Blender itself, including the introduction of the Material and Composite Node editor and the render pipeline refactor, which appeared in Blender 2.42. The release log for that release can be found at www.blender.org/development/release-logs/blender-242. The Orange project's production blog can be found at http://orange.blender.org.

Figure 1.1

A still from
Elephants Dream

Big Buck Bunny

After the success of Orange, a precedent was set to name projects after fruits. Aside from this similarity, the next Blender Foundation project, code-named Peach, could not have been more different from *Elephants Dream*. The goal of the Peach project was, in part, to experiment with a more directed, premeditated way of making a movie than had been used with *Elephants Dream*. There were a few technical goals for the software as well, in particular the development of better tools for creating, editing, and rendering hair and strand particles, as you can see from the still of the film in Figure 1.2. This and the desire to do something completely different from *Elephants Dream* led naturally to the idea of having animal characters in a funny, lighthearted setting. The result was the lush, colorful, and not a little twisted romp *Big Buck Bunny*.

The Peach project was supported by several nonprofit and corporate sponsorships, including support from the Dutch foundation Digitale Pioniers, rendering by Sun Microsystems, hardware from Maqina Computersystems, and sound facilities from Wavemage. *Big Buck Bunny* was also released as an open movie under the Creative Commons Attribution 3.0 license. It can be found at www.bigbuckbunny.org.

Figure 1.2

Improved hair rendering functionality in a still from *Big Buck Bunny*

Yo Frankie!

Although Blender has always been first and foremost an animation and modeling application, game creation and prototyping is an important aspect of its functionality. These sides of Blender got their day in the sun with the Apricot project, whose goal was to create a fully fleshed-out, industry-quality game prototype. In order to advance the project as rapidly as possible, character designs and 3D assets were recycled and modified from the *Big Buck Bunny* project. Whereas previous projects had focused on Blender as the central tool, the Peach project also attempted to incorporate development on the Crystal Space open source game engine as a primary goal.

Partners and sponsors of the Apricot project included Grupo Ikusnet, Dutch Game Days Foundation, Amsterdams Fonds voor de Kunst, Maqina Computersystems, Paravizion, Redfish, Nyquist Art + Logic, and Tarent. *Yo Frankie!* was released as an open game under the Creative Commons Attribution 3.0 license and is available at www.yofrankie.org.

A screenshot of the game play can be seen in Figure 1.3.

Figure 1.3

A screenshot from
Yo Frankie!

Professional Training Products

A secondary goal for all of the Blender Foundation projects has been to produce top-quality Blender training material, and each of the projects has contributed to the production of at least one training DVD. These include Bassam Kurdali's rigging and animation training DVD *The Mancandy FAQ*, Andy Goralczyk's intensive modeling and texturing over-the-shoulder course *Creature Factory*, William Reynish's advanced character animation course *Learning Character Animation with Blender,* and Pablo Vazquez's eye-popping *Venom's Lab* training DVD, which covers a wide variety of advanced topics, from materials and compositing to sculpting, as shown in Figure 1.4. All of these DVDs are available commercially from the Blender e-shop and feature intensive tutorials on professional techniques for Blender users. All of the training DVDs are released under the Creative Commons Attribution 3.0 license and are part of the ongoing series of releases in the Blender Foundation's Open Workshop.

Durian and Blender 2.5

Two long-awaited projects are advancing rapidly as I write this: the Durian project and the finalization of the Blender 2.5 release. These two Blender Foundation projects go hand in hand. Durian promises to be the most ambitious short film produced by the Blender Foundation yet, with realistic designs, action, heavy use of physics, and simulation, including newly developed features for fire and smoke. The production is underway, and concept sketches such as the one in Figure 1.5 have been released on the project's blog. The Durian project promises to go even further than previous projects in proving the quality of work that Blender is capable of.

Figure 1.4

Pablo Vazquez's charming Korno character teaches you how to sculpt on the *Venom's Lab* training DVD.

Figure 1.5

David Revoy's concept sketch of the heroine of Durian

Final WIP paintover - artwork: David REVOY (c) copyright Blender Foundation : http://durian.blender.org Creative Commons Attribution 3.0

The Blender 2.5 version has been under active development now for more than a year, in parallel with regular updates of the 2.4*x* series, development of which is now frozen. As I write this, Blender 2.5 is in an advanced alpha stage for debugging by the community. Blender 2.5 brings a complete overhaul of the event system and interface, eliminating a number of problems that had been deeply embedded in the code of previous versions of Blender. For professional users of other 3D applications who have considered switching to Blender, one of the most attractive aspects of Blender 2.5 is its greatly enhanced capability for customization, accomplished by use of tightly integrated Python scripting. Users can now freely map their keyboard shortcuts, add their own tools to a quick-access tool shelf, and integrate custom scripts more fluidly into the interface. Splitting and uniting windows is now a single mouse movement, and it is possible to render and animate simultaneously while working with changing values and 3D content in the viewport. The overall look and feel of the interface is both familiar and strikingly different, as you can see from the screenshot of the development version in Figure 1.6.

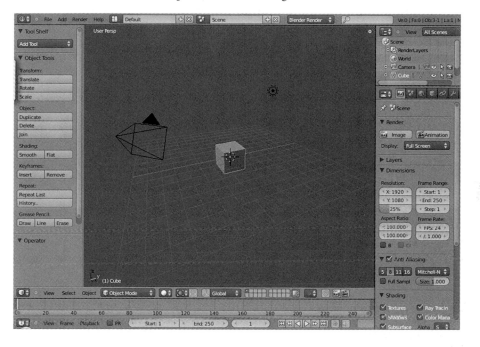

The combined result of the Durian project and the completed push for Blender 2.5 promises to be another big step for Blender into the world of high-end animation studios. The release logs for the Blender 2.5 alpha release can be found at `www.blender.org/development/release-logs/blender-250`.

Studios around the World

As important as these focused Blender Foundation projects are to keeping Blender honed with use, they are far from the only place where Blender is used in an industrial-grade studio setting. 3D-content-creation houses around the globe use Blender for artistic and commercial projects.

Asia

For Malaysia's Vision Animation studio (`www.visionanimation.net`), Blender is an important component in the production pipeline, particularly when it comes to modeling and texturing. Vision Animation did the animation for the TV series *Rip Smart* (Figure 1.7), for which all the modeling was created in Blender. Rip Smart was produced in Malaysia by the production company Creative License (`www.creativelicence.net`).

Figure 1.7

Rip Smart

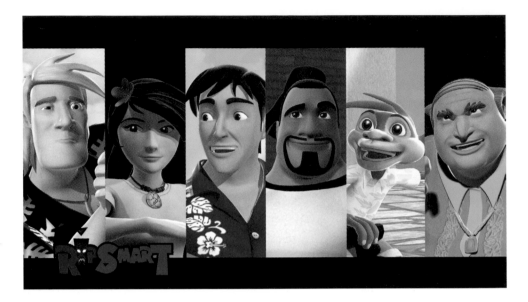

North America

Spiral Productions of Washington is a general media solutions provider whose services range from branding and product demos, to keynote and trade show media, to training videos and entertainment. It's a company that is clearly not afraid to venture beyond its comfort zone, which may explain its involvement in one of the most ambitious Blender projects around, the live-action science fiction adventure feature film *Project London*, for which Blender has played a central role in the creation of 3D CG visual effects. Giant robots, spacecraft, and breathtaking cityscapes were all created in Blender, enabling this low-budget independent film to have visual effects that are often on par with much more expensive Hollywood fare. Figure 1.8 shows a promotional still from the film.

Oceania

Sydney, Australia's RedCartel (formerly ProMotion Studio) is a collaborative CG studio that creates world-class 3D content for the advertising, game, TV, and film industries. RedCartel has made heavy use of Blender alongside other applications in advertisements for high-profile products such as Bridgestone tires, Kraft macaroni and cheese, and Stride Rite Nickelodeon Slimers shoes. Their Blender-made short film *Lighthouse*, written and directed by Exopolis for Liberty Mutual's Responsibility Project, was a finalist at the Australian Effects and Animation Festival in November 2009 and came in second out of 88 films in the iiNet Get Animated film festival in January 2009.

RedCartel is currently using Blender to develop an animated comedy series called *Kajimba*, featuring a gaggle of hard-drinking ne'er-do-well talking animals in the Australian outback. Figure 1.9 shows the cast of *Kajimba*.

Figure 1.8

Spiral Productions' *Project London* features CG effects that were created in Blender and composited into live-action scenes.

Figure 1.9

The cast of RedCartel's *Kajimba*

Welcome to Licuadora Studio

Outside of the Blender Foundation itself, perhaps no single studio has a higher concentration of Blender-specific expertise than Licuadora Studio of Buenos Aires, Argentina. Licuadora Studio was founded by Claudio Andaur, Manuel Perez, Ivan Hoffmann, Juan Redondo, and Diego Borghetti. Claudio, Manuel, and Ivan had previously worked together as Manos Digitales Studio on the Blender-made feature film Plumiferos, where they met Juan and Diego. During their work with Plumiferos, the team developed a unique level of expertise in working with Blender in a professional movie production pipeline. In terms of length and budget, Plumiferos remains the largest-scale animation project undertaken with Blender as a primary tool. Plumiferos premiered in Buenos Aires in February, 2010, receiving national media attention as Argentina's first ever entirely 3D CG-animated feature film.

Although it's a young studio, Licuadora has been busy. The team has done commercial work creating real-time content for product visualizations for clients such as the U.K. company Paravizion, and did visual effects (VFX) using Blender and the Voodoo Camera Tracker for the live-action Argentine movie Los Superagentes, which premiered in Buenos Aires in 2008. The studio also organized the Che! Blender conference, which brought together Blender users and developers from throughout Latin America.

The currently under production *Mercator* short film is Licuadora's flagship project. It is planned to be a short, exciting, high-seas epic inspired by imagery from Romanticism and its darker 19th-century descendants. This book will focus on the process of creating *Mercator*.

The Blender-Based Animation Studio

Licuadora uses nearly all aspects of Blender at some point in its pipeline, from video sequencing to the game engine (although only on a technicality—Blender's rigid body physical simulation functionality is accessed via the game engine). But Blender alone is not enough to build an entire animation studio on. Other software plays a part in numerous tasks in the animation pipeline. Mostly, Licuadora Studio opts for open source software wherever possible.

A Studio's Foundation

The computer operating system, networking tools, and asset and revision management systems provide the software foundation of a project such as *Mercator*. Workers at Licuadora Studio work on PC workstations connected to a single central server via wired Ethernet. The machines run the latest 64-bit Ubuntu Linux. Ubuntu is a distribution of the free and open source Linux operating system based on the Debian distribution. Ubuntu is known as a user-friendly and fully fleshed-out distribution. Installing and running the Ubuntu desktop is straightforward and in most cases no more complicated than installing any major commercial OS such as Windows or Mac OS X. A standard installation of Ubuntu includes the Synaptic Package Manager, a powerful tool for choosing and installing from a huge plethora of open source tools. If you are new to the world of open source software, the variety of software available through the Synaptic Package Manager may be daunting in itself. You can choose what you need and install it as necessary. Ubuntu Linux can be downloaded and installed from www.ubuntu.com.

Every project needs a way to coordinate and control the contributions of individual artists. For Licuadora, the software that supports this collaboration is the free and open source version-control system Git. Git is a fast and versatile application that is broadly similar to other version and revision control systems such as CVS, Subversion, and Perforce. Such programs are fundamental to any mid- to large-scale software development project, but their use extends to any project for which digital assets need to be managed, previous versions need to be accessed, or multiple workers need to have their contributions coordinated. With Git, a central repository is created that holds the current state of the project and all prior states in an efficient and accessible way. Users create a local "clone" of the repository to work on. When they are satisfied with their local changes, they commit the changes locally and then "push" the changes to the central repository, where the changes will become available to other users when they update their local clones. If there are conflicts between what contributors have done, the software flags them so they can be reviewed and resolved. Git is the version-control system of choice for numerous large-scale software development projects including the Linux kernel, Perl, and Android. Git is available for all major operating systems. In Ubuntu, you can install Git directly through Synaptic; otherwise, you should download Git from http://git-scm.com and follow the instructions for your own operating system.

Licuadora Studio has made things even easier for the team by deploying an in-house graphical user interface (GUI) for Git called LicuaTools (Figure 1.10), developed by Diego. LicuaTools lets users easily create and manipulate repositories on the server in an even more intuitive way than the traditional Git command line. LicuaTools also adds a few extra checks to minimize conflicts that may be specific to the 3D production pipeline.

Content-Creation Software

In addition to Blender, several other content-creation applications are employed on the *Mercator* project for non-3D work.

2D Artwork

For concept art, textures, and matte painting, GIMP and MyPaint are used. GIMP is the GNU Image Manipulation Program, the most widely used open source raster graphics editor. GIMP is available on all major platforms and can be downloaded from www.gimp.org. GIMP is a stable and powerful alternative to proprietary applications such as Adobe Photoshop for raster image manipulation. MyPaint is more specifically geared to creating painterly and fine-art styled images.

Figure 1.10

LicuaTools Git GUI

All members of the *Mercator* team use Wacom tablets, which are supported by all of the graphics applications mentioned so far, including full pressure support in Blender, which is especially useful for sculpting.

Audio/Video Editing

Blender's video sequence editor may well be the best free and open source cross-platform video editor available, but it has limitations that make it insufficient for the audio/video (A/V) editing needs of a professional production pipeline. Its biggest weakness in the context of the Licuadora Linux-based pipeline is in handling sound. Although it includes a multitrack audio editor, it lacks a lot of the necessary functionality that a full A/V suite enables, and its handling of multichannel audio has playback glitches as of Blender version 2.49. And audio is far from a mere afterthought. Even in the visualization stages early in the production, creating 2D animatics with music and temporary dialog (if applicable) is an absolute must to get a sense of the pacing and emotional effect of the visuals.

Widely used proprietary tools are available for all aspects of A/V editing, and if your pipeline includes these tools, it is straightforward to work with output from Blender in your compositor or video editor. Blender can support whatever video codecs you have installed on your computer, including proprietary codecs, and Blender supports a wide range of render output options. So if you do your video editing in, for example, Avid Media Composer, you should have no problems working with Blender-created content. Blender supports the open-standard high dynamic range (HDR) EXR format, and in particular multilayer EXR, enabling you to work with Blender output in high-end compositing software such as Digital Fusion. Blender itself also has a lot of basic (and a few advanced) compositing tools, so a lot of compositing work can be done directly in Blender without the need to render full animations first.

Good open source alternatives also exist. An appealing alternative is the use of the Ardour audio editing package alongside Blender. Ardour is available under the GPL for Linux and Mac. No port exists for Windows at present. If you are working on one of the supported platforms, you can download Ardour from `http://ardour.org`. For a discussion and tutorial on using Ardour alongside Blender as a unified A/V editing suite, follow the links from the following BlenderNation article:

`www.blendernation.com/blenderardour-a-truly-powerful-combination`

For the present, Licuadora Studio has settled on the use of Cinelerra for editing of audio with video or adding subtitles. Cinelerra is a Linux-based A/V editing program with full HD support and some basic compositing functionality. Cinelerra has been a staple of Linux-based A/V content creation for years and provides a full-featured editor to meet most studios' needs. Like Ardour, however, it is limited in the platforms it can run on, being available only on Linux. Note that although these applications are limited to running on the Linux platform, if you use Windows or Mac, you can take advantage of them by using virtualization software such as VirtualBox to install a virtual Linux machine that runs right on your desktop.

Conceptualizing and Writing

Licuadora's script was written in OpenOffice.org Writer, the premier open source word processing application, using a screenplay formatting extension to conform to industry screenplay standards. Writer can be downloaded from `www.openoffice.org`, and the screenplay formatting extension is available at `http://extensions.services.openoffice.org/project/scr2`.

Much of the initial visual conceptualization for *Mercator* was done using images scoured from various sources on the Internet. Photographs and artwork of people, clothing, buildings, and scenes can be used to provide inspiration and ideas. For collecting and viewing a database of such images, Licuadora's scripting guru, Ivan, coded some special in-house tools.

Working with Blender Development

One of the potentially tricky aspects of working with Blender is the apparently rapid pace of development of the software. In truth, Blender doesn't change any faster than any other software, proprietary or free, of similar scale. But the fact that Blender is open source means that new builds with potentially interesting features and bug fixes are available on essentially a daily basis. This can leave some users feeling that the latest stable release of Blender is obsolete long before the next version is ready. And with every new version of Blender offering significant and exciting new functionality, users often find themselves chomping at the bit for development builds that may not be stable enough for professional use.

At the time of this writing, this conundrum is compounded by the much ballyhooed upcoming release of Blender 2.5, which both promises and threatens to *change everything* in the Blender world. With release schedules as fluid and (let's face it) unpredictable as they are, it's reasonable to give some serious thought as to how to integrate Blender into a professional pipeline without being inconvenienced by ongoing developments.

There are a couple of approaches a studio can take regarding Blender development. The simplest is to begin with the most recent official stable release of Blender and stick with it until the end of a project. Assess your project's functionality needs at the outset and assure yourself that the stable version of Blender meets these needs. Find out about the latest versions by reading the appropriate release notes at `www.blender.org/development/release-logs`. Because there are no licensing costs associated with Blender, you can always download more than one version, including development versions (available at `www.graphicall.org`) to experiment with. Of course, any professional studio keeps backups of all work, but it is especially important to make copies of anything you intend to open in an alternate version of Blender. Although Blender generally has excellent backward compatibility between released versions, sometimes problems can arise, particularly with developmental builds. This is another reason why it is so important to work with version-control software such as Git or Subversion. Changes to the way a `.blend` file is saved could render your experimental files incompatible with stable Blender releases, so always be sure to sandbox any work you do with unofficial Blender builds. Likewise, when it comes time to upgrade to a newly released official build, make sure that the project is completely backed up before migrating to a new version. The migrated project should be thoroughly tested before the previous one is abandoned. All in all, the process needn't be any more complicated than upgrading proprietary software. Mainly it's just cheaper.

There's another approach you could take that truly makes the most of the freedom of free software, and that is to regard Blender *not* as a no-cost off-the-shelf option but as your own instant in-house software. This is the ideal approach for studios with the resources for it, and it's where Blender really shines.

Licuadora Studio does not use the official Blender branch. Rather, the studio maintains its own in-house branch of Blender called LicuaBlender. The LicuaBlender splash screen is shown in Figure 1.11. This enables Licuadora to quickly add desired features without having to go through the rigorous process of feature verification and testing necessary to add functionality to the official Blender trunk. As of this writing, LicuaBlender is a branch of the official Blender 2.49 version. Official Blender Foundation development on Blender 2.49 has been frozen now, with focus having shifted to Blender 2.5, so LicuaBlender no longer needs to be updated from the official trunk. Fixes or feature additions are mostly in-house only at the moment. When the official release of Blender 2.5 is ready, LicuaBlender will integrate its own newly developed functionality with Blender 2.5 to create an in-house version of Blender 2.5. The migration from the previous version to the next will be gradual, and for a time both applications will be used as appropriate.

Figure 1.11
The LicuaBlender splash screen

Some of the changes introduced in LicuaBlender will be of specifically local use, but other changes may be of interest to the wider public. In that case, Licuadora can commit some of its changes to the official Blender trunk and in that way contribute to the worldwide Blender community. It's important to realize that there is no requirement to make your modified GPL software public. The GPL requires only that if you *do* make modifications available publicly, you also release the source code for the modifications under GPL. It is perfectly permissible to use Blender as a private in-house tool indefinitely, without ever releasing a single line of your own code. However, the relationship with the community that is fostered from being an active contributor to the Blender trunk has a value in itself, so it's a great idea to do so when possible.

Using Blender in this way gives a studio total control over its tools, a luxury that is usually reserved for only the biggest and best-financed studios in the world. Of course, in order to take advantage of this, it is necessary to have in-house technical support that is fluent in Blender source code. The best place to post a job opening for someone with these skills is on www.blendernation.com, the primary news source for the Blender community. There are Blender developers all over the world, and it's very likely that one near you would jump at the opportunity to help your studio become the master of its own tools.

In the following chapters, you'll get an up-close view of how Licuadora Studio has created its short film *Mercator* in a Blender-based professional studio environment. I hope this will give you a sense of how each part of the pipeline fits with the others, and inspires you to push the limits of what you can do with Blender in your own professional work.

CHAPTER 2

Planning and Preproduction

In this chapter, you'll begin your voyage into the dark and stormy world of Mercator. The earliest stages of creating a movie like this one require harnessing the wild ideas and imagery that inspired the project to begin with, and forging them into a cohesive narrative. This chapter gives an overview of this process from the perspective of the Licuadora Studio open source production pipeline. Much of the earliest conceptualization involves still images and story ideas, and Licuadora uses various in-house and off-the-shelf software tools to assist in working with these. Already, at the relatively early stage of creating a 2D animatic, Blender itself also plays a central role, as you will see in the last section of this chapter.

CHAPTER CONTENTS

- **Conceptualizing the Movie**
- **Designing Characters**
- **Storyboarding**
- **Pacing the Story with a 2D Animatic**

Conceptualizing the Movie

Mercator is the project name of a short film by Claudio Andaur about love, death, poetry, and madness. It is inspired by the imagery of late 18th and 19th century Romanticism, in works such as Samuel Taylor Coleridge's *The Rime of the Ancient Mariner* and especially Edgar Allan Poe's *The Narrative of Arthur Gordon Pym of Nantucket*, with their themes of seafaring explorers. The earliest inspiration to create such a movie arose from an image that Claudio created in Blender, shown in Figure 2.1. You can read about the creation of this image in the following work-in-progress thread on the BlenderArtists forum, where members of the Blender community have commented extensively:

```
http://blenderartists.org/forum/showthread.php?t=134269
```

Fascinated by the mystery and potential of the scene, Claudio began to imagine a broader context for this lone lighthouse at the edge of the world.

Figure 2.1

An early inspira-
tion for Mercator
was this image cre-
ated by Claudio in
Blender.

Searching for Inspiration

The initial inspiration is the spark, but it won't grow into a robust creative project without some kindling. There are many tricks and techniques for stoking your creativity and
fomenting ideas, and a great one is through searching the Web. Running Google and
Flickr searches for key words related to the ideas and atmosphere you want to represent is
a terrific way to build up a library of images and visual references that can help you refine
your own vision of the project. In the case of *Mercator*, numerous images were collected
as references for ocean scenes, ships, skies, clothing, characters, moods, and visual styles.
The images range from pictures of classic artworks to independent snapshots to stills
from Hollywood blockbusters. All of them can help to fashion a completely original final
look for the movie.

Organizing a library of images according to criteria that's meaningful to your project
is a useful thing to be able to do. At Licuadora, the in-house application Salsa is used to
help manage the library of collected images and make it searchable by properties that
are useful for *Mercator* artists. Figure 2.2 shows some collected images of Botticelli's *The
Birth of Venus* (one of many inspirations for the Virginia character, in addition to being a
reference for nautical themes) displayed in the Salsa viewer. You can also see the tag cloud
displayed, with tags scaled according to the number of items with that tag.

Images themselves can be tagged with arbitrary types of information. In Figure 2.3,
you can see some images tagged (in Spanish) with terms including *sea*, *boat*, *ocean*,
magenta, *high contrast*, *3D*, and *sky*. Color, subject matter, and thematic or visual emphasis (such as in the case of a starkly foreshortened image labeled as *3D*) may all be important criteria for artists to be able to search on.

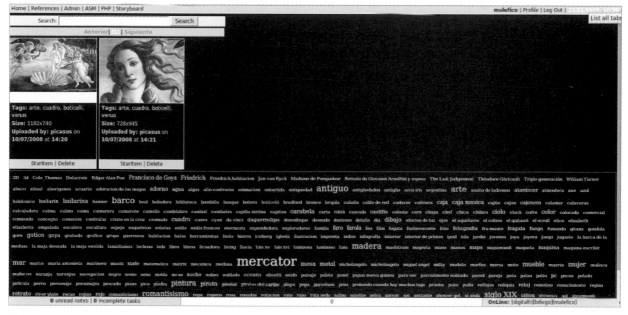

Figure 2.2

Licuadora's in-house application Salsa helps to organize reference pieces and inspirational art collected from the Web.

You may not have an in-house solution that's completely tailored to your studio's specific needs. A nice off-the-shelf application for managing collections of images is XnView. XnView is primarily a tool for batch processing of images (if you ever need to convert 100 TIF files to JPEG, this is definitely the tool for you), but it also enables you to add descriptions and tags to the image files and you can search and display images according to these criteria. You can quickly build a website or print a contact sheet with an arbitrary selection of images. XnView is proprietary software and is free-of-charge only for noncommercial use.

Writing the Story

At some point, you're going to need a script for your movie. A good, solid, well-paced script with strong dramatic tension is the foundation of any movie that seeks to engage an audience. Depending on the project, the script may be developed well in advance of the visual conceptualization or it may be inextricably linked

Figure 2.3

Images can be tagged with a variety of information.

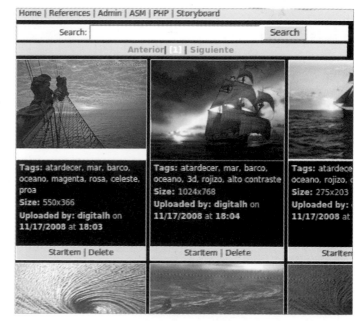

with the conceptualization phase. Writing a good script is an involved process, and going into any kind of discussion on it is well out of the scope of this book. There are numerous books on screenwriting for feature and short films, and anyone who wants to write movies of any kind should read more than one or two of such books.

In terms of open source resources for screenwriting and story development, OpenOffice .org is a good place to start, as mentioned in Chapter 1, "Blender in the Studio." In addition to the screenwriting templates available for the Writer word processor, OpenOffice also includes spreadsheet software that can be used to plan scenes and sequences, if you're comfortable working that way.

Another excellent freely available application, Celtx, is entirely dedicated to screenwriting and story development. Celtx is available at `http://celtx.com` and provides a sophisticated editor and formatter for screenplays, theater plays, audio dramas, comic books, and more, as well as tools for scheduling, character development, storyboarding, and much more. Although Celtx is not used by Licuadora, it's well worth being aware of if you are interested in building an open source software-based preproduction pipeline.

Creating Original Concept Artwork

Concept artwork is where the unique look and atmosphere of the project begins to take shape. Concept artists work with the director of the movie (in a studio as small as Licuadora, they may *include* the director of the movie) to synthesize the various collected inspirational works and to develop an original expression of the director's vision. Concept artworks serve multiple purposes. Images such as the one shown in Figure 2.4 work as both character studies and as evocations of the overall mood of the movie.

Figure 2.4
A character sketch can express the visual essence of the movie.

There is really no limit to the kinds of tools that a concept artist might use. Traditional 2D artwork with ink, paint, or other media is common, as is traditional 3D artwork in the form of models or sculpted clay. As in all areas, digital techniques have become ubiquitous for their versatility and the ease with which they can be produced.

The 2D raster graphics editor GIMP and the 2D vector drawing program Inkscape are two staples in the world of open source 2D graphics and concept art. Licuadora Studio uses both of these in creating its concept art, as well as MyPaint, an open source painting application. MyPaint is a good choice for art-styled graphics. Figure 2.5 shows a selection of some of the brushes available in MyPaint; traditional media styles such as watercolors, pastels, and charcoal are easy to mimic with a default installation of MyPaint. (GIMP also enables a wide variety of brush styles as plug-ins, but these are not available "out of the box" with GIMP.) The MyPaint workflow is also simple and fluid, making it the tool of choice for many concept art tasks at Licuadora.

Figure 2.5
Some brush options in MyPaint

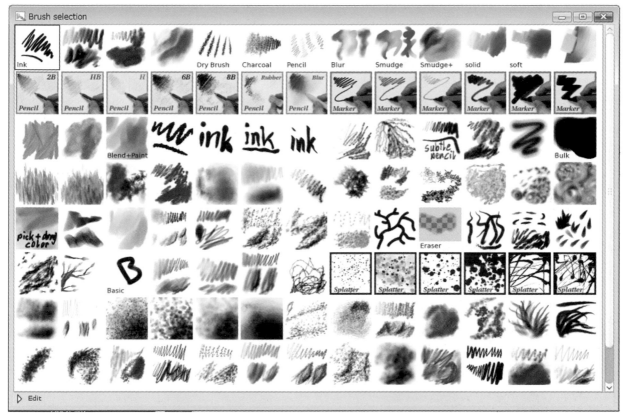

Concept art varies greatly across different projects, depending on the artists and the needs of the project. Generally, though, good concept art tends to be simple and expressive, as in the example in Figure 2.6, rather than highly polished. In this sense, concept art is different from illustration. Although more-illustrative work such as the image shown in Figure 2.7 also has a place, much of the concept art is likely to be far rougher. Even a short movie requires that many pieces of concept art be produced in a short span of time; making a movie is time-consuming enough without spending an undue amount of time on pieces of art that no one outside the production will probably see. Characters, settings, props, and scenes from throughout the movie need to be envisioned. In some cases, an important sequence of shots will warrant a complete concept-art treatment, as shown in Figure 2.8. In many cases, the concept art will also serve the purpose of storyboards and occupy a space in the 2D animatic. When studio resources are tight, it's important not to reduplicate efforts unnecessarily, and studio resources are always tight.

Figure 2.6
Good concept art
is often simple and
expressive.

Figure 2.7
A more polished
piece of concept art

Figure 2.8

Visualizing mood and lighting for a sequence of shots

Figure 2.8

(continued)

With digital tools such as GIMP, it is easy to recycle images where necessary. In the previous example sequence, the captain's face being lit up by the beam from the lighthouse is an important detail to represent in the concept art. Because only the lighting changes, the effect is best accomplished by simply painting over the original face. GIMP's layering functionality enables you to do this kind of painting on a transparent layer that lies over the original image, as shown in Figure 2.9. Using layers in this way is convenient and can also be used to represent more-complex sequences in a single file, as you will see later in this chapter.

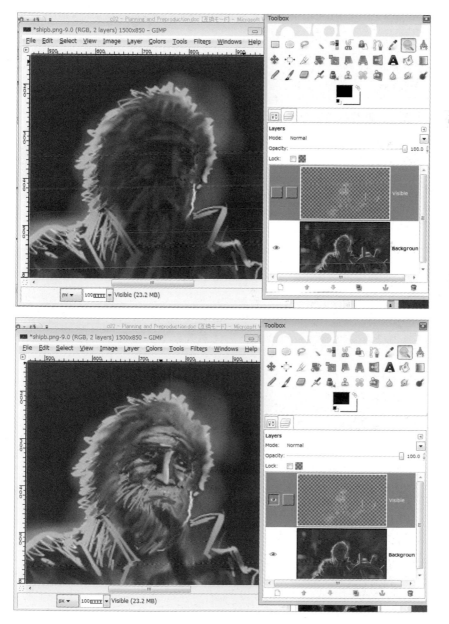

Figure 2.9

Using layers in GIMP to minimize duplicated effort

Designing Characters

A very important subtask of conceptualization for a movie is character design. Characters are originally created in the script, but their physical appearance and style of rendition must be developed by artists. A CG animated movie has particular requirements from its character design. The characters must be thoroughly thought out from all dimensions, and resulting concept artwork should include orthographically drawn portraits from the front and direct side views for use by the modelers.

For the character of Virginia in *Mercator,* images from Romantic and Renaissance art as well as photos of contemporary actresses in various period roles helped to guide the design. Different ages and moods were experimented with, as you can see in Figure 2.10.

The look of the captain was also synthesized from a combination of contemporary and canonical imagery. Some concept art pieces for the captain character are shown in Figure 2.11. Notice how a simple paint-over technique was used to add age to the first image. Just as in the previous example, the light from the lighthouse was added on a separate layer. The gray in the captain's beard and hair can be easily displayed or removed by using a separate layer.

Figure 2.10

Designs for Virginia

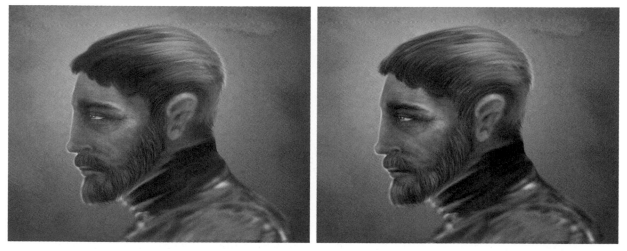

Figure 2.11
The captain, young
and older

Clothing design is an important part of character design. Particularly in the case of a period movie such as *Mercator*, the clothing plays a major part in establishing the characters and action in an historical setting. In Figure 2.12, you can see how different outfits establish the setting in different ways. Consider what the clothing tells you about the character.

Figure 2.12
Sketches for the
captain's clothing

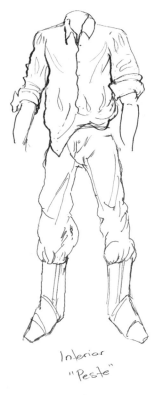

Exterior Antarctic

Interior
Antarctic

Interior
"Peste"

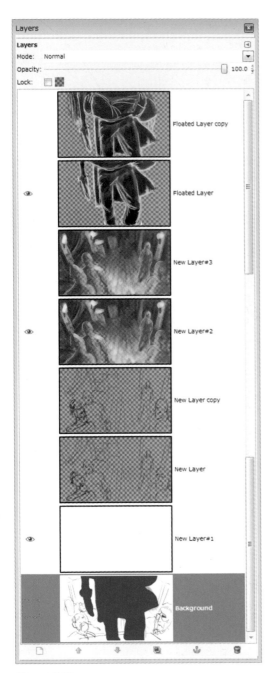

Figure 2.13

GIMP layers can be used to represent time passing.

Storyboarding

Storyboarding is a crucial part of the preproduction phase of most movie projects, be they live action or animation. Storyboards are sequentially arranged, hand-drawn sketches of individual shots. Some shots with significant movement, particularly camera movement, may require multiple sketches; other times movement can be represented within a single shot. In addition to individual sketches being a necessity for planning shots, having all the sketches placed sequentially in a static storyboard enables the director to take a broad view of the movie by seeing all the action (or significant portions of the action) at once, in order. It's customary to print out and arrange storyboards on large walls, where many shots can be seen at once. At this stage, several important decisions about the film already need to be made. In particular, the aspect ratio of the finished film should be decided, so that the storyboard artist and the director can frame and block the work accurately from the beginning.

As simple as it may sound, storyboarding is crucially intertwined with the work of the director, and there is a great deal to know about how to create good storyboards that read well and depict the unfolding action in a way that makes it possible to envision the final rendered shots. Of the books available about storyboarding, far and away the best one I know of is *Prepare to Board!* by Nancy Beiman (Focal Press, 2007). It's incredibly informative and thoroughly enjoyable to read, and I highly recommend it for anybody involved in any stage of animation preproduction or production.

As in previous examples, GIMP layers can be used to make the storyboard creation task easier. In the case of storyboards, it's important to be able to represent time passing from one still to the next. Changes within a scene can often be well represented by layers laid one over the next. You can see in Figure 2.13 the Layers window for a single GIMP file that is used to produce multiple storyboard stills. Figure 2.14 shows several of the resulting stills.

For organizing its storyboards, Licuadora once again takes advantage of its in-house technical savvy to produce its own tools. The Story Mosaic software, shown in Figure 2.15, is a part of the Salsa suite that enables images to be displayed in order and rearranged by dragging and dropping. The number of stills available in the system and the number of stills already used in the storyboard are displayed. Optionally, dialog text and description fields for each frame can also be displayed. In Figure 2.16, you can see the storyboard with description fields displayed.

Figure 2.14

Characters' movement is represented by making different layers visible in GIMP.

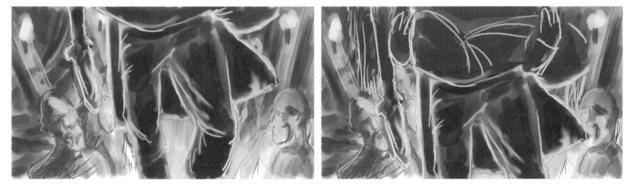

Figure 2.15

Licuadora's in-house Story Mosaic is used to arrange the storyboard.

Figure 2.16

Story Mosaic with dialogs toggled on

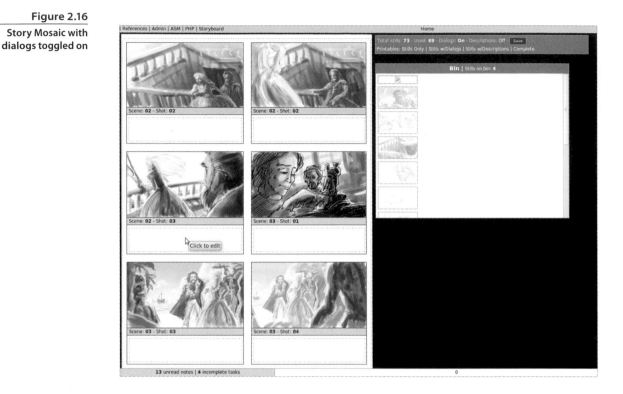

As I mentioned previously in connection with script writing, Celtx is an excellent open source alternative for many preproduction tasks including storyboarding. A series of images from *Mercator* are shown in Figure 2.17 imported into Celtx's storyboarding functionality. Like Licuadora's Story Mosaic, storyboards can be shuffled around with the mouse, and there is a field for descriptions for each still.

An attractive aspect of Celtx is the way all the different areas of functionality are integrated with each other. Scene titles, character information, and other details can all be accessed for use in generating reports and populating drop-down menus throughout the software as you go. Celtx even enables you to play back your storyboards as slideshows, shown in Figure 2.18, creating a simple 2D animatic automatically. The length of time that each frame is displayed can be adjusted to give an idea of the pacing of the final work. In some cases, this may even be enough for a 2D animatic. In cases where a more sophisticated 2D animatic is needed, you can use Blender in conjunction with other tools, as you'll read about in the next section.

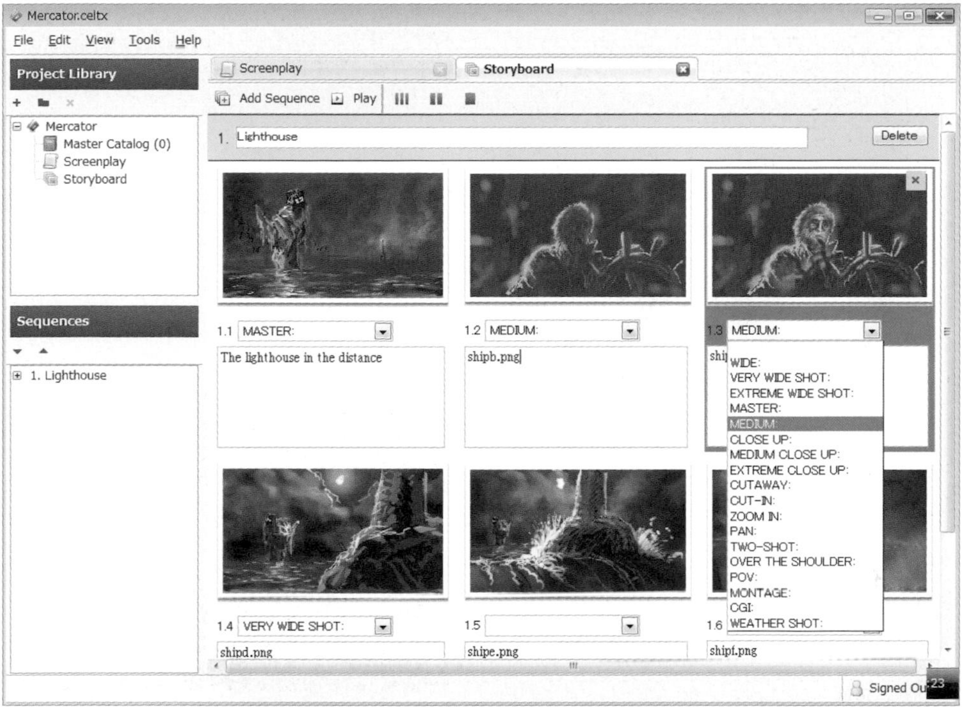

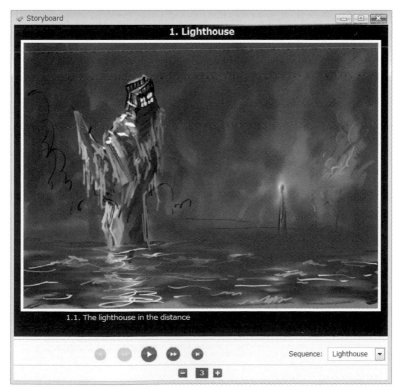

Figure 2.17
Celtx is an excellent
open source option
for storyboarding
and other prepro-
duction tasks.

Figure 2.18
Celtx can also be
used to create a sim-
ple 2D animatic.

Pacing the Story with a 2D Animatic

With storyboards, it's possible to stand back and look at whole sequences of the movie at once. You can see the framing of shots side to side and get a sense of how they will cut together, and get an overall sense of how the pacing works. However, there's a limit to how accurate a feeling for pace and timing you can get from statically arranged images. Movies are a temporally dynamic medium, and the speed with which changes happen on-screen is fundamental to how movies work on their viewers. In short, you've got to see your shots sequenced in time to really understand what the movie will be like.

In animation, the term for a rough sequence of frames played one after another is *animatic.* For a 3D CG movie such as *Mercator,* it is typical to create two separate animatics. The first is a 2D animatic, used to establish the pacing of the movie. Drawn stills representing shots or parts of shots are arranged to reflect the length of the shot or the timing of significant movement in the shot. Music, preliminary recorded dialog, and significant sound effects may also be included where appropriate. This animatic may be little more than a temporally arranged storyboard such as those produced by Celtx, or it may give more information about the movements of objects and the camera. After the 2D animatic is finished, the director should have a very good idea of the kind of length to shoot in his shots for the movie.

The 3D animatic is the next step after the 2D animatic. In the 3D animatic, rough stand-ins for characters and props are used to establish blockings and concrete details such as camera angles and lens values. You'll read about *Mercator*'s 3D animatic in the next chapter.

Stills for the 2D animatic may be taken directly from storyboards or concept art. In the eight-and-a-half-minute *Mercator* animatic, there are 12,863 frames composed of 403 separate images. As in other preproduction steps, effective artwork must be created rapidly. As Figure 2.19 shows, polish and detail are not the order of the day for the 2D animatic. The stills need to convey the important elements of the shot and their framing, and not a lot else.

One of the most important things for the 2D animatic to convey is how multiple shots cut together. In the example shown in Figure 2.20, four drawings are used to represent two shots. The first shot shows the characters together, and the woman reacting to what she sees. The second shot cuts to the view of the ship wedged on the top of an iceberg, and the camera zooms in to reveal a gruesome scene on deck. When the images are viewed in sequence, the director can see the effect of cutting the shots together: It's immediately clear that the shot of the ship is meant to show us what it is that the woman has seen.

Figure 2.19
Creating representative images quickly is important when making a 2D animatic.

Figure 2.20
A sequence of storyboards showing several shots

Creating a 2D Animatic with the Blender Sequence Editor

Although Blender's primary duty is as 3D software, it has a robust set of tools to support many parts of the animation pipeline, including a very useful video-sequence editor that especially shines when working with collections of still images. This makes it a nearly ideal tool for creating the 2D animatic. Blender's weak point in this regard is its limitations in working with sound. Licuadora solves this problem by using the Linux-only open source video editing application Cinelerra to edit audio for the Blender-produced 2D animatic video.

Blender has different default screen setups that correspond to different workflows. The default screen setup that appears when you open your freshly installed Blender is number 2, the Model screen setup. You can see this from the drop-down menu in the User Preferences window header labeled SCR:2-Model. SCR:4 is the Sequence screen setup, which can be selected by using that same drop-down menu. The Sequence screen setup is a good one to start from when working with the Sequence Editor, because most of the windows you need are open in that setup by default. Figure 2.21 shows the *Mercator* 2D animatic opened in a slightly modified Sequence screen configuration. The windows you see here (not including the hidden User Preferences window) are as follows: the upper-right window is a Sequence Editor window, set to Image Preview display mode. This option for the window can be found in the drop-down menu shown in Figure 2.22. To the right of this window is a Buttons window displaying the Sequencer buttons subcontext of the Scene buttons context (accessed by pressing the F10 key). In this window, the Edit panel and the Input panel are visible. Below these windows is another Sequence Editor window, this time in the Sequence display mode. The Sequence display mode is the mode that displays the nonlinear audio/video sequence-editing functionality itself, as you can see in the figure. The sequence strips you see in the image are color-coded by their content, which you'll read more about in the next section. Below the Sequence Editor is the Timeline window, and below that is another Buttons window, this time set to the Render buttons subcontext of the Scene context, where the final animated resume can be executed.

The Sequence Editor has features for quickly navigating through sequences. Markers can be placed at any point along the Timeline, as shown in Figure 2.23. Setting, naming, and editing markers can be done through the Marker menu in the Sequence Editor header, as shown in Figure 2.24. Navigating along the Timeline to the next or previous marker can be done in the View menu of the Timeline window header, as shown in Figure 2.25, or with the Page Up (next marker) and Page Down (previous marker) keys.

Figure 2.21

The 2D animatic in
the Sequence Editor

Figure 2.22
The Image Preview display mode of the Sequence Editor
window

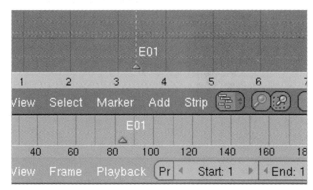

Figure 2.23
Markers on the Sequence Editor and Timeline

Blender enables information to be imprinted, or *burned in*, to frames as they are outputted. This functionality is accessed in the Stamp panel of the Render buttons area, as shown in Figure 2.26. As you can see from the buttons on that panel, there are a number of data values that can be output automatically, such as the timestamp and the frame number. The Note field enables you to include an arbitrary note to be printed on the frames. The burn-ins used in the Licuadora 2D animatic print out the frame, marker, and sequence strip data for each frame. The resulting burn-ins are shown in Figure 2.27.

For more information on using the Blender Sequence Editor for audio/video editing, you can refer to my book *Mastering Blender* (Sybex, 2009), which includes chapters covering video editing and compositing in considerably more depth than is presented here. The techniques required to create a 2D animatic are not particularly sophisticated, so for the purposes of this chapter, it's enough to go through a simple example of putting together a dynamic animatic shot.

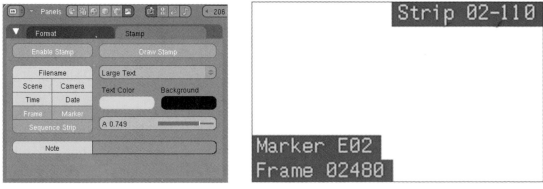

Figure 2.24
Adding a marker in the Sequence Editor

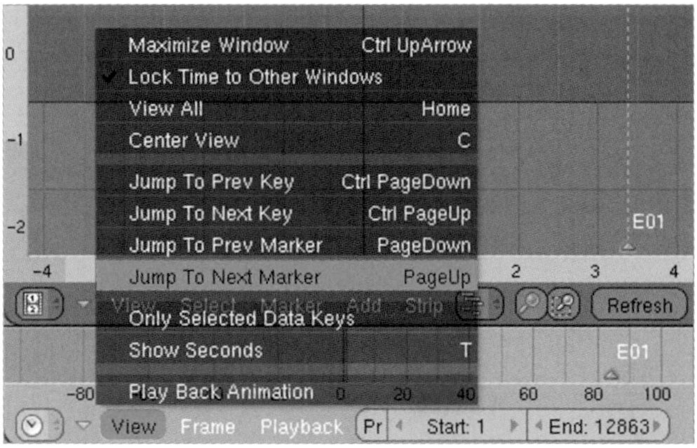

Figure 2.25
Navigating from marker to marker in the Timeline View menu

Figure 2.26
Setting burn-ins with the Draw Stamp option

Figure 2.27
Burn-in labels outputted by the Sequence Editor

Sequencing a Dynamic Animatic Shot

In the following example, you'll see how to use the Sequence Editor to put together a simple but nontrivial 2D animatic shot that includes a camera pan effect, a convincing illusion of depth, and a camera zoom effect. To follow the steps, you will need to find the files in the panning-example directory on the DVD that accompanies this book. I suggest you copy the directory and files to some place on your hard drive. In that directory, you'll find three images, shown in Figure 2.28. The first and second images in the figure, paneo-capa1.jpg and zoom.jpg, are JPEG files with no alpha transparency. The third image, paneo-capa2.tif, is a PNG file with alpha transparency. In the figure printed here, the transparent portions of the image are shown with a grid background.

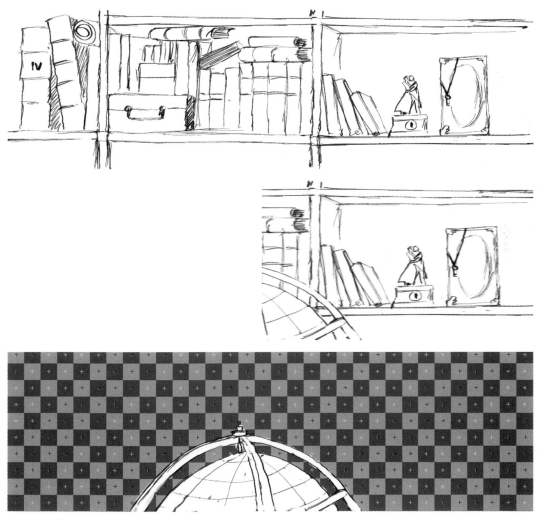

Figure 2.28

The shot is made up of three images.

In the directory on the DVD, will also find the file `paneo.blend`, which contains the completed sequence. You can check that file if you run into any trouble creating the sequence from scratch according to the following instructions. First, though, start up a fresh Blender session and follow these steps to set up the sequence yourself:

1. From the drop-down menu in the Info window header at the top of the screen, select 4-Sequence to display the Sequence editing screen configuration as shown in Figure 2.29. When you do this, your desktop will change to that configuration and display the windows most used during sequence editing tasks. Of course, it's not strictly necessary to use preset screen configurations like this one, but it's easier than splitting up and reassigning all the windows by hand.

Figure 2.29

Choosing the Blender Sequence screen

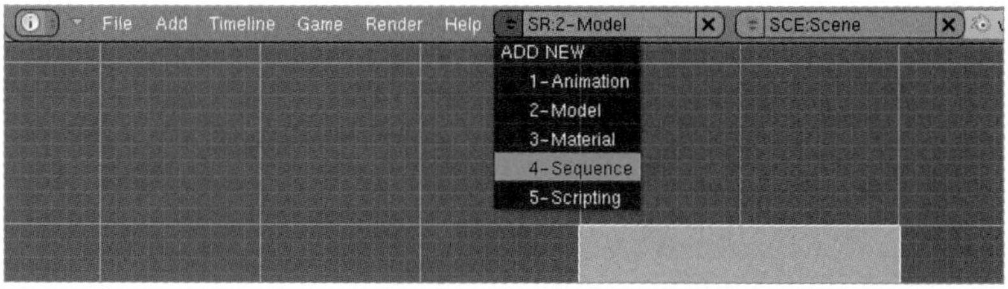

2. Add an Image sequence strip by pressing the spacebar over the Sequence Editor window that runs across the middle of your workspace and selecting Image Sequence from the Add Sequence Strip menu shown in Figure 2.30. A file browser will open, and you should select the file `paneo-capa1.jpg` from your hard drive. When you've added the strip, it will appear as shown in Figure 2.31. The strip will follow your mouse when it first appears, so set it at frame 1 on channel 1 of the editor (the lowermost horizontal gray lane in the figure). Left-click to fix the strip in place. Note that although you've selected only a single image, the strip is 50 frames long. This is convenient for creating 2D animatics. You can leave the length of the strip as it is for the time being.

3. In the Format panel of the Render buttons, click the PAL 16:9 button to set the resolution of the project to the PAL preset. If you wanted to set up a different frame rate, now would also be the time to do that in the same panel, but for this example, the default 25 fps will be fine, so leave it at that.

4. In order to simulate the effect of a rightward camera pan, you'll make the image gradually move to the left. This is accomplished using a Transform sequence strip associated with the Image sequence strip. First select your Image sequence strip by right-clicking it in the Sequence Editor window. Then once again press the spacebar and select Transforms from the menu, as shown in Figure 2.32. The resulting Transform sequence strip will appear as shown in Figure 2.33.

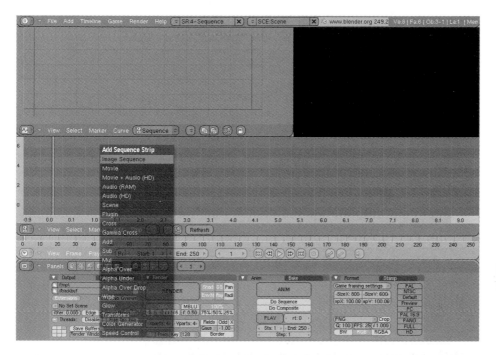

Figure 2.30
Adding an Image sequence strip

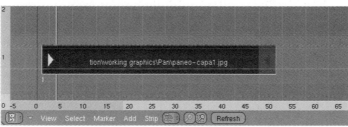

Figure 2.31
The Image sequence strip

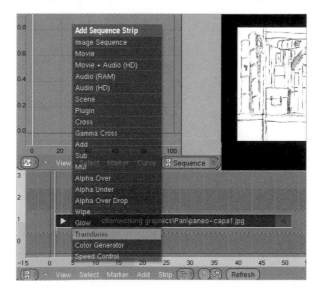
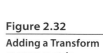

Figure 2.32
Adding a Transform sequence strip

Figure 2.33

The Transform sequence strip

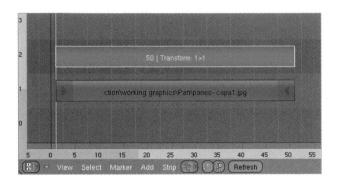

5. You need to set the values for the transform in the Sequencer buttons panel of the Scene context (F10) as shown in Figure 2.34. These values determine the state of the frame at the beginning of the transform and at the end of the transform, either in terms of raw pixel sizes or, as in this case, in terms of percent of the original input values of the frame. First, set both xScale Start and xScale End to be **2.00**. This will stretch the image out horizontally. Notice in the viewer that the original long image has been compressed horizontally to fit the size of the frame. Doubling the xScale value will return it to its original long shape. This won't change over the course of the strip, so the value at the start and the value at the end are equal. The only thing that will change over the course of the strip is the location of the image, which will be shifted to the right and then gradually move leftward. To set this up, enter **50.0** in the x Start field and **−50.0** in the x End field. Other values you can leave as they are.

Figure 2.34

Values for the Trans-form sequence strip

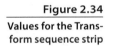

6. You've entered values for the beginning and the end of the transform, but you haven't yet told Blender how to get from the first value to the last. Like anything that's animated in Blender, this is done by using Ipo curves (or, in the newer 2.5 terminology, F-curves). Go to the Ipo Curve Editor window in the upper-left corner of the screen. Make sure the drop-down menu in the window header displays Sequence as the type of curve. Hold down the Ctrl key and left-click to create a new Ipo curve. The curve will be flat and will appear as shown in Figure 2.35. Press the G key to move the Ipo around and place the point you created near the <0, 0.0> origin point of the

PACING THE STORY WITH A 2D ANIMATIC ■ 43

graph. Ctrl+left-click again near the <100, 1.0> point in the graph so that the curve is as shown in Figure 2.36. The curve is shown in Edit mode. As with other editable assets in Blender, you can toggle into and out of Edit mode by using the Tab key. This Ipo represents the degree to which the transformation has been applied (y axis) as a function of the percentage of the strip's distance that has been covered (x axis). Having the first point at <0, 0.0> and the second point at <100, 1.0> means that the strip begins with the values you input in the Start fields previously and ends with the full values you input in the End fields. You can enter the Ipo point location values numerically by hand by pressing the N key to open up the Transform Properties window, as shown in Figure 2.37. When you've done this, play the strip by pressing Alt+A. You should see the image move leftward as though there is a camera pan to the right, as shown in Figure 2.38.

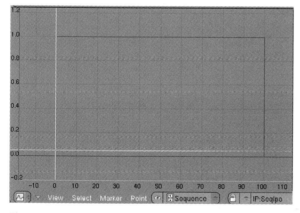

Figure 2.35
Adding a Sequence Ipo curve

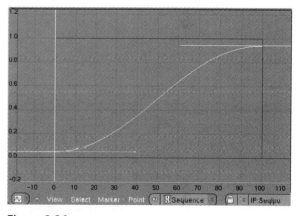

Figure 2.36
Creating the second point on the curve

Figure 2.37
Adjusting curve point values

Figure 2.38

The curve controls
the pseudo-camera
pan effect.

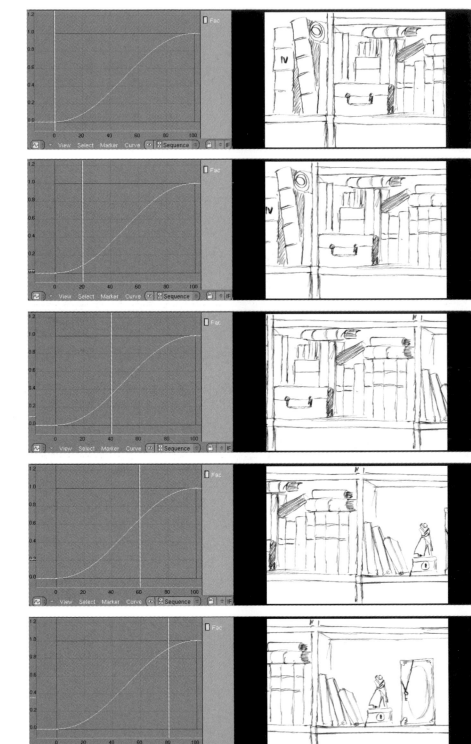

7. Meta-strips are a way to combine multiple strips into a more compact and manageable bundle that can be manipulated like a single strip. Image strips that are being modified by Transform strips are good candidates for creating meta-strips, because the two strips remain aligned regardless, whether they take up one channel or two. To create a meta-strip, select both strips and press M, bringing up the confirmation box shown in Figure 2.39. The resulting meta-strip is shown in Figure 2.40. You can unpack a meta-strip by selecting it and pressing Alt+M. You can edit a meta-strip without unpacking it by toggling into Edit mode with the Tab key.

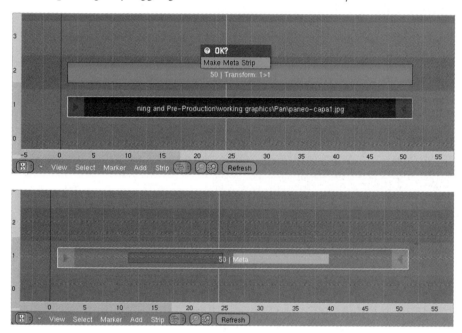

Figure 2.39

Creating a
meta-strip

Figure 2.40

The meta-strip

8. Add the globe image in the file paneo-capa2.tif, in the same way you added the first image, by pressing the spacebar and finding the file on your hard drive. Place the strip at frame 1 in channel 2, directly above the meta-strip you just created, as shown in Figure 2.41. As you see in the figure, the alpha channel of the PNG is displayed as black in the viewer, and channel 1 is concealed. As you did with the previous Image strip, add a Transform strip to this one too, as shown in Figure 2.42.

9. As you did previously in step 5 for the panning of the background, you need to enter the transform values that will move the globe. The values are shown in Figure 2.43. Once again, the x scale of the image is doubled to stretch the image back into its original shape. However, in this case, the Start x value is **100** rather than **50**. The End x value is the same as previously, **−50**. This results in the globe moving somewhat faster than the background, which gives an illusion of depth to the scene. As you did in step 6, you need to set an Ipo curve to control the transform. The strips and Ipo you should wind up with are shown in Figure 2.44.

Figure 2.41

Figure 2.41

Adding the globe
Image strip

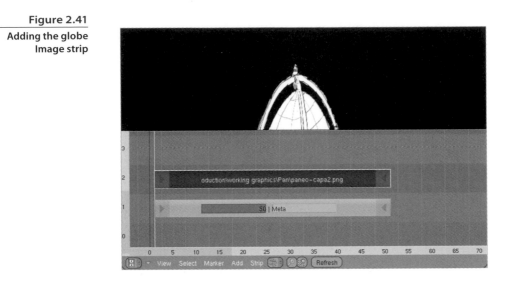

Figure 2.42

Adding a Transform strip to the globe

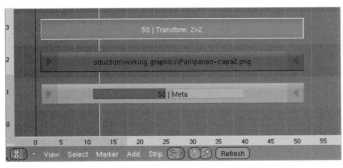

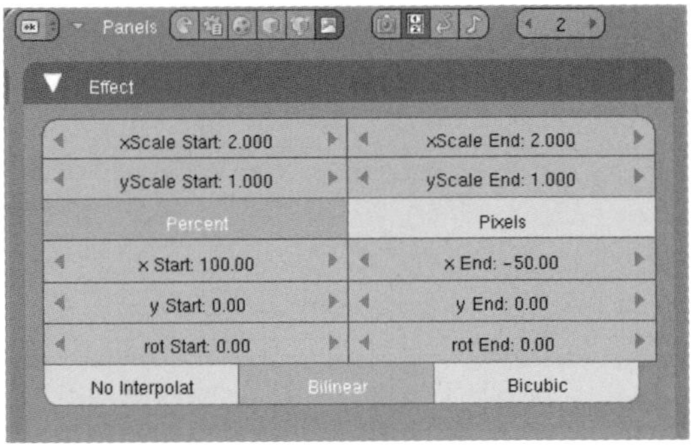

Figure 2.43

Transform values for the globe

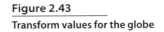

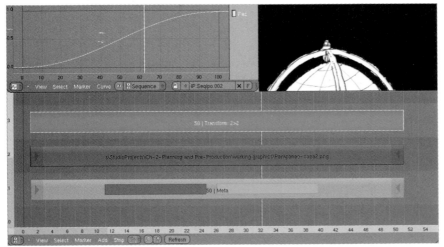

Figure 2.44

The animated transform

10. Create a meta-strip from the globe Image sequence and the Transform as shown in Figure 2.45. Select it and then Shift+right-click on the first meta-strip in channel 1 to select them both. Press the spacebar to add a sequence strip and choose Alpha Over Drop, as shown in Figure 2.46. The result is shown in Figure 2.47. As you see, the globe is now in the foreground of the bookshelf.

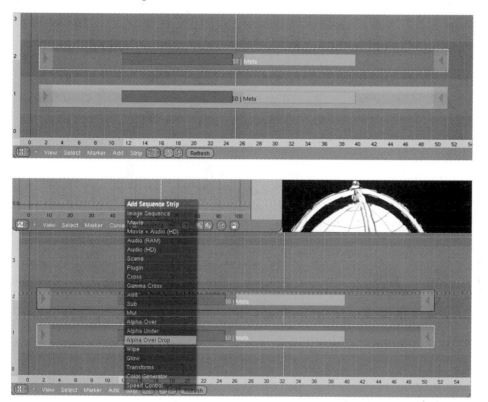

Figure 2.45

Creating a meta-strip

Figure 2.46

Adding an Alpha-Over-Drop strip

11. The next step is to add the zoom image. This image is created by rendering the last frame of the previous composited sequence, and doing that will give you the best results. If you use the zoom.jpg image from the disk, you may see a slight jump in the location of the globe at that frame. In either case, load the image in the same way you have loaded the others, but this time place the strip flush against the rightmost edge of the previous strip on channel 1, as shown in Figure 2.48. Add a Transformation strip as shown in Figure 2.49.

Figure 2.47

The composited strips

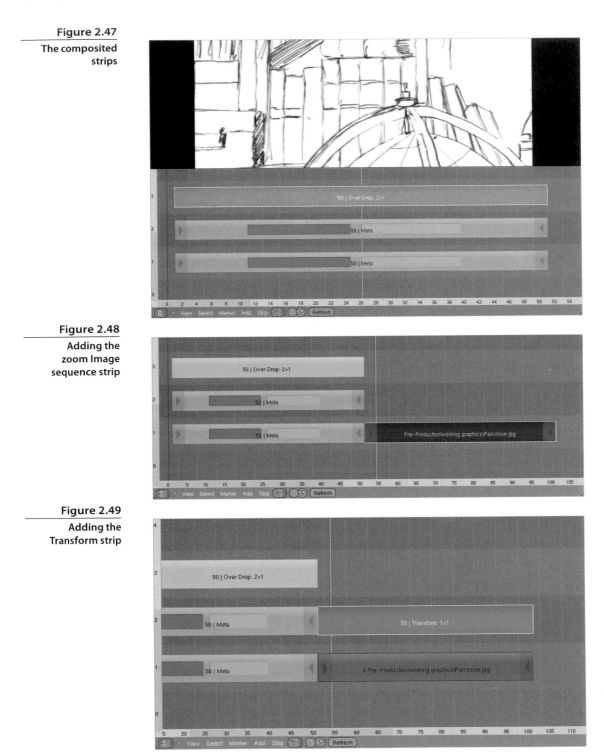

Figure 2.48

Adding the zoom Image sequence strip

Figure 2.49

Adding the Transform strip

12. The zoom transform values are shown in Figure 2.50. The Start values are all unchanged from the original frame. Create an Ipo as you did in steps 6 and 9. The End values for both x and y scale are **1.5**, so the image will scale up over time. Because of this scaling, the x location value needs to change as well, to hold the center point of the image fixed. For this reason, the x End value is set to **−16.79**.

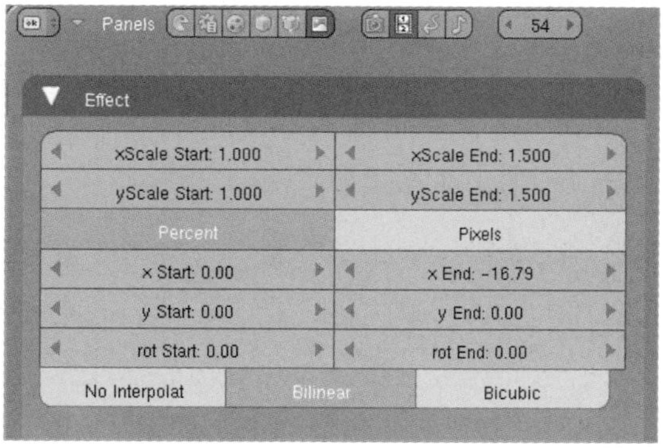

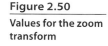

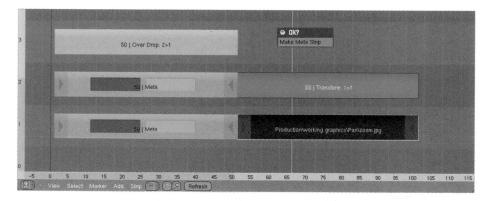

Figure 2.50

Values for the zoom transform

13. When you've finished this, you can create meta-strips for the zoom Image and Transformation strips as shown in Figure 2.51, and then combine the pan meta-strips into another meta-strip as shown in Figure 2.52. The completed sequence is shown in Figure 2.53. The length of either of these meta-strips can be easily adjusted by dragging the ends of the strips. The Ipo value extends the length of the strip regardless of the actual number of frames the strip covers up to the original length of the strip. If you extend the strip by dragging the right end of the strip out, the last frame will be frozen for the duration of the extended part of the strip, but the transform effect will not be extended.

Figure 2.51

Creating a meta-strip for the zoom strips

Figure 2.52

**Creating a
meta-strip for
the pan strips**

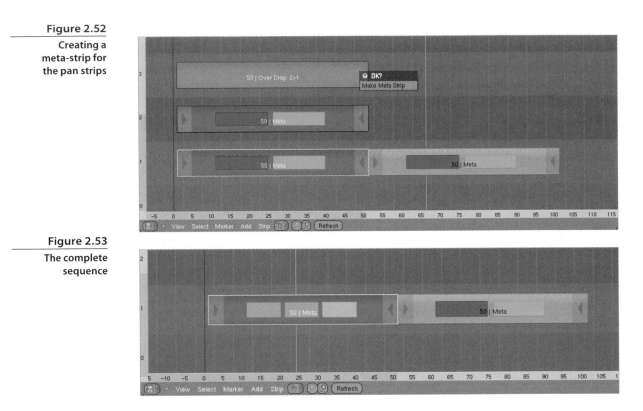

Figure 2.53

**The complete
sequence**

Finishing the Animatic

As of this writing, Blender still has some weaknesses in dealing with sound that make
it not optimal as a sole A/V editing tool in a production environment. But sound is an
important part of a 2D animatic, particularly music, which can make an enormous difference in getting a sense of the pacing and emotional impact of the images. Licuadora
Studio addresses this by exporting the animatic video from Blender and finishing the
job with sound in Cinelerra, as shown in Figure 2.54. This is a good solution for studios
with Linux support, but Cinelerra is not available across platforms and therefore other
solutions must be sought. Proprietary solutions are the most common and reliable for
the task of general production-quality audio and video editing. The good news is that
Blender has improved by leaps and bounds in its ability to handle sound, and the day
when it will hold its own as a complete A/V editing solution may be approaching.

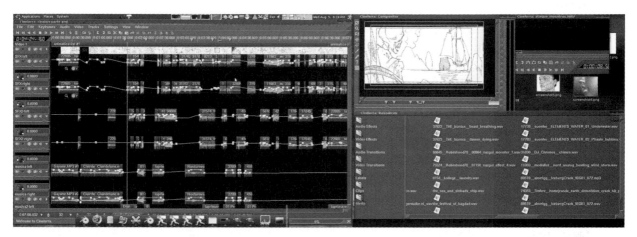

All that said, Blender's primary focus has never been video editing or 2D compositing. The primary focus of Blender is 3D animation. In the next chapter, you'll step into Blender's real comfort zone and take a look at how the process of producing specifically 3D animation begins.

Figure 2.54
Editing the animatic together with sound in Cinelerra

CHAPTER 3

Creating a 3D Animatic

This chapter discusses the preparations and organization necessary to create a useful 3D animatic. The 3D animatic takes the 2D animatic as its guide for framing and timing of shots and sequences, but adds further information about blocking and camera setups and movements in the 3D space. This is where Blender's natural strength as a 3D animation environment will really begin to be exercised. The 3D animatic will form the basis for all the subsequent animation work for the movie, so it is very important to plan it well and to carry it out in a way that maximizes its usefulness. As always, avoiding extra wasted time and effort is a priority.

CHAPTER CONTENTS

- **Working with an Asset Library**
- **Organizing Sequences and Shots**
- **Animating and Rendering the Animatic**

Working with an Asset Library

After the shots and their timing have been planned out satisfactorily using the 2D animatic, it's time to begin work on realizing the story in 3D. For this, a 3D animatic is created to do blocking and to plan camera setups. This is a crucial step in creating a 3D animated movie, because the final animation will be based closely on this animatic, to the extent that actual animation curves may be recycled from the 3D animatic.

Throughout the production, managing 3D assets such as models, textures, lights, and animation curves is an important part of the job. Assets often need to be in "two places at once" in the sense that several strands of work may be going on in parallel that use the same assets. Animators may need to animate a character at the same time that texture artists work on textures for the same character. Even in a small, one-person project, it will not do to try to keep multiple distinct copies of an asset up-to-date. It is necessary to have a centralized library for the character model that can be accessed and modified by everyone who needs it without disrupting anybody else's work.

When you begin to work on the 3D animatic, this kind of organization takes a central role. It will become even more important during the production of the finished animation, as the number of assets increases and their complexity grows.

Organizing Files

The first thing you need to do when using asset libraries is to put them somewhere. It's important that all files are located in a place where they will be accessible to everyone who needs them. For maximum portability, Blender's linking system is capable of making use of relative paths for library files. This implies that the locations of the libraries and the files that use them are constant with respect to each other. If this is not the case, the links in the .blend files will be broken. The best approach is to make sure that all libraries and scenes that require them are grouped together in a meaningful way in a single directory.

On the *Mercator* project, the directory for the 3D animatic is located inside the main project directory and is named animatic-3D. Inside this directory are the directories lib, shots, and render. As you can guess from their names, these hold the libraries, the shot files, and the rendered output of the 3D animatic, respectively. Inside the lib directory, the .blend files containing props and scenes are stored. A subdirectory in lib, called personajes, stores the characters. Another subdirectory, textures, contains the textures used throughout the 3D animatic.

The shots directory contains the .blend files used to create the actual shots of the 3D animatic. Each shot is a separate .blend file. These shots will be rendered to corresponding subdirectories of the render directory, and eventually edited together using the Blender Sequence Editor.

Linking and Appending

There are two main functions of Blender for transferring assets from one .blend file to another and for working with shared assets from multiple files. These are appending and linking. The simpler of the two is appending. Appending enables you to bring a copy of an asset from one .blend file into another. When you append an asset from one .blend file to another, the two files become independent of each other, each with its own copy of the asset. In the case of linking, however, the linked object can be edited only in the original resource .blend file. Furthermore, the linking file must have correct path information for the original resource file. If this information becomes corrupted, as can happen, for example, if one of the files is moved or if the resource file is deleted, then the data will be lost.

The following steps will walk you through the process of appending assets from one
.blend file to another. For a resource file, you can use any file that has a couple of objects
in it. If you like, you can use the file bailarina.blend from the DVD accompanying this
book, which is where the examples in the figures come from.

For appending a 3D object, the process is very simple:

1. To begin with, you need the library file and the object that you will append. Any
   ordinary .blend file will do as a library file, and no special treatment or preparation
   is necessary to append objects. Figure 3.1 shows the ballerina figurine from the file
   bailarina.blend provided on the DVD. The figurine is actually made up of several
   separate objects, including meshes for the base, the keyholes, the figurine's body, the
   head, and some other small meshes. In addition, an empty is used as a parent object
   to rotate the figurine. In this example, you will append only single objects one at a
   time. If you use a different file as your library file, create some recognizable objects
   to append elsewhere.

Figure 3.1

**Objects in a
library file**

2. Open a second .blend file to use as your destination file. This is the file into which you will append the object from the previous file. You don't need to do anything special to this file either. However, when you append the asset, you will be given the choice to use absolute or relative path information to locate the library. If you use relative path information, Blender needs to know the location on the hard disk of both files. This means that you must save your destination .blend file before you can append anything with relative path information. In any case, you're going to have to save your file eventually, so you may as well save it now. It doesn't matter where you save it, but again, if you plan to use relative paths, you will be restricted in the future to keeping this file and the library file in the same position relative to each other, so bear this in mind when choosing a place to save.

3. In your destination file, press Shift+F1 or choose Append or Link from the File drop-down menu, as shown in Figure 3.2. When you do this, Blender's File Browser window opens. When appending or linking, the file browser treats other .blend files like directories, with assets divided into subdirectories within them. You can navigate .blend files in the file browser just as you would other directories and file systems. When you open up the file browser to append, Blender makes a guess about which .blend file you want to access. By default, it will open the last .blend file that was opened previously. In this case, the file browser should display something similar to Figure 3.3. If it shows another directory, that's fine; you simply navigate to the library .blend file you want on the hard disk.

Figure 3.2
The Append or Link menu item

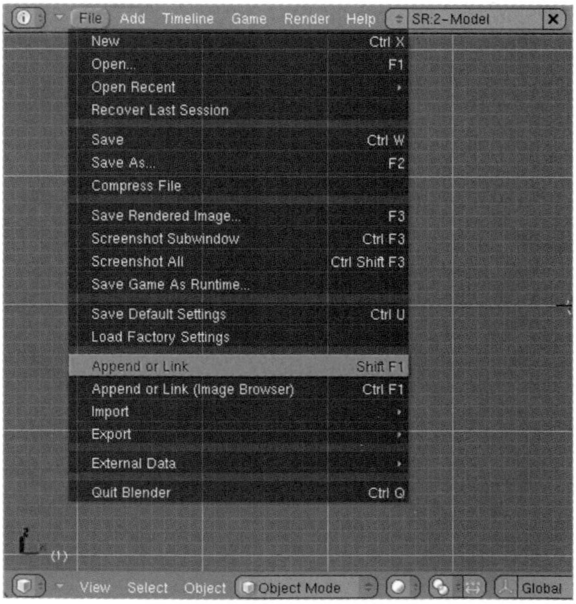

4. Click the Object subdirectory of the library .blend file. This opens the .blend subdirectory containing the 3D objects in the .blend file. Note that you did not enter the Mesh subdirectory. That subdirectory contains Mesh datablocks without 3D object information such as location, rotation, and scale. You can append those assets too if you want, but they will not appear in the 3D space in your target .blend file unless you associate them with an object. If you're not clear about the distinction between datablocks and objects, you might want to refer to an introductory book such as my *Introducing Character Animation with Blender* (Sybex, 2007), which discusses this distinction in detail. For now, stick with appending an object. Select the base object as shown in Figure 3.4. Click Load Library, and you're finished. The base object appears in the 3D space of your destination .blend file, as shown in Figure 3.5.

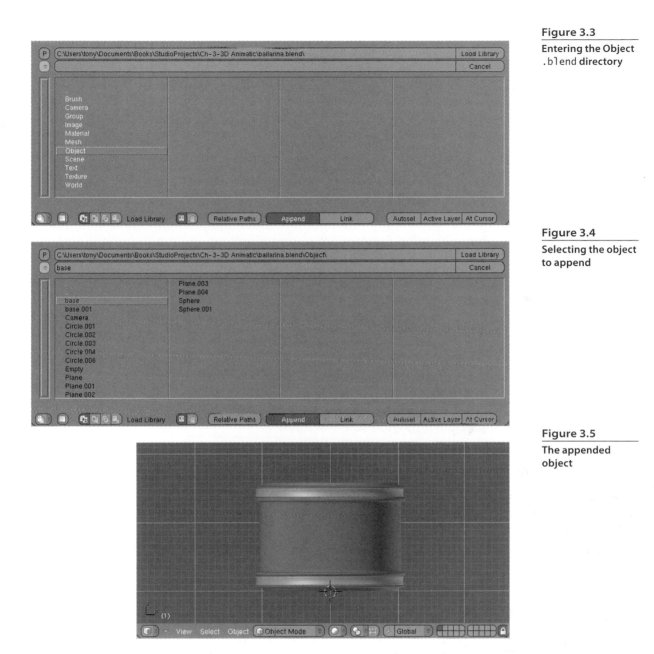

Figure 3.3
Entering the Object
`.blend` **directory**

Figure 3.4
**Selecting the object
to append**

Figure 3.5
**The appended
object**

Groups

Appending an object is a simple and common operation. But there are many cases in which it is not the most convenient way to go about things. Suppose your intention is to append the complete figurine from the `bailarina.blend` file—base, figure, empty, and all?

If you append by object, you will need to go through the steps from the previous section again and again for each object. Instead of doing this, it is much easier to place a collection of objects into a group and then append the group. The following steps show you how to do this:

1. Once again, begin by opening up the library .blend file, bailarina.blend, or whatever file you've decided to use as your library. This time, before you do the actual appending, you will need to prepare the data in the library by creating a group and assigning the objects you want to it. Select the base object in the 3D viewport. In the Object and Links panel of the Object buttons area (F7), choose Add New from the Add to Group drop-down menu, as shown in Figure 3.6. In the GR: text field that appears, type in the name **ballerina** to name the group, as shown in Figure 3.7. Check the 3D viewport. The base of the figurine should have a green outline around it, indicating that it's a member of a group. In wireframe, it will appear as shown in Figure 3.8.

2. One by one, add the remaining objects in the figurine to the group. Do this in the same way that you added the base, except that instead of choosing Add New from the drop-down menu, choose Ballerina. Alternately, select all the pieces and press Ctrl+G with the mouse over the 3D viewport to bring up the group context menu and group all the objects at once. The objects will all be outlined in green when you finish and will look as shown in Figure 3.9 in wireframe. Don't forget the empty shown selected in Figure 3.10. That also needs to be part of the group. Be sure to save the library file after adding the objects to the group.

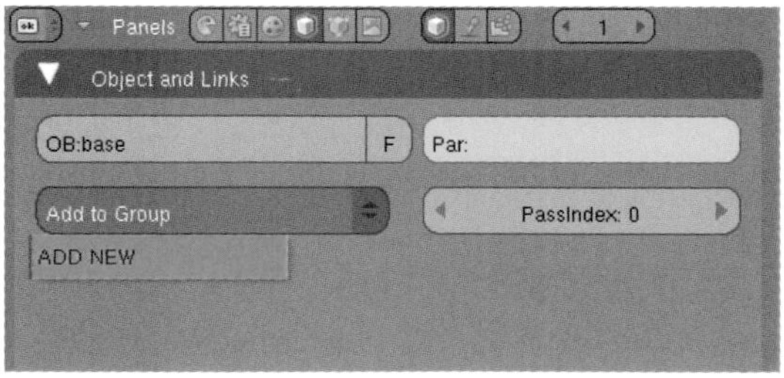

Figure 3.6
Creating a new group

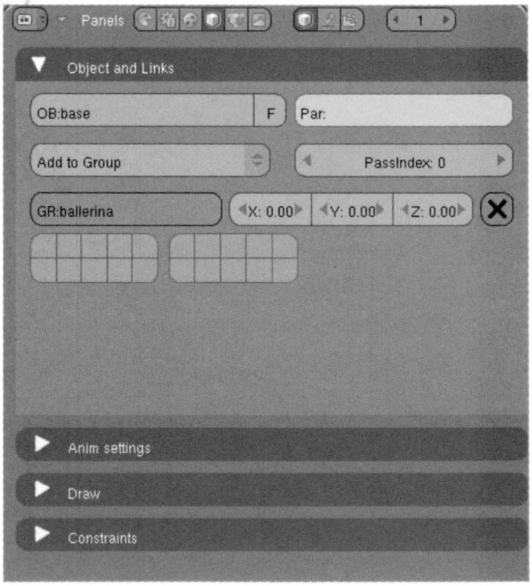

Figure 3.7
Naming the group

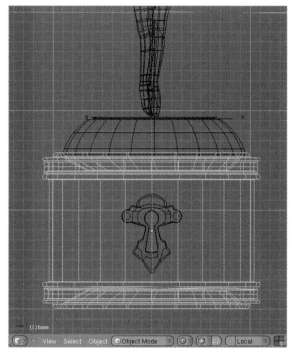

Figure 3.8
The grouped object in Wireframe view

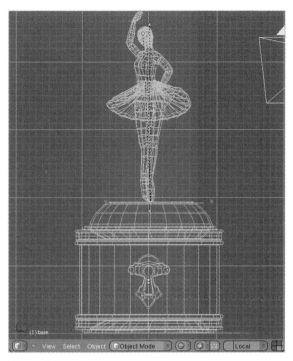

Figure 3.9
All the grouped objects

Figure 3.10
The empty also belongs to the group.

3. In the destination .blend file, choose Append or Link from the File menu. In the file browser, navigate to the Group subdirectory of the bailarina.blend file, as shown in Figure 3.11. Inside this directory, you'll see the group name that you just created listed, as shown in Figure 3.12. Select the group name and click Load Library. The full figurine will appear in the 3D window of your destination file, as shown in Figure 3.13.

Figure 3.11

The Group .blend subdirectory

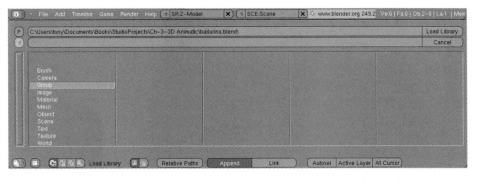

Figure 3.12

Selecting the group name

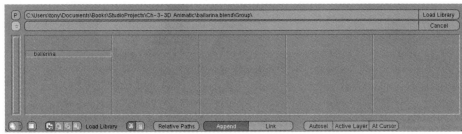

Figure 3.13

The figurine in the destination .blend file

Appended objects are complete and independent copies of the library objects and belong entirely to the destination .blend file. As such they can be moved, animated, edited in Edit mode, or otherwise altered with no regard for the original copy.

Linking

Like appending, linking also enables you to work with a copy of a library object in a separate .blend file, but to a more restricted extent. With linking, the destination .blend file refers to the library .blend file for the data afresh every time it is opened. Linked objects cannot generally be transformed or edited; they receive their data entirely from the original library. The power of linking lies in the fact that the original library object can be updated or altered even while it is being used in a destination .blend file, and the changes will automatically appear in the destination file the next time it accesses the library data.

The process of linking objects is identical to appending objects except that the Link option rather than the Append option is selected in the file browser header. However, there are some subtle differences with linking groups. Follow these steps to go through the process of linking a group:

Figure 3.14

The Select Grouped menu

1. Assuming you started with the same destination file that you used in the previous example of appending a group, first delete the group of objects you just appended. You can easily select a group of objects by selecting one of the objects and pressing Shift+G to bring up the Select Grouped menu, as shown in Figure 3.14. Choose Objects in Same Group, and then press the X key and delete the objects, as shown in Figure 3.15. Note that even after you've deleted the objects in the group, the group itself will remain inside the .blend library instantiated as an empty. To completely remove the group, you have to add it again to the 3D viewport and delete the empty. When you save and reopen the file, the group will be gone.

2. Just as you did previously, choose Append or Link from the File menu and navigate to the Group directory to find the Ballerina group. Make sure that Link is selected in the header of the file browser, as shown in Figure 3.16. Click Load Library.

Figure 3.15

Deleting the appended group

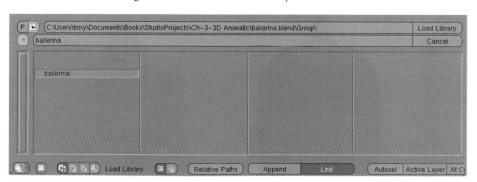

Figure 3.16

Linking the group

3. Unlike in the case of appending groups or linking objects, the group of objects you linked will not appear in the 3D viewport. Linked group data is treated in a somewhat more complex way than simply as a collection of linked objects. In order to position the linked group in the 3D space, press the spacebar to bring up the Add menu just as if you were adding a new object. Choose Group → Bailarina → Ballerina, as shown in Figure 3.17. The figurine will appear as shown in Figure 3.18. Note the light gray outline around the solid view and the gray-colored wireframe. This represents linked objects in the Rounded Blender theme. If you are using the Default Blender theme, this outline will be in pink. None of this can be selected in the destination file. However, also note the white empty at the base of the group. This empty was not present in the original library group, and it can be used to manipulate the linked group in the 3D space.

Figure 3.17

Adding the linked group object to the 3D scene

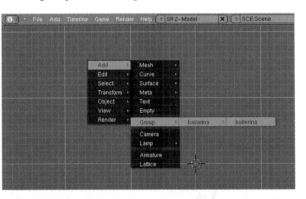

Figure 3.18

The linked group

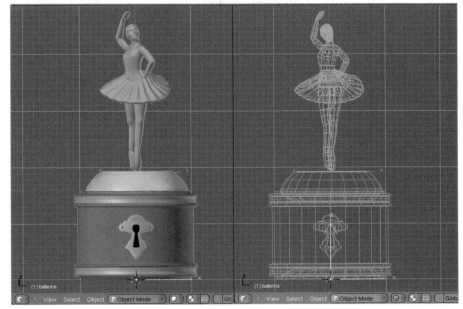

4. Select the empty and experiment with it a bit. You can rotate, translate, or scale the empty, and the entire linked group will be transformed accordingly, as shown in Figure 3.19. Take a closer look at the empty. In the Edit buttons, the Link and Materials panel shows the options you have for visualizing the empty, as shown in Figure 3.20. By default, the empty is visualized with three arrows. You can visualize it as a cube, a sphere, a cone, or an intersection of three orthogonal lines. You can also adjust its display size.

5. To see the significance of linking, open the original library .blend file. Make some changes to the original library objects. Rotate the empty that controls the figure's rotation by selecting the empty, pressing the R key followed by the Z key, and rotating so the figure turns as shown in Figure 3.21. Then select the gray platform at the top of the base. Enter Edit mode and edit the object as shown in Figure 3.22. To do this, select the middle edge loop by holding Alt and right-clicking on an edge in the edge loop. Then scale the loop down by pressing the S key and scaling with the mouse. Save the changes as shown in Figure 3.23.

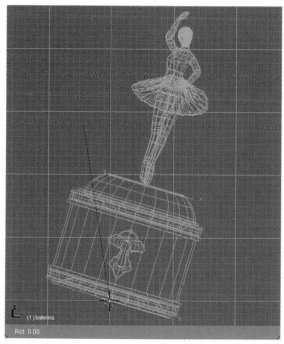

Figure 3.19
Rotating the linked group object

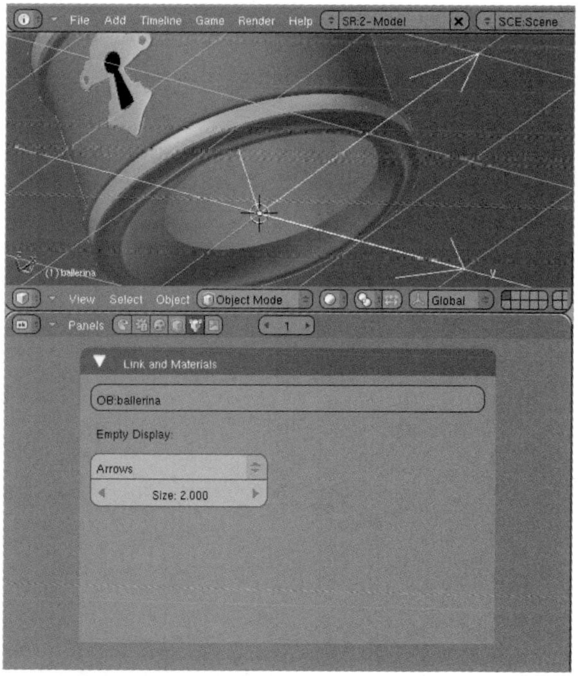

Figure 3.20
Options for visualizing the empty

Figure 3.21

Rotating the empty

Figure 3.22

Editing the top of
the base

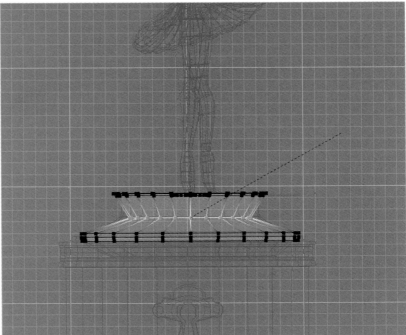

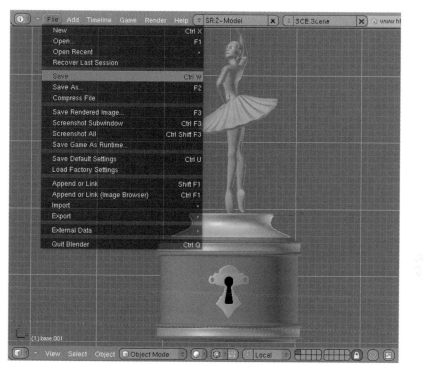

Figure 3.23

Saving the changes

6. The objects in the library group are no longer synced with those in the destination file, as you can see in Figure 3.24. To sync them, you'll need to reopen the destination file. This can be done easily by simply selecting Open Recent from the File menu (Ctrl+O). If you've saved the current file, it will always be the topmost item on the recent files list. Save first to avoid making a mistake and losing data, and then open the file from this list, as shown in Figure 3.25. The results are shown in Figure 3.26. As you can see, the two groups and their objects are now identical in both .blend files.

In this example, it is desirable to be able to look at two .blend files at the same time. Blender is not designed to enable multidocument editing, so it is necessary to run multiple instances of Blender. This is no problem in Windows or Linux—simply click on a .blend file, and the file will open in its own instance of Blender—but it is forbidden in Mac OS X, which allows only one instance of any application to run at a time. Unfortunately, there are no elegant solutions to this problem. You can close one .blend file to look at the other, or you can install two completely distinct installations of Blender 2.49 and place two separate icons for them in your dock, or you can run Blender from the command line, which does not have this problem. There does not seem to be any workaround that will enable you to click a .blend file open while another is already open on a Mac. Readers who know otherwise are invited to contact me and tell us how.

Figure 3.24

The library and destination files unsynced

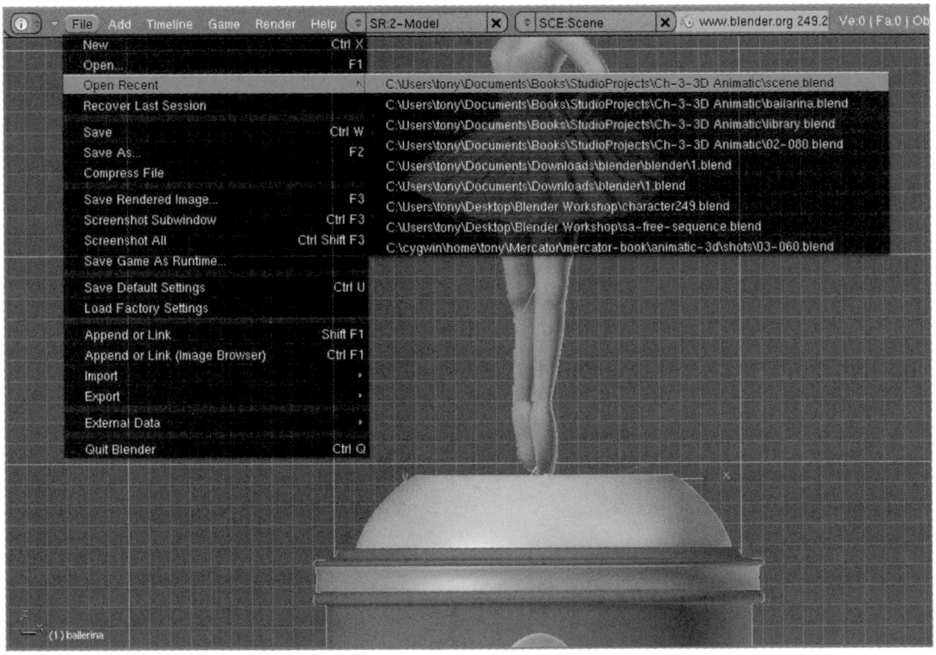

Figure 3.25

Reopening the current file

Groups are used in many situations. Even a fairly simple single object such as the figurine is made up of several different objects. Likewise, the ship shown in Figure 3.27 is made up of numerous grouped objects. Snow on a part of the deck is a separate object from the deck itself, as shown in Figure 3.28. These situations require using groups.

Figure 3.26

The library and destination files synced

Figure 3.27

A ship made up of numerous grouped objects

Figure 3.28

Snow modeled separately and grouped with the deck

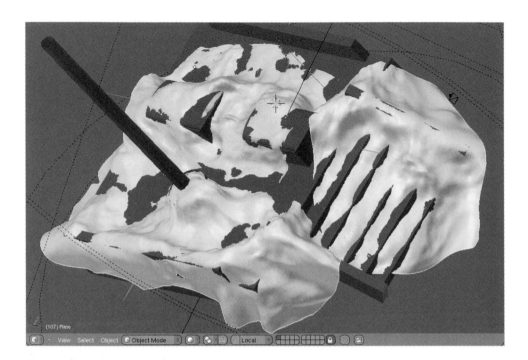

Animating with Proxy Objects

Linking is an excellent way to maintain consistency between files, by restricting changes to assets to a single library file, and updating assets in the various places they are used elsewhere. Using grouping, you can transform groups as though they were freely transformable objects in the destination file.

However, simply being able to rotate, scale, and translate 3D objects may not be sufficient for the animator's needs. An important example is in the case of character animation, in which armature data needs to be accessible and changeable in Pose mode. Ordinary object and group linking does not make any special provisions for armature animation. For this, you need to use Blender's proxy object system, which was designed especially with this use case in mind.

To see an example of the proxy object system in action, follow these steps:

1. Find the capitan_dummy.blend file on the DVD that accompanies the book. Open it to check that the rigged character is prepared for group linking, as shown in Figure 3.29. This is a dummy rig that will take the place of the captain in the 3D animatic. All of the objects in this character rig are grouped into a group called Capitan (be careful of the Spanish spelling). The character rig is based on Nathan Vegdahl's biped rig, created during the *Big Buck Bunny* production, and is an example of how Creative Commons licensed content can be reused in other projects. You can close this file after you've looked it over. There's nothing more you need to do here.

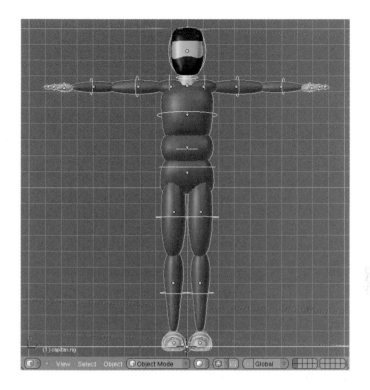

Figure 3.29

The captain character dummy rig

2. Start a new Blender session and save the new destination file so that you can use relative paths to link the assets. As you did in previous examples, choose Append or Link from the File menu and navigate to the Capitan group in the Groups .blend subdirectory of the capitan_dummy.blend file, as shown in Figure 3.30.

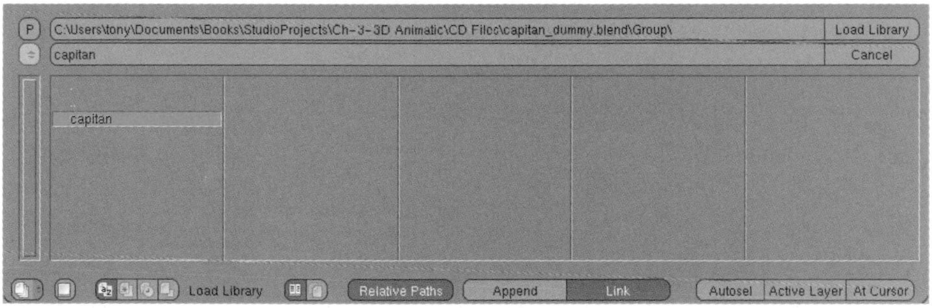

Figure 3.30

Linking the Capitan group

3. In the 3D viewport, press the spacebar to bring up the Add menu and choose Group → Capitan_dummy → Capitan, as shown in Figure 3.31. The captain rig will appear as an uneditable linked group, as shown in Figure 3.32. Note that the armature object is not visible.

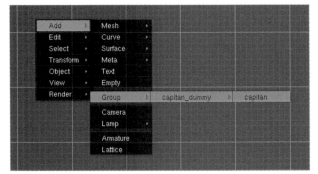

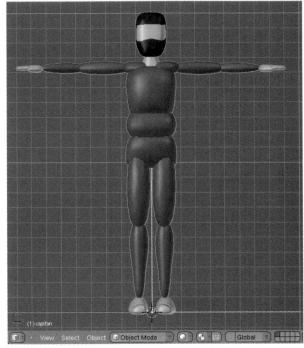

Figure 3.31
Adding the captain rig to the scene

Figure 3.32
The linked group of the captain rig

4. Make a proxy object for the armature by pressing Ctrl+Alt+P to bring up the Make Proxy menu and selecting Capitan.rig from the menu, as shown in Figure 3.33. When you have done this, the proxy armature will appear as shown in Figure 3.34.

5. The proxy armature is a special case of linking. You can't edit it in Edit mode; however, you can pose it. Enter Pose mode as you normally would, using the drop-down menu on the header (Ctrl+Tab), as shown in Figure 3.35. You can pose the model freely now, as shown in Figure 3.36. I also suggest object parenting the linked group empty to the proxy armature, so that when you move the armature object, the rest of the rig follows along. This is not automatic.

> As of the release of Blender 2.50 alpha, currently available as of this writing, the process of appending, linking, and creating proxy objects is slightly different from what is described here. One difference is that Append and Link are now two separate entries in the File menu and have different keyboard shortcuts. Another difference is that adding objects in the 3D window (including group instances) is not currently accessed via the spacebar by default. Instead, you add new 3D objects with Shift+A. Finally, when adding an instance of a group from the Add menu, the menu entry to choose is called Group Instance, rather than simply Group.

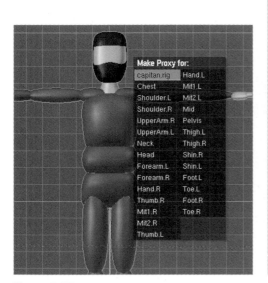

Figure 3.33
Making the proxy armature

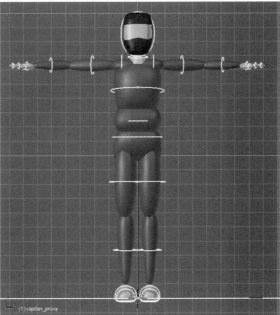

Figure 3.34
The rig with the proxy armature shown

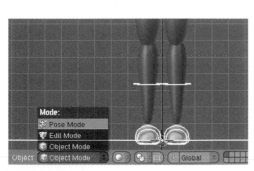

Figure 3.35
Entering Pose mode

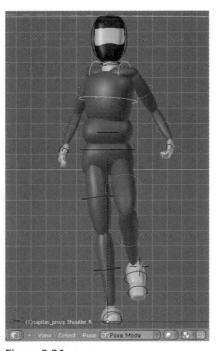

Figure 3.36
Posing the captain rig

Figure 3.37 shows an example 3D animatic clip in which two characters are used. These are the captain and the Virginia character rigs. Both of them are proxy linked into the scene as just described. You can see also that each rig includes a set of IK/FK sliders for controlling the arms and legs by forward kinematic (FK) posing or inverse kinematic (IK) posing.

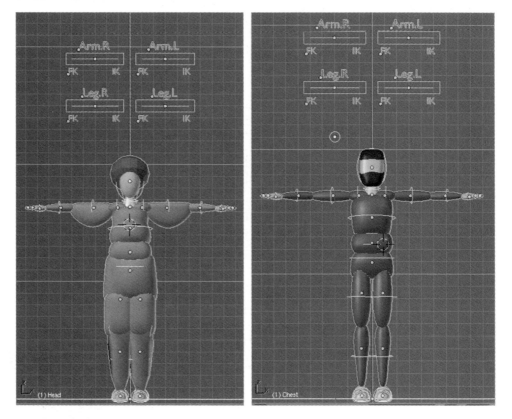

Organizing Sequences and Shots

Like the 2D animatic before it, the 3D animatic must be clearly organized in terms of scenes and shots so that the subsequent production can be carried out without confusion. In filmmaking terms, a *shot* is an unbroken sequence of frames taken from a single camera setup. A *scene* is a sequence of shots held together by some concrete, unifying factor, often a shared location and a single thematic trajectory that makes up a part of the larger story of the movie. Scenes can be composed of any number of shots.

The 2D animatic uses markers in the Sequence Editor to demarcate scenes, as shown in Figure 3.38. Shots are represented by meta-sequences. When a single camera shot is composed of multiple image sequences in the 2D animatic (as in the pan and zoom example you saw in Chapter 2, "Planning and Preproduction"), a meta-sequence strip is created to keep the sequence strips corresponding to shots.

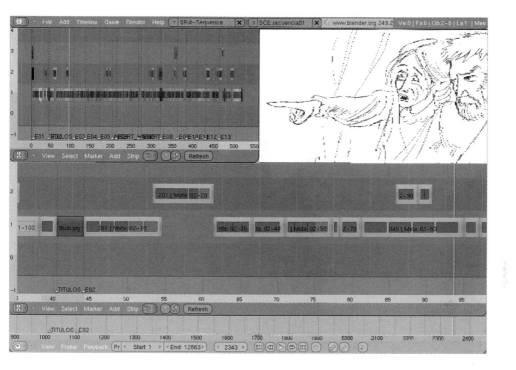

Figure 3.38

The 2D animatic
organized into
scenes and shots

Unlike the 2D animatic, the 3D animatic is too resource intensive to be created entirely in a single .blend file. Blender does have an internal concept of scenes, and these can be useful in a variety of ways, but for actual movie production, it is unlikely that you will use Blender scenes to correspond to anything like a movie scene. A much more sensible way to organize multishot Blender animations is to store each individual shot as its own .blend file. Each file has its own camera setup and animation, and each file's assets are linked from a common library. Each file can be set to save its rendered animation to a specific render directory, and the renders can then be imported as sequence strips in a final sequence edit .blend file. This method of organizing .blend files is appropriate for organizing both the 3D animatic and for the final production animation.

The *Mercator* project files are organized in this way. The .blend files corresponding to all the shots in the movie are stored in the shots subdirectory of the animatic-3d directory. The naming of the .blend files reflects their scene and shot number, with the scene first, followed by the shot number represented in multiples of 10 (that is, shot 3 is represented as 030). The 3D animatic shot included on the DVD with this book is the eighth shot of the second scene, so its filename is 02-080.blend.

The 3D animatic needs to give a full sense of the blocking, camera angles and movement, and animation timing in a 3D environment as close to the final production scene as possible while still being quick to create and render. As you can see in Figure 3.39, the models and sets are as simple as these requirements allow.

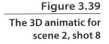

Figure 3.39

The 3D animatic for
scene 2, shot 8

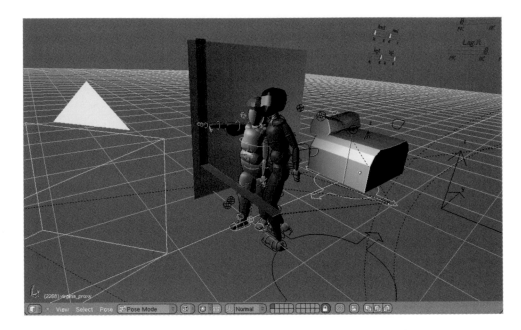

The timing for the 3D animatic is based on the timing of the 2D animatic. Indeed, a primary reason for creating the 2D animatic was to efficiently establish the timing for the movie's animation. Although rough in appearance, the timing of the 2D animatic should be very close to the desired timing of the animation. Likewise, the framing of the 2D animatic should also be a reliable guide for the framing of the 3D animatic. With a well-framed, well-timed 2D animatic as the basis, the work of constructing the 3D animatic is greatly eased.

Blender's 3D viewport background image functionality enables you to refer directly to the 2D animatic on a frame-by-frame basis while constructing the 3D animatic. If you have used background images for modeling, you are familiar with the general idea, but rather than using single still frames, it is possible to use animated sequences. Specifically, the 2D animatic (or rather, the relevant sequence within the 2D animatic) itself will be the background image.

In the example of 02-080.blend, included on the DVD, the entire relevant sequence of the 2D animatic is also included on the disk. You can find these images in the directory Animatic/animatic-2d/render/jpg. The names of these files range from animatica-002269 .jpg to animatica-002374.jpg, representing the span of frames from frame number 2,269 to frame number 2,374. These are the same frames that will be used in the 3D animatic. In this way, the 3D animatic can be synced properly with the 2D animatic, and the rendered frames from the 3D animatic will be numbered to correspond with their place in the full movie.

To add an animated background image while working with a 3D animatic, first enter Camera view by pressing 0 on the number pad. You must be in one of the axis views or in Camera view to see the background image, but for the purposes of using an animatic guide, the meaningful view is Camera view. Select Background Image from the View menu in the 3D viewport header, as shown in Figure 3.40. In the floating window that opens, click Use Background Image and click on the file selection menu to open the file browser. Navigate the browser to the location of the rendered 2D animatic and select the first image of the sequence, animatica-002269.jpg, and then click Select Image. The image will appear in the background, which you can see when you toggle into Wireframe view. Set the values in the Background Image floating window as shown in Figure 3.41: Select Sequence and in the Frames field enter **2374**. Leave the offset (Offs) value at 0 and the start frame (StartFr) value at 1.

With the models in wireframe, you can see the background image clearly in Figure 3.42. Note that the actual current frame of the animation as shown in the Timeline is the same as the frame number displayed on the stamp on the rendered 2D animatic frame. If you skip back to a frame before the earliest image frame, the background image will disappear, and likewise it will disappear if you skip forward to a frame after the end of the sequence.

Figure 3.40

Adding a background image

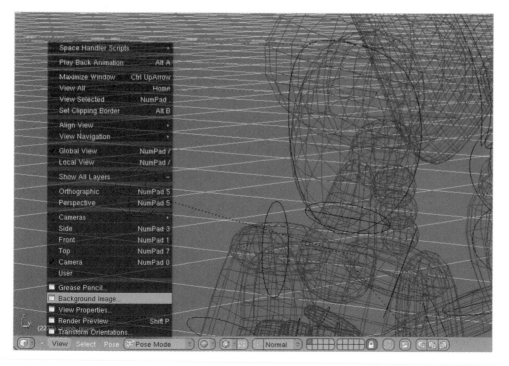

Figure 3.41

Settings for the
background image
sequence

Figure 3.42

The background
image is visible in
wireframe view.

The animation in the 3D animatic is then carried out to follow the timing of the 2D animatics. Although it is composed of just two images, the 2D animatic indicates the point at which the character raises her arm, which is then animated in a smooth but simple 3D animation, as shown in Figure 3.43.

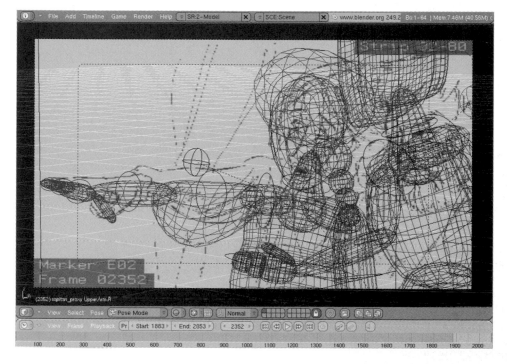

Figure 3.43

The 3D animation follows the timing of the 2D animatic.

The same pair of frames is shown in Figure 3.44 in Textured Display mode to show the way in which the 3D animatic also can be used to capture some of the lighting and atmosphere that will play an increasingly important role in the movie as the production continues. Like modeling, lighting is not the focus here and is rudimentary, but (also as in the case of modeling) it's not too early to get a basic notion of how the lighting will ultimately be set up.

Figure 3.44

The animated gesture shown in Textured Display mode with lighting

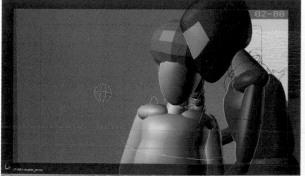

Animating and Rendering the Animatic

The animation used in the 3D animatic is much more rudimentary than what will be used in the final production shots. Nevertheless, the basic techniques are the same. Unlike the 2D animatic, the 3D animatic makes use of much of the key functionality of the Blender animation tool set. Figure 3.45 illustrates the use of actions and the Ipo curves for animating the Virginia armature. In the Action Editor, you can see that there are four key channels: Control, FK_Control, Sliders, and IK_Control. These correspond to four different groups of keyable bones. The Control channel consists of the main control bones, which behave the same whether IK posing or FK posing is activated. In Figure 3.46, this channel is shown unfolded to display the keyed bone channels beneath it.

Figure 3.47 shows the FK_Control, Sliders, and IK_Control channels unfolded to display the names of the bone channels. The bone channels are color coded according to each bone's theme color set. The FK control bones are used to pose the portion of the armature that is set to forward kinematic posing, and the IK control bones are used to pose the part of the armature set to inverse kinematic posing. The Sliders channel contains the keys on the IK/FK sliders themselves, enabling the animator to create smooth transitions between IK posing and FK posing for each limb.

Figure 3.45

Actions and Ipo curves for the 3D animatic

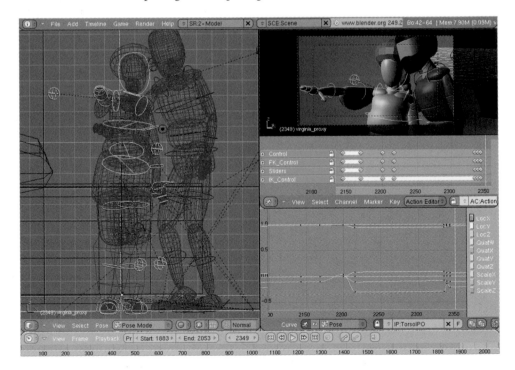

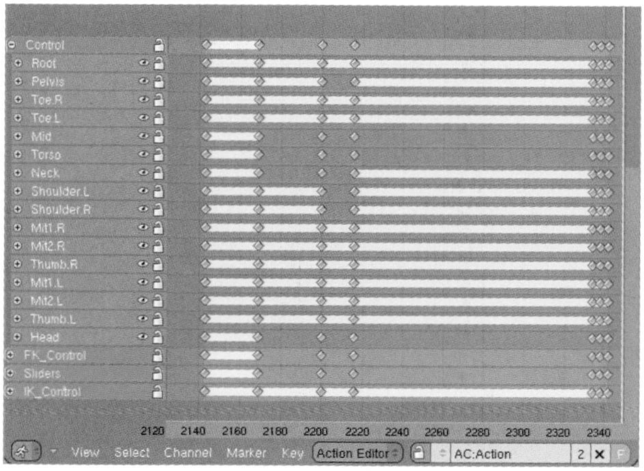

Figure 3.46
Control bone channels

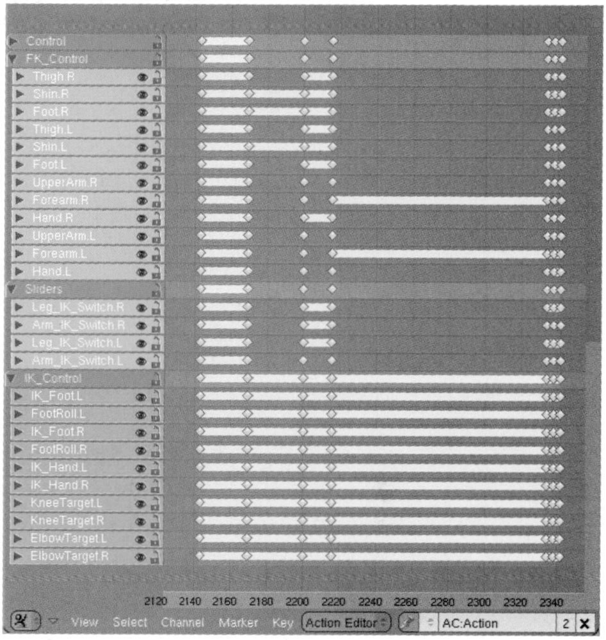

Figure 3.47
FK, Slider, and IK control bone channels

You can drill down even further and open up the individual bone channels to reveal channels for each individual Ipo curve associated with that bone. This enables you to see not only which bones have keys on them, but which specific Ipos are keyed. In Figure 3.48, you can see this view for the right upper arm bone (UpperArm.R) revealing that location, quaternion rotation, and scale have all been keyed. The figure also shows the corresponding Ipo curves themselves in the Ipo Editor. Note the correspondence between keyframes. Some of these keys were clearly not strictly necessary; it's clear that none of the bones change scale, so the scale doesn't really need to be keyed. But the LocRotScale option for keying is a very convenient way to key bone poses and ensure that you have made at least enough Ipos to represent the movement.

The FK/IK sliders enable smooth transitioning from FK to IK style posing and vice versa. This is important to give characters a complete range of posability. As a general rule, limbs that swing or move freely from their base, such as an arm winding up to pitch a baseball, should be posed using FK posing, whereas limbs that are constrained at their tip, such as feet on the ground when a character is walking, should be posed using IK posing. FK enables you to pose your characters similarly to how you pose a doll; moving the upper arm automatically moves the lower arm in a wider arch. IK enables you to pose limbs by placing a target for the limb to reach to, and then calculating the angles and position of the bones of the limb leading from its base to the target. Cases in which a limb goes from constrained to free-swinging or vice versa represent cases in which IK/FK switching is necessary.

Figure 3.48
Ipo view

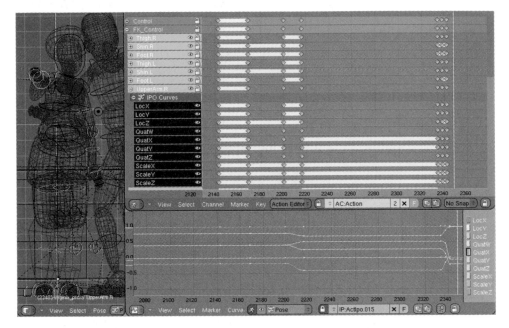

The character movement in Figure 3.49 is a good example of the need for IK/FK switching. In this animation, the character first props herself up on a window sill with her (IK-animated) hand and then steps back, letting her (FK-animated) hand drop to her side. Note the pose of the character, and note the change in position of the slider on the Arm.L IK/FK control in the lower-right window of the figure. Note also that it is the only slider in the Action Editor whose keys are not connected by a thick yellow line, indicating that its value is different between the two keyframes, whereas the values remain constant between the other channels' keyframes.

A final important part of animating a 3D animatic is working with the camera. Framing, camera angle, and the camera's angle of view/focal length must be represented as accurately as possible in the 3D animatic. The camera's movements must also be keyed to give a good indication of how the camera is working with the subjects in the 3D space. You can see two camera positions and the keyframes that unite them in Figure 3.50. In fact, two types of Ipo are shown here. The top Ipo Editor in the figure shows the Object Ipos, which govern the location, rotation, and scale of the camera. The bottom Ipo Editor window shows the Camera values in the drop-down menu. The Camera Ipos show the animation of the camera's angle of view or focal length.

Figure 3.49
FK/IK switching

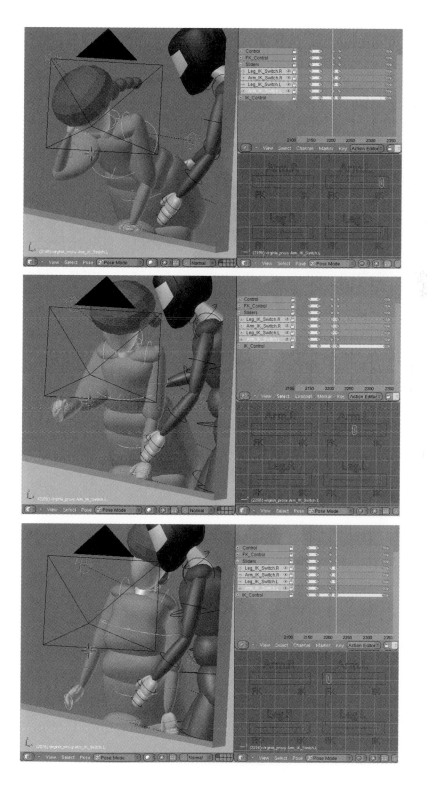

Figure 3.50

Camera animation

In order to keyframe these camera values, simply press the I key over the buttons area with a Camera object selected, which will raise the option box shown in Figure 3.51.

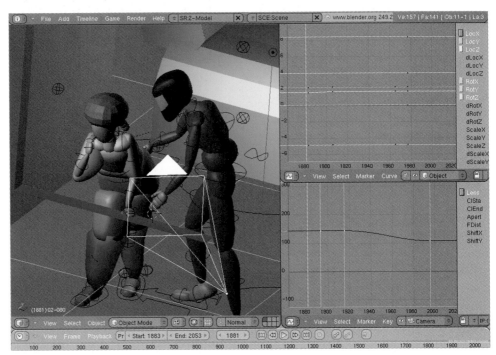

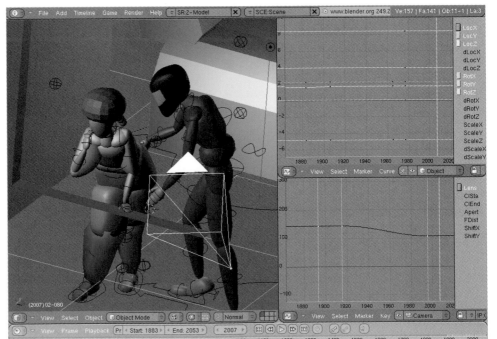

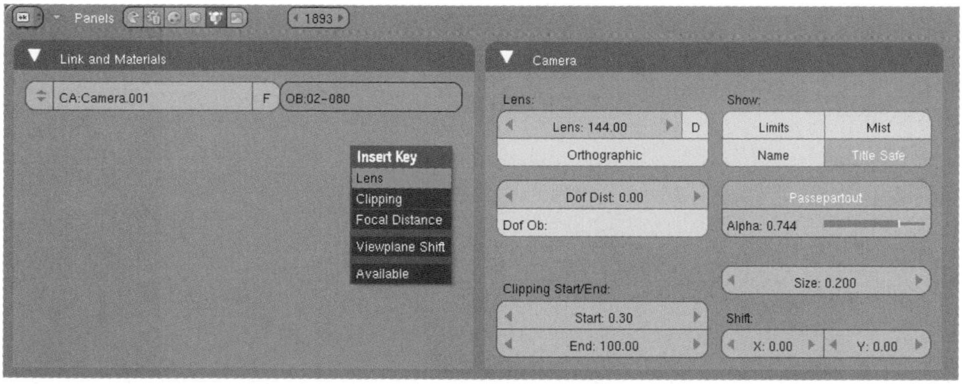

Figure 3.51

**Keying Camera
attributes**

Camera positioning and movement are important parts of conveying drama and emotion in the movies. A 3D animatic is an excellent way to make sure that the camera work, framing, timing, and other aspects of direction are working together to maximize the clarity and impact of the movie's emotional message, because everything is carried out using faceless, emotionless dummies rather than highly animated virtual actors. You might be surprised by the range of emotions that can be expressed by these totally blank dummies, given the right movements of the camera. A slow zoom, a barren long shot, or a close-up on some casual gesture can carry a great deal of resonance even at this raw stage in the production, so never underestimate the importance of the 3D animatic.

In the next chapter, you'll see another necessary step in preparing for a full-fledged animation, namely the mesh modeling of the characters and props.

CHAPTER 4

Modeling

The modeling stage of creating a CG animated movie is where the project really begins to take shape, literally! This chapter follows the development of the *Mercator* production as the mesh models for the characters and props are created. Licuadora Studio uses several interesting techniques for building organic and inorganic models, which are sure to be welcome additions to your workflow.

CHAPTER CONTENTS

- **Organic Modeling Techniques**
- **Cloth and Clothing**
- **Inorganic Modeling**

Organic Modeling Techniques

In Chapter 3, "Creating a 3D Animatic," you looked at how the 3D animatic is made. The 3D animatic is a rough representation of the finished animation, with an emphasis on the relative positions and movements of the characters, props, and camera. Just a quick look at the animatic is enough to see that there is a lot of work left to be done to create the finished product. One of the most obvious things that has not yet been done is modeling. In this chapter, you'll look at some of the methods used to replace the ovoid dummies in Chapter 3 with fully modeled mesh characters like those shown in Figure 4.1.

Modeling Methods

Mesh modeling is a huge topic in itself. Moreover, it is a skill that requires practice and firsthand experience to master. Nevertheless, there are many techniques to learn that will help you to improve your work. Blender has numerous tools that can be employed to create realistic or stylized mesh models. Some of the tools—such as cutting tools, vertex operators, and sculpting—are explicitly regarded as modeling tools. Other tools, such as cloth simulation and armatures, also offer powerful modeling functionality.

Figure 4.1

Rigged mesh models of the captain and Virginia

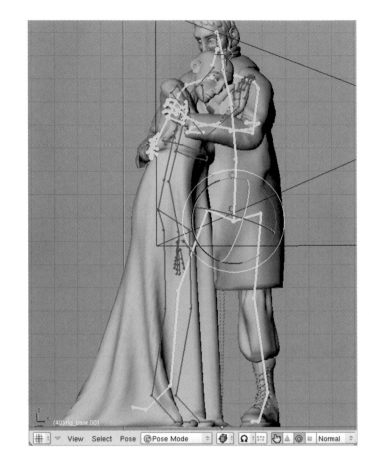

View   Select   Pose   ⊕Pose Mode   Normal

If you haven't done any mesh modeling before, this chapter is not going to be the most fruitful place to start. The focus here is on intermediate and advanced uses of the tools. You can find beginner-friendly introductions to organic character modeling with Blender in *Introducing Character Animation with Blender* (Sybex, 2007) or some of the available online tutorials. Montage Studio's DVD series on modeling the human head and body (http://montagestudio.org/dvds) is also an excellent place to start if you prefer video tutorials. After you understand the basics of Blender modeling, you can learn a great deal from general mesh modeling books and tutorials, such as the *D'Artiste* series from Ballistic Publishing. To learn about using the sculpting functionality in Blender, please refer to my book *Mastering Blender* (Sybex 2009), which includes an in-depth introduction to sculpting, Retopo, and normal map baking. If you are interested in inorganic modeling, an excellent intermediate to advanced resource is Robert Burke's freely available PDF document *Precision Modeling: A Guide to Modeling Parts and Components Accurately Using Blender*, which you can download from the following site:

http://homepage.ntlworld.com/r.burke2/precision_modeling1.html

Blender's mesh modeling functionality can be broadly broken down into three main categories: traditional mesh modeling, in which the modeler directly manipulates vertices, edges, or faces (or selected groups of the same); sculpting, in which the modeler uses tools that operate on the shape of the mesh in a way analogous to clay sculpting, with less or no regard for the underlying topological structure; and the use of modifiers and simulations, which include a wide variety of operators of varying complexity that can be applied to meshes. It's fairly rare that any of these categories of modeling is used entirely on its own. Even in introductory mesh modeling tutorials, modifiers such as the Mirror modifier and the Subsurf (subdivision surface) modifier are used.

Poly-by-Poly and Box Modeling

Traditional mesh modeling is often divided into two styles or categories: poly-by-poly and box modeling. In general, *poly-by-poly* refers to a style of modeling that takes a single vertex or plane as its starting point and extrudes edges and faces from there, gradually building up the shape in that way. *Box modeling*, on the other hand, takes a box or a simple, blocky mesh shape as its starting point and refines the shape by using cutting and smoothing tools and adjusting vertex positions.

A comparison of the two approaches can be seen in Figure 4.2. The first image shows an early point in box-modeling a human head: Loop cutting and the knife tool were used to create the shape from a cube. The second image shows what the same head might look like if the model was begun using poly-by-poly modeling, with an emphasis on extrusion and filling in faces. The distinction is a bit arbitrary, and it is rare that a complex model would be modeled entirely with methods from one or the other style.

At times one approach may be better than another, however. For example, when preparing a mesh to be used as the basis of sculpting, a simple base shape can usually be quickly created using box-modeling techniques. If you plan to sculpt and retopo the model anyway, it would be a waste of effort to do poly-by-poly topology modeling for the

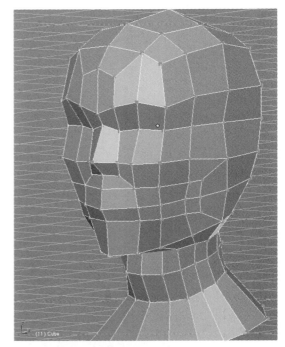

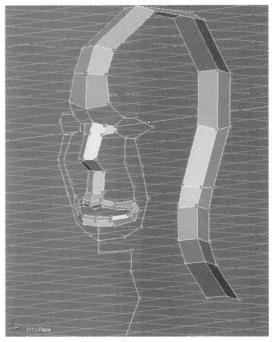

Figure 4.2

The early stages of modeling similar human heads with box modeling and poly-by-poly modeling

base shape. On the other hand, when using the Retopo tool to improve the topology of a sculpted mesh, a poly-by-poly approach may be the only option that will give you sufficient control over the placement of vertices.

The operators accessible via the Mesh Specials menu (W key in Edit mode) all fall into the category of traditional mesh modeling tools.

Sculpting

Blender's sculpting functionality enables very direct and intuitive modeling, particularly when coupled with a pen tablet or tablet monitor interface, as shown in Figure 4.3 (the model shown is not from the *Mercator* project). When sculpting, the user uses the pointing device (ideally a stylus, but the mouse can also be used) to affect the surface of the 3D object by depressing it, pulling it, pinching it, inflating it, smoothing it, or carrying out any of several other operations.

Figure 4.3

Sculpting with a pen tablet monitor

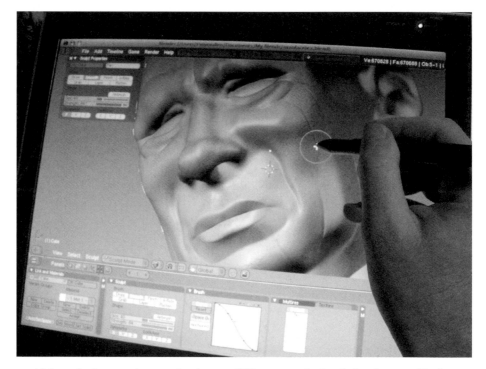

Although the user interaction is very different, sculpting is fundamentally the same as traditional mesh modeling in that it is basically the manipulation of vertices. For this reason, finely sculpted detail requires a very dense mesh. When sculpting, edge-loop topology is far less important than sheer vertex density. This is at odds with the needs of many other areas of functionality such as animation, rendering, simulations, and indeed traditional modeling, which all favor less-dense meshes with better-organized topology. This is dealt with in Blender in two ways: First, multiresolution modeling can be used to add levels of topological density in a nondestructive way. Second, the retopo and normal map baking workflow described in detail in *Mastering Blender* enables the appearance of finely sculpted detail to be transferred from a dense model to a lower-poly mesh in the form of a normal map texture.

Figure 4.4 shows a new mesh being created over the sculpted mesh by using the Retopo tool. The resulting mesh is less detailed than the original sculpted mesh, as you can see in Figure 4.5, but by baking a normal map from the sculpted object and using it as a texture for the new mesh, you can achieve the appearance of a very similar level of detail, as shown in Figure 4.6.

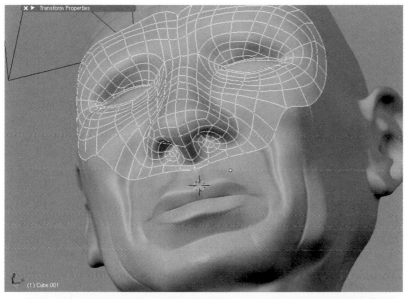

Figure 4.4

Using the Retopo tool to create a deformable mesh

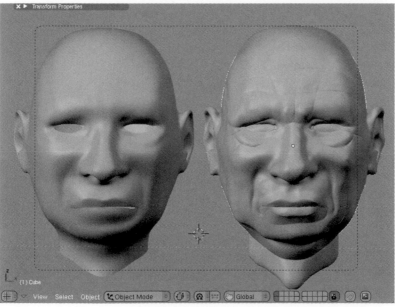

Figure 4.5

The retopo mesh and the original sculpted mesh

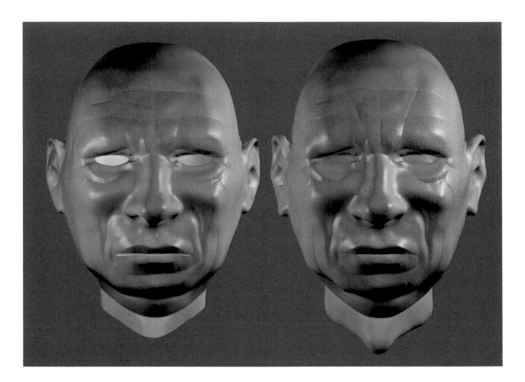

Modifiers and Simulations

The third category of mesh modeling includes the operators available in the modifier stack, shown in Figure 4.7. Modifiers take a mesh as an input and alter it in some nondestructive way. The modifier stack applies modifiers in a linear fashion; the output of one modifier is the input to the next modifier.

Commonly used modifiers in modeling include the Mirror modifier, which mirrors the mesh along a chosen axis or set of axes, and the Subsurf modifier, which subdivides the mesh in a nondestructive way, commonly to round off the corners of a mesh. Other modifiers include Armature modifiers, which represent armature deformation as an operation on the modifier stack, cloth and soft body simulations, Array modifiers, Smooth modifiers, and Cast modifiers, which force the mesh to conform to varying degrees to some target shape. All of these can be used for modeling. You'll see an example of using cloth simulation in conjunction with an armature to model realistic clothing later in this chapter.

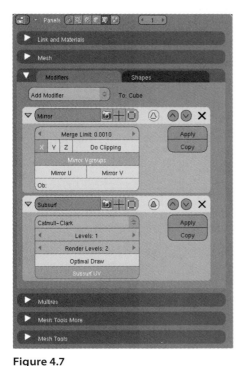

Figure 4.7

The modifier stack with a Mirror modifier and
a Subsurf modifier active

Topology

In mesh modeling terminology, two terms are often used to refer to the structure of a mesh. The *geometry* of the mesh refers to the locations of the vertices. Modifiers and matrix transformations use this information to generate new mesh geometry, altering the size, shape, or location of the mesh's parts. The *topology* of the mesh refers to how the vertices are connected by edges and faces.

Topology is often more important than it looks. It is possible for two 3D objects that appear the same to have different underlying topological structures to their meshes. The different topologies may not matter if the mesh does not deform, but for animation it is often necessary for meshes to deform. The wrong topology can make deformations problematic. This focus on topology is one difference between organic modeling, for which deformable topology is often vital, and inorganic modeling, for which objects are less likely to need to deform.

An excellent discussion of mesh topology by Alexander Martis (Toontje) can be found at the following site:

```
http://blenderartists.org/forum/showthread.php?t=93651
```

This discussion includes lucid explanations and clear illustrations of key concepts. Several of the ideas brought up in those threads are central to the following discussion, and we highly recommend that anybody interested in mesh modeling spend some time with that thread.

Vertices, Edges, and Faces

Vertices form the geometric foundation of 3D objects. Vertices are connected to one another by edges, and edges can be connected by faces. In Blender 2.49, faces can be made up of three or four vertices. The former are called triangles, or *tris*, and the latter are typically referred to as *quads*.

Tris and quads have different areas of functionality. In real-time graphics, tris are the norm because they provide the most basic geometric representations of planes. In offline rendered graphics such as animated movies, quads are preferred because Catmull-Clark subdivision performs better on quads than on tris. Catmull-Clark subdivision (available in Blender as the default option for the Subsurf modifier) is an important method of creating rounded surfaces out of sharply angled meshes, without too much added computational expense. Although the algorithm works on triangles, the results are more appealing when the model is made up primarily of quads.

You don't always need to avoid triangles, and by the same token, modeling with quads will not necessarily result in acceptable subsurfacing and deformations. You should limit the use of triangles to areas of the mesh that will not have much visible deformation, and the triangles should be as uniformly proportioned as possible. Likewise, deformations work best when quads are roughly the same size and proportionately shaped. This also facilitates texturing by making it easier to create seams and unwrap the mesh to UV coordinates and simplifying the process of texture painting. Carefully arranged quad topology also can help to map procedural textures uniformly and to reduce stretching of UV textures. Avoid creating meshes with many long, narrow quads or with too much drastic variation in quad sizes.

Poles

Vertices where three, five, or any number greater than five edges meet are known as *poles*. Figure 4.8 shows examples of poles with three edges (three-poles) highlighted in orange with the Grease Pencil tool, and poles with five edges (five-poles) highlighted in green. Poles are unavoidable in modeling; all closed meshes have poles. It's important to be aware of them, however, because poorly placed poles can cause problems for deformation and subsurfacing. Furthermore, a good understanding of poles and how to work with them will give you more control over the loop flow of your models.

As a rule, avoid placing poles in areas where you plan to have a lot of mesh deformation, and avoid having multiple poles placed too close together. There are a few tricks for eliminating poles or moving them around.

Figure 4.8

A simple mesh with three-poles (highlighted in orange) and five-poles (highlighted in green)

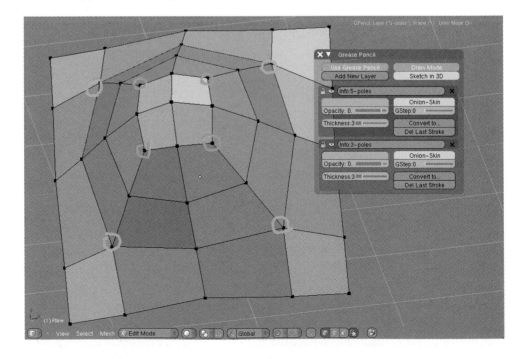

Loops

Loops are unbroken, nonforking strips in the geometry of a mesh. There are two basic kinds of loops: edge loops and face loops. An edge loop is a series of edges connected end to end with each edge crossing exactly two edges at each vertex. You can think of an edge loop as a road with nothing but four-way intersections. An example of a cyclic edge loop is shown in Figure 4.9. Despite the word *loop*, edge loops needn't be cyclic. In the noncyclic case, an edge loop extends to the edge of a mesh (or to a hole in the mesh), as shown in Figure 4.10, or to a pole, as shown in Figure 4.11. You can select edge loops by holding the Alt key and right-clicking on a single edge in the edge loop. An edge loop on a human head is shown in Figure 4.12. Note how it follows the form of the model.

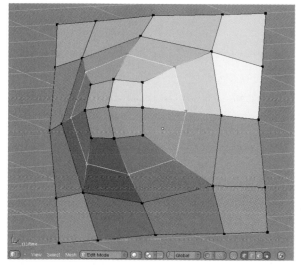

Figure 4.9
An edge loop

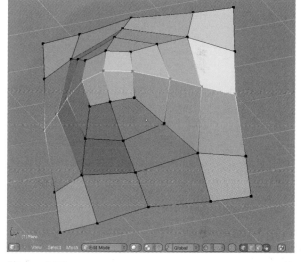

Figure 4.10
An edge loop ending at the edge of the mesh

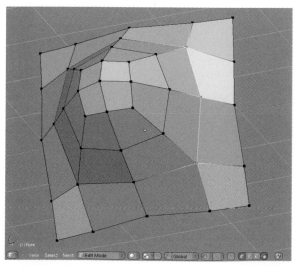

Figure 4.11
An edge loop ending at two five-poles

Figure 4.12

An edge loop
on a model of a
human head

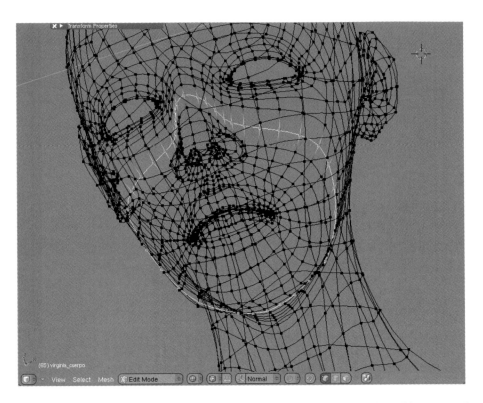

A face loops is a sequence of faces; each vertex in a face loop is shared by two and only two faces in the loop. An example of a cyclic face loop is shown in Figure 4.13. Like edge loops, face loops are not necessarily cyclic. Figure 4.14 shows a face loop that extends to the edges of the mesh. Figure 4.15 shows another face loop at the edge of the mesh. Note that the face loop does not extend around the corners of the mesh here. The vertices on the inner corner of the four corner faces are shared among more than two faces each (they are five-poles), so this is not a cyclic face loop. A face loop on a model of a human face is shown in Figure 4.16.

Figure 4.13

A cyclic face loop

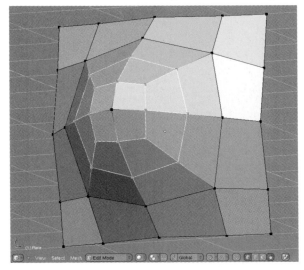

The importance of loops in organic modeling is hard to overstate. Loops enable you not only to control the base shape of your model, but also to control how the model deforms when it is animated. In organic modeling, loops are sometimes referred to as *muscle loops* because having loops follow the shape of the subject's muscles is the best way to ensure natural deformations. For this reason, a basic knowledge of anatomy is particularly valuable when modeling for animation. You can see in Figure 4.17 several face loops highlighted on a human head model. These loops are arranged to ensure smooth and natural deformations for facial animation.

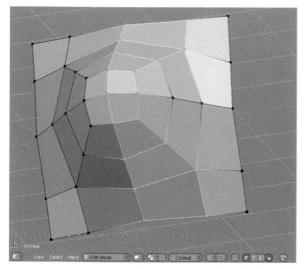

Figure 4.14

A face loop extending to the edges of the mesh

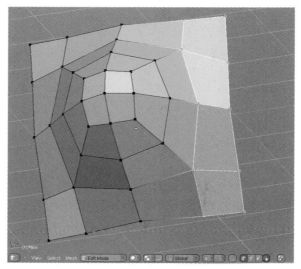

Figure 4.15

A noncyclic face loop

Figure 4.16

A face loop on a human face

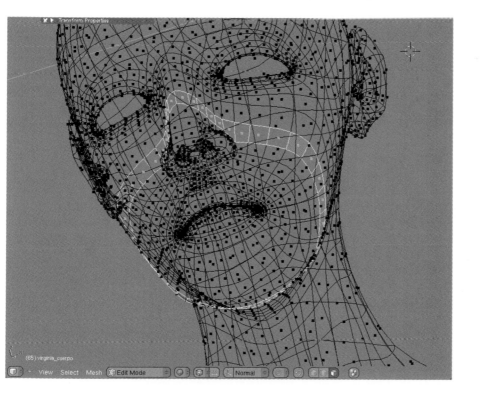

Figure 4.17

Well-placed face loops should follow the expected deformations of the face.

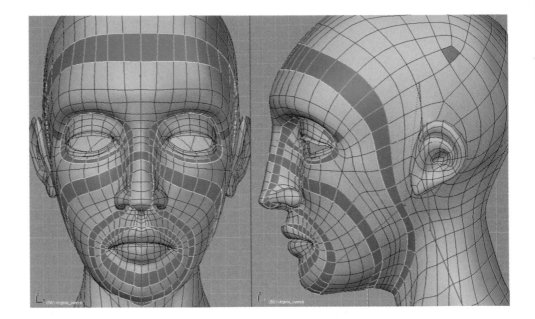

Poles and loops interact in important ways. If you master working with poles so that you can place them where you want them on a mesh, you will also find that you can easily control exactly where your loops are. An in-depth treatment of working with poles and loops is beyond the scope of this book, but the BlenderArtists.org discussion thread mentioned previously contains a wealth of information on this topic. The thread has also been made available as a PDF document, thanks to Yves Poissant, and is available as a download in the forum thread itself and also at www.tonymullen.com/PolesAndLoops.pdf. Anybody who wants to get serious about organic modeling should study this valuable document.

Retopo

The Retopo function enables you to re-create the shape of a mesh by using new topology. As mentioned previously, this is very useful when dealing with sculpted meshes. It is also useful for improving the topology of models created by traditional modeling means. A modeler may choose to do a "quick-and-dirty" model the first time through, focusing on getting the shape of the model just the way it should be, without worrying about the proper deformability of the mesh for animation. Later, the modeler can use this original mesh as a target mesh for editing a new retopo mesh. The model from *Mercator* in Figure 4.18, for example, is the basic shape of the head mesh for the captain character. It was originally modeled without a great deal of attention to the flow of the edge loops. Using Retopo, a new mesh with more carefully positioned poles and loops can be created, as shown in Figure 4.19.

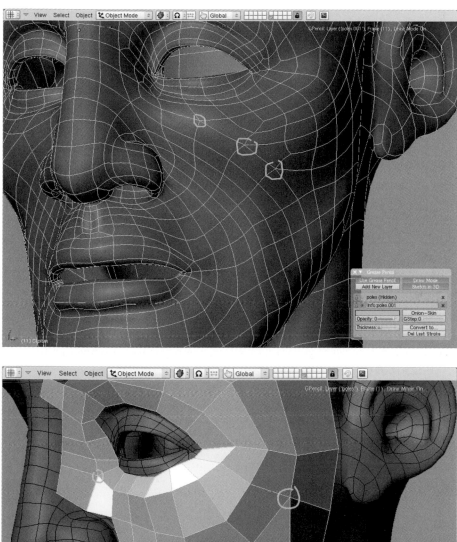

Figure 4.18
The original base model of the captain's face

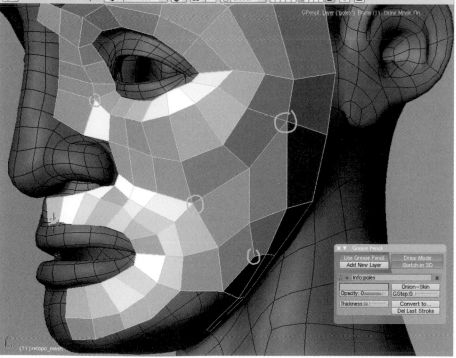

Figure 4.19
Improved topology with Retopo

In order to use Retopo, you need to create a new Mesh object. Position the center of the new object at the same place as the center of the original Mesh object, whose shape you want to re-create. You'll be editing the new mesh in Edit mode, and you can begin by simply deleting all of the vertices. In Figure 4.20, the sphere is the original mesh, and the mesh being edited is the retopo mesh. The Retopo option must be activated in the Mesh buttons panel, as highlighted in the figure. Also, X-ray should be selected in the Draw panel of the Edit buttons area. This makes the mesh visible. Otherwise, the vertices will be visible at the surface of the target mesh, but the edges of the retopo mesh will be concealed beneath the surface of the target mesh.

Figure 4.20

Settings for working with Retopo

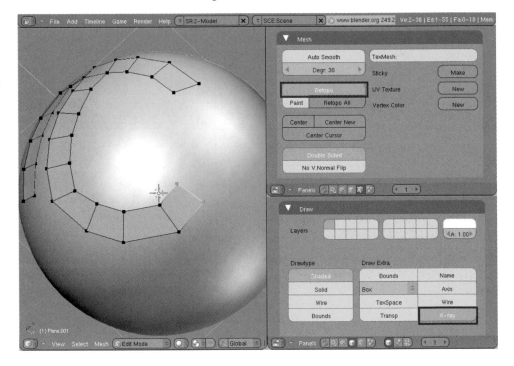

Cloth and Clothing

Creating clothing for animated characters is a very important and often poorly understood aspect of organic modeling. Furthermore, in addition to the traditional mesh tools at your disposal in Blender, you also have a powerful cloth simulation solver, which is capable of creating highly realistic cloth perturbations with relatively little effort. It's important to understand how to get the most of it.

Some clothing articles are best modeled in the traditional way. A good example of this is the boot model shown in Figure 4.21. Boots are stiff objects and can be best modeled by hand, and then rigged directly to the armature. Other items of clothing, such as the dress in Figure 4.22, may require a cloth simulation to be active on at least part of the mesh during the entire time they are animated. The flowing portions of the dress need to be accurately responsive to each movement of the character.

When animating cloth simulation, there are several issues to be aware of. You need to ensure that any potential areas of penetration are avoided or concealed. You need to make sure that the movement of the cloth is doing what you want it to, and avoid wrong behaviors such as the cloth squirming when it should be resting motionlessly. Finally, you need to be prepared to bake full-quality simulations for every animated sequence involving the cloth, which can be resource intensive. If that's what it takes to animate the clothing object the way you need it, then that's what it takes. But in many cases, it's not necessary.

Figure 4.21
Stiff clothing articles such as boots can be rigged as normal.

The most common kind of clothing resides somewhere between these two extremes. Most clothing is made of cloth, after all, and has characteristic wrinkles and perturbations whenever it is worn. However, the perturbations in ordinary-to-tight-fitting clothing do not change drastically in response to a character's movement. The wrinkles behind the knee in a pair of jeans, for example, do not substantially change their arrangement when a person's knee bends. The captain's clothing shown in Figure 4.23 is also an example. You can take advantage of this by using Blender's cloth simulation functionality not as an animation tool but as a modeling tool. Using cloth simulation, you can create a static mesh that can be rigged in the ordinary way, resulting in highly realistic clothing without the extra challenges of animated cloth simulation.

Figure 4.22

A flowing dress may need cloth simulation frames baked for each animated sequence.

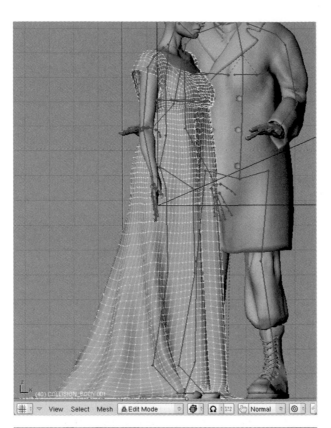

Figure 4.23

Cloth deforms, but the wrinkles maintain their general arrangement.

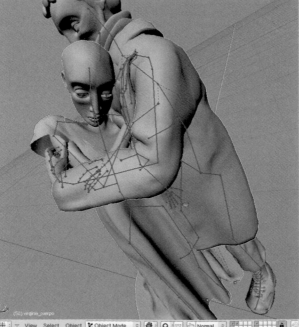

One trick that the *Mercator* team has made considerable use of in creating clothing is to model clothing piece by piece, almost as might be done when actually sewing clothing, and then stitch it together in a separate modeling phase. In this way, rather than model an entire shirt at once, cloth simulation and all, the team would model sleeves separately from the torso portion of the shirt, and then put them together afterward. For modeling purposes, a dummy body model is used to get the shape right. When the final model is rigged, the underlying body rig is deleted, and the clothing makes up the hull of the model.

The following tutorial will show you how to use cloth simulation along with an armature-rigged base body mesh (in this case, just an arm) to create a sleeve. You can extrapolate what you learn here to create the rest of a shirt or any other piece of clothing.

In order to follow the steps, you'll need to prepare a bit. If you don't want to model and rig the base mesh and armature yourself, you can append the group Arm_Rig from the file arm_sleeve.blend found on the DVD that accompanies this book. If you are comfortable with basic mesh modeling and rigging and would prefer to model and rig the starting point yourself, refer to Figure 4.24 for the topology used. Your model doesn't need to be identical, but it should be a nicely modeled arm that will deform well. Note that the polygons are fairly uniform in their size and proportions. The armature used is shown in Figure 4.25. Parent the mesh to the armature and select Create from Bone Heat, as shown in Figure 4.26. The arm should deform nicely, as shown in Figure 4.27. To minimize clutter, put the armature in Stick View mode by selecting Stick under Display Options on the Armature buttons panel, shown in Figure 4.28. If you're working from the file, the mesh is on layer 10 and the armature is on layer 20. The mesh is already parented to the armature, and the armature is visible in Stick View mode.

Figure 4.24

Three views of an arm model

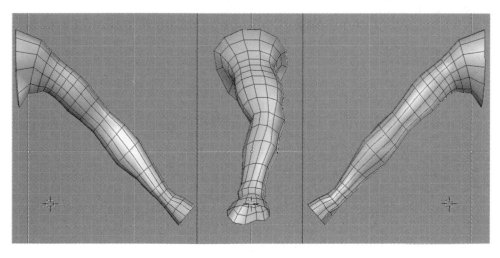

Figure 4.25

Figure 4.25

Adding an armature

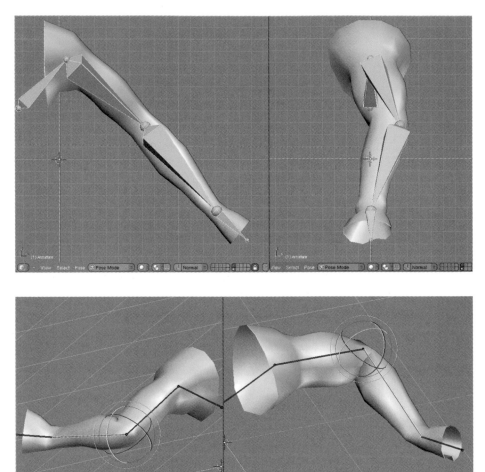

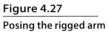

Figure 4.26

Rigging the arm with bone heat-based weights

Figure 4.27

Posing the rigged arm

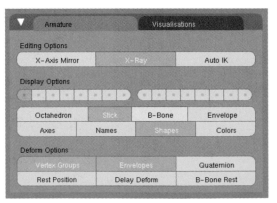

Figure 4.28

Settings for the armature

After you've either appended the group or modeled and rigged an arm of your own, follow these steps to create the shirt sleeve:

1. The sleeve will begin its life as a lowly cylinder. Add a cylinder to the scene by pressing Shift+A and choosing Add → Mesh → Cylinder from the menu, as shown in Figure 4.29. Make it eight vertices around by editing the Vertices field, and ensure that Cap Ends is not selected in the dialog box, as shown in Figure 4.30. Then click OK. [AU: Just a style issue; reserve "press" for the keyboard. CE]The cylinder should appear something along the lines of Figure 4.31. If you placed it somewhere other than at the center of the Armature object, press Alt+G and Alt+R to clear any translation and rotation. In this particular example, it doesn't matter much whether all the objects have their centers at the same place, but it's a good habit to get into. There's no reason these objects should have their centers scattered around.

2. Tab into Edit mode. Select all the vertices of the mesh by pressing the A key. Then rotate the cylinder by pressing the R key followed by the Z key and entering **90**. Press the G key and move the cylinder so that it begins at the shoulder, as shown in Figure 4.32. Scale as necessary by pressing the S key. Select the rightmost loop of the cylinder and translate, rotate, and scale it to where the wrist is, as shown in Figure 4.33.

3. Press the K key to bring up the Loop/Cut menu and select Loop Cut, as shown in Figure 4.34 (this can also be accessed with Ctrl+R). Use your mouse wheel to increase the number of cuts, as shown in Figure 4.35. This example uses eight cuts, but the important thing is to try to keep the polygons close to evenly sized squares. When you finalize the loop cut, the mesh will look as shown in Figure 4.36.

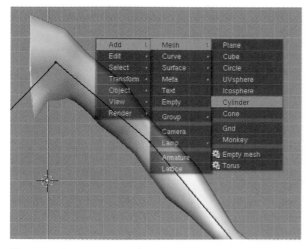

Figure 4.29
Adding a cylinder

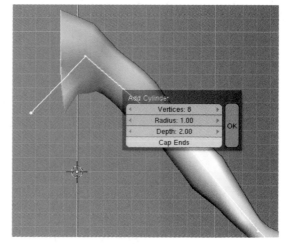

Figure 4.30
Parameters for the cylinder

Figure 4.31

The new
cylinder mesh

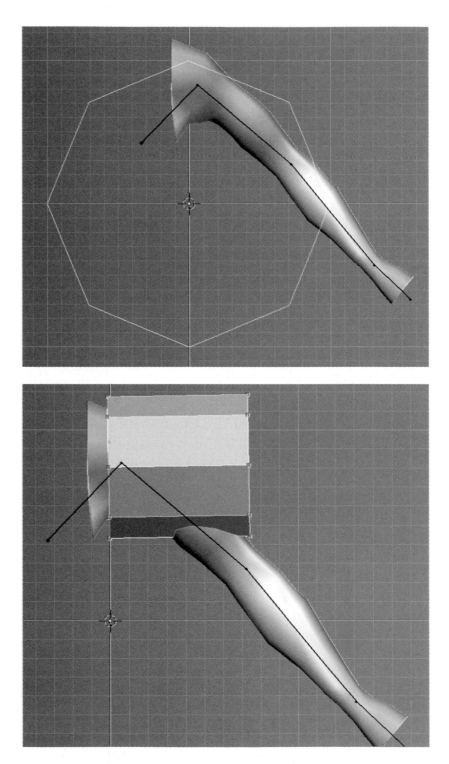

Figure 4.32

Rotating, scaling,
and placing the
cylinder

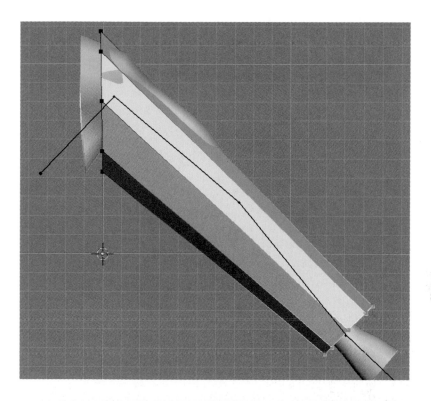

Figure 4.33

Extending the cylinder into a sleeve shape

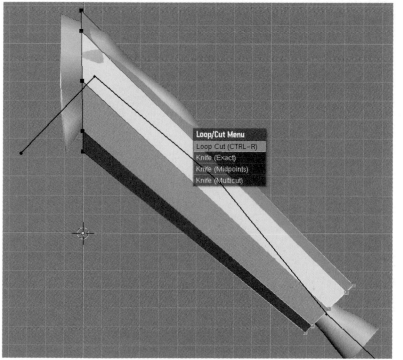

Figure 4.34

Activating the Loop Cut tool

Figure 4.35

Adjusting for
multiple cuts

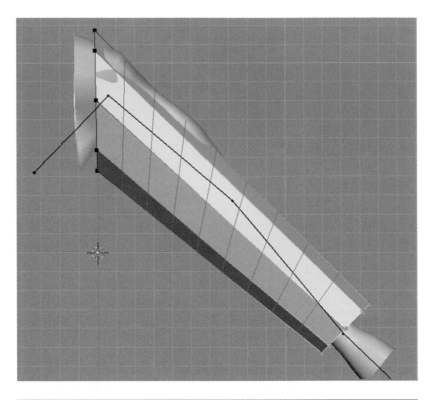

Figure 4.36

The mesh with new
loops cut

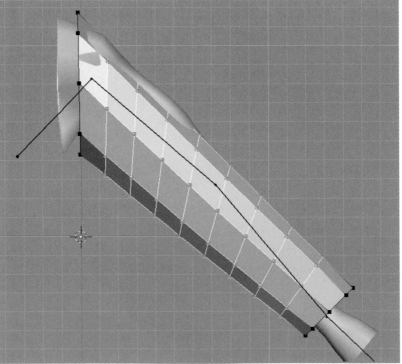

4. Turn on proportional editing by selecting it the 3D viewport header menu, as shown in Figure 4.37. Select some loops in the middle of the sleeve and translate them as shown in Figure 4.38. Adjust the influence range of the Proportional Editing tool displayed as a circle) by using the mouse wheel. The goal here is to ensure that the sleeve covers the arm without penetration. Move the loops as necessary to get the results shown in Figure 4.39.

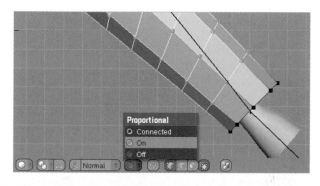

Figure 4.37

Activating proportional editing

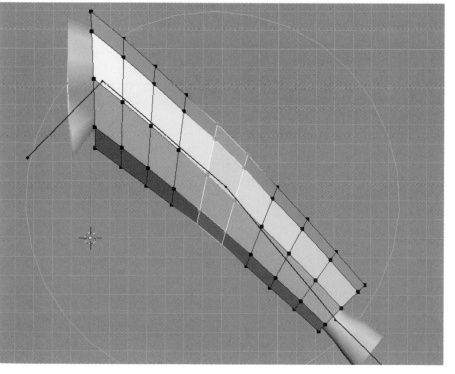

Figure 4.38

Adjusting the mesh with proportional editing

Figure 4.39

The adjusted sleeve mesh, without penetration from the arm

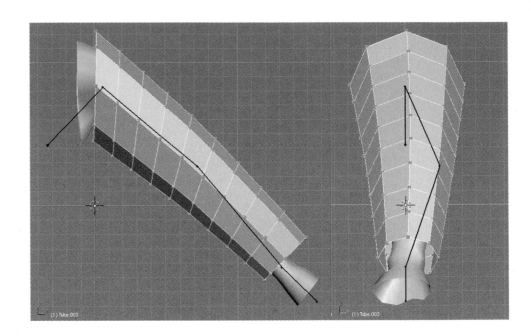

5. Go to the Add Modifier menu on the Modifiers tab, shown in Figure 4.40. Select Shrinkwrap from that menu, as shown in Figure 4.41. The Shrinkwrap modifier panel appears, as shown in Figure 4.42. In the Ob field, enter the name of the arm object, in this case **Arm**. Increase the value of Offset. This value determines the distance from the surface of the target mesh (the arm itself) to the shrinkwrapped mesh (the sleeve). This will directly impact how tightly or loosely the sleeve fits. The resulting modified mesh should look something like Figure 4.43. Apply the modifier by clicking the Apply button on the Modifiers panel.

6. Model the shoulder seam and the cuff of the sleeve by hand. Use the E key to extrude, and S, G, and R keys to scale, translate, and rotate as appropriate. The shoulder seam should look similar to Figure 4.44. The cuff should look like Figure 4.45.

Figure 4.40

The Modifiers panel

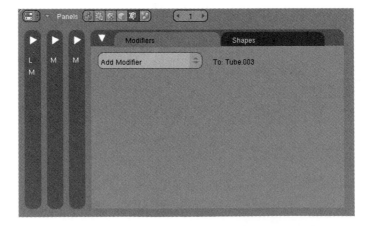

Figure 4.41
Adding a Shrinkwrap modifier

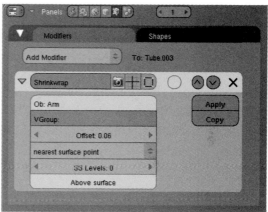

Figure 4.42
Settings for the Shrinkwrap modifier

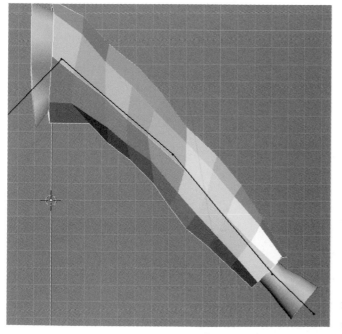

Figure 4.43
The Shrinkwrap-modified
sleeve mesh

Figure 4.44

Editing the shoulder
seam by hand

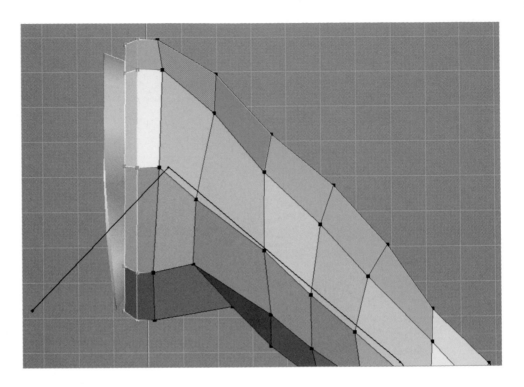

Figure 4.45

Modeling the cuff of
the sleeve

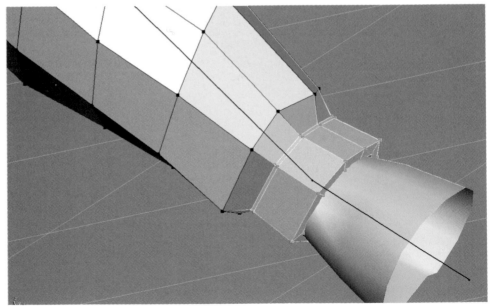

7. The shoulder seam and the cuff area cling to the body and should be completely static. Neither area should be affected by the cloth simulation. To ensure this, you'll use a vertex group to pin the cloth when the time comes. Now, you need to create the vertex group. On the Link and Materials panel shown in Figure 4.46, click New under Vertex Groups. Name the new vertex group **Cloth**. Select the second loop from the shoulder seam and then enter a value of **0.50** in the Weight field and click Assign, as shown in Figure 4.47. Select the topmost loop of the sleeve (the seam loop itself) and the entire cuffs and assign them a weight of **1.0**, as shown in Figure 4.48. To check your weights, enter Weight Paint mode from the menu on the 3D viewport header. You should see the mesh displayed, as shown in Figure 4.49. Most of the mesh is blue, but the cuff and the shoulder seam are red. The loop nearest the shoulder seam is green.

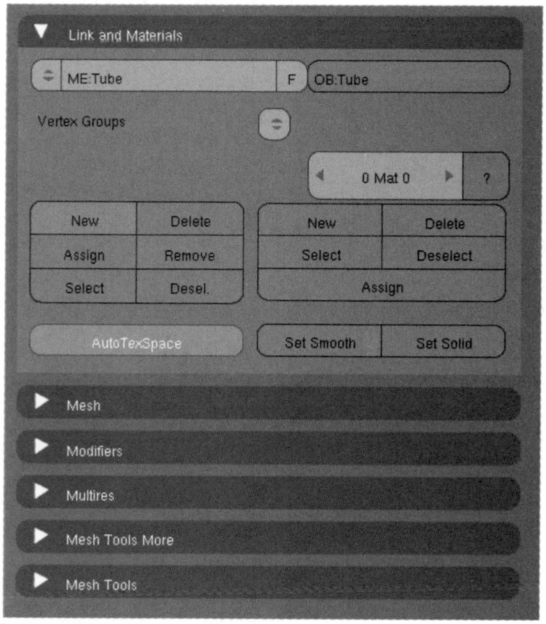

Figure 4.46
The Link and Materials panel

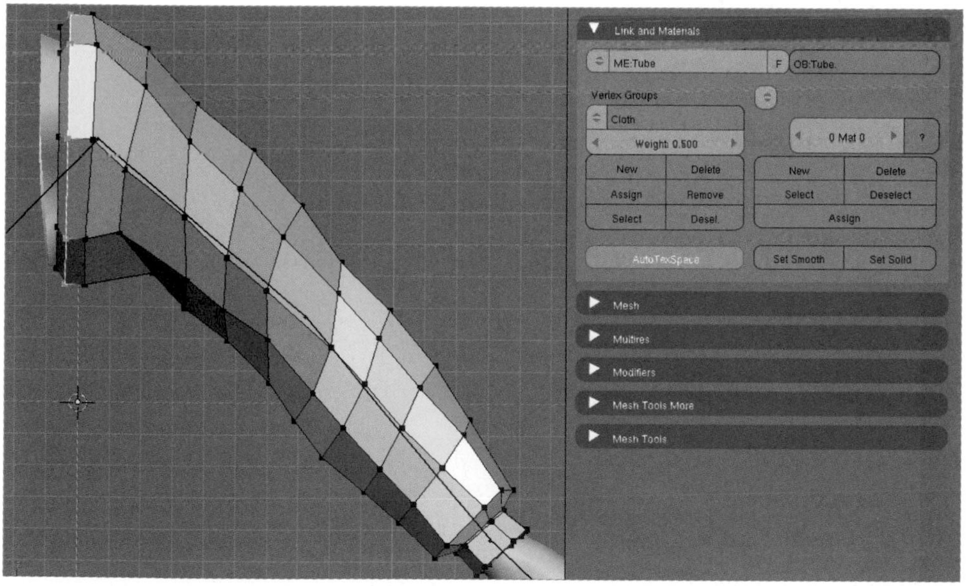

Figure 4.47
Setting vertex weights for the loop near the seam

Figure 4.48

Setting vertex
weights for the
seam and the cuff

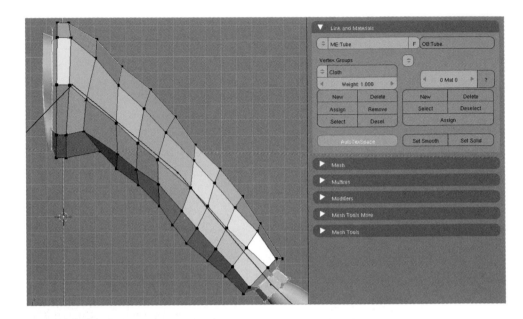

Figure 4.49

The sleeve in Weight
Paint mode

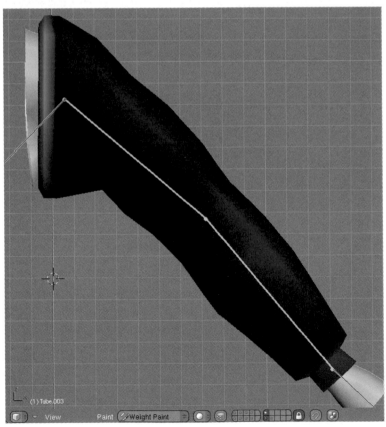

8. Enter Object mode and rig the sleeve. Select the sleeve and the armature (in that order), press Ctrl+P to create the parent relationship, select Armature as shown in Figure 4.50, and choose Create Vertex Groups from Bone Heat, just as you did previously with the arm itself (if you rigged your own). The sleeve can now be posed with the armature.

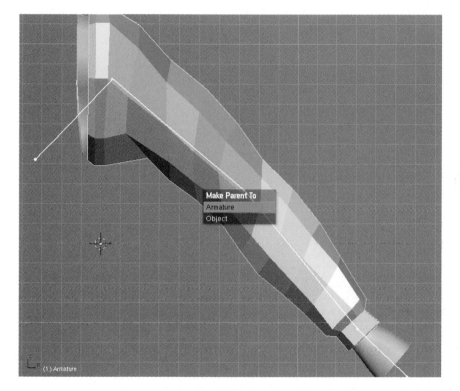

Figure 4.50

Rigging the sleeve

9. A good way to get interesting-looking cloth wrinkles is to run the cloth simulation over a posed model set up as an obstacle to the cloth. The cloth effects can be even more dynamic and convincing if, rather than using a statically posed model, you animate the model into the pose and let the cloth simulation play out over the animated mesh. To do this in this example, animate the arms from the outstretched pose shown in Figure 4.51 to the bent-arm pose shown in Figure 4.52. You'll want to have an Action Editor open to see the locations of your keyframes. Pose the bones in frame 1 and press the I key to keyframe location and rotation. Then pose the bones again in about frame 60. This will ensure that the motion is slow enough to prevent any unnecessary problems with cloth penetration, even at low cloth-quality settings.

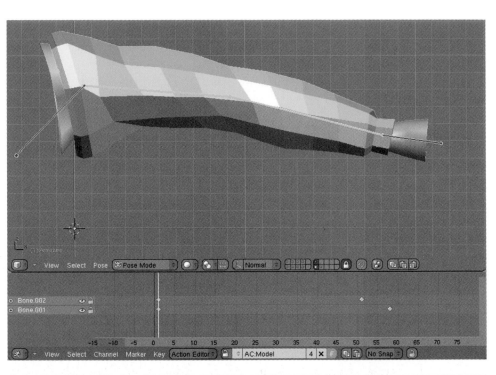

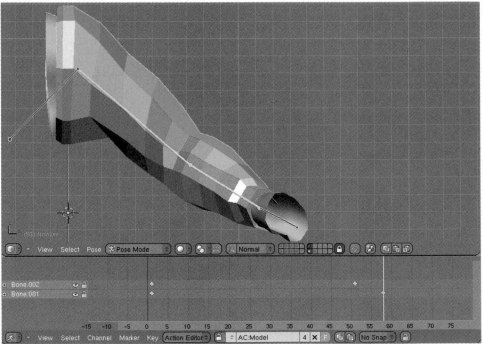

10. Add a Subsurf modifier, as shown in Figure 4.53. Set the Levels value to 2, as shown in Figure 4.54. Click Set Smooth on the Link and Materials buttons panel to give the model a smooth surface. The Subsurf modifier is important. The cloth simulation will work on the subsurfed mesh vertices, giving it much more detail than you would get with an un-subsurfed mesh. If you want even more detail in your cloth simulation, you can set the Levels even higher, but this will slow down the cloth simulation.

11. Set the arm object to be a Collision object on the Collision panel in the Physics buttons area, as shown in Figure 4.55. You can leave the default values as they are. This will ensure that the arm behaves as an obstacle for the cloth, so that the cloth will conform to the shape of the arm. Without this setting, the sleeve would fall right through the arm.

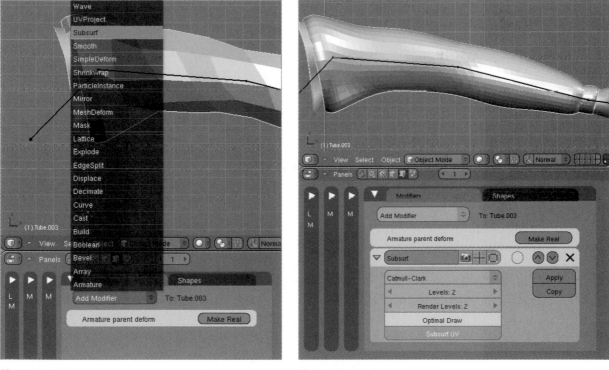

Figure 4.53
Activating the Subsurf modifier

Figure 4.54
Settings for the Subsurf modifier

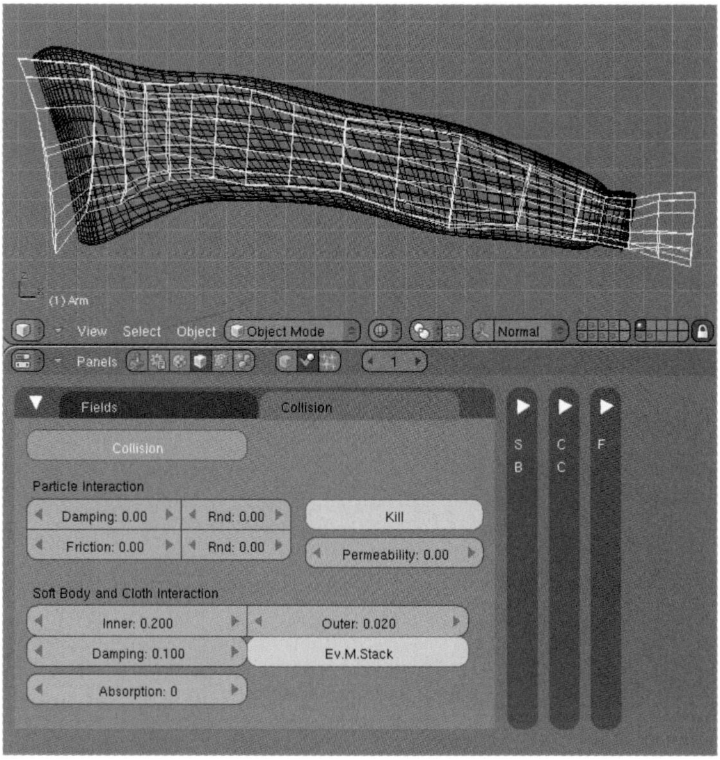

Figure 4.55

Setting the arm as a
Collision object

12. Select the sleeve and activate cloth simulation by clicking the Cloth button in the Cloth panel in the Physics buttons area, as shown in Figure 4.56. You can leave the defaults for the parameter values. Activate Pinning of Cloth and select the Cloth vertex group. This will ensure that only the portions of the mesh that were blue in the previous Weight Paint view are enabled as cloth simulations. Turn to the Collision tab, shown in Figure 4.57. Baking for 250 frames is a waste of time here, so set an End value that's just a second or so past the end of the arm animation, at around frame 80. For this specific example, you probably won't need to activate self-collision at the bottom of this panel. However, if you have a looser sleeve than the one in the example, or if you are working at a higher subsurf level, it's possible that the cloth could collide with itself. If this happens and Enable Selfcollisions is not activated, the cloth will pass right through itself. Don't activate self-collision unless you need it, but if you get self-penetration problems with the cloth, then activate it. When you have the settings as you want them, click Bake to bake the cloth simulation. This will take some time, so be patient. Figure 4.58 shows the mesh at various points along the bake process. Notice that the arm is bending according to the armature animation, and that the cloth is following it naturally. It's important to remember that the Collision object and the Cloth object must be on the same layer, or else they won't collide at all.

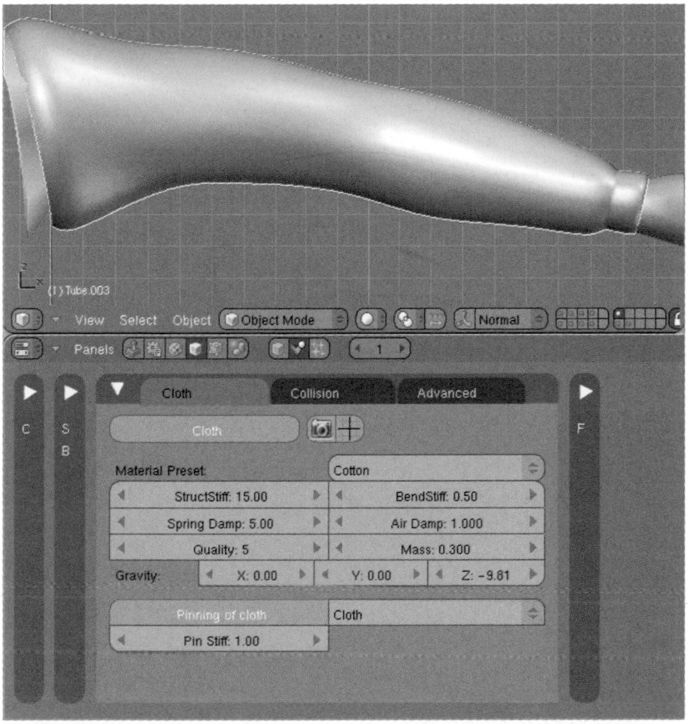

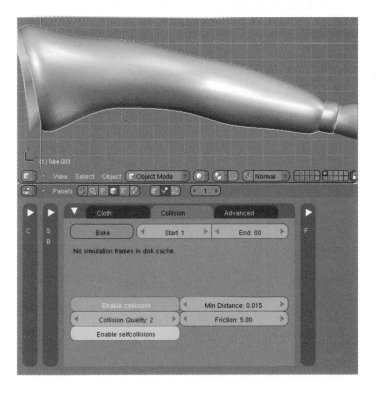

Figure 4.56

Cloth simulation
settlngs

Figure 4.57

Collision panel
settings

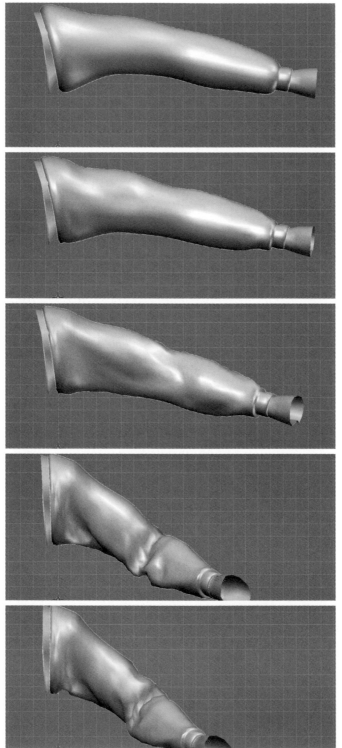

Figure 4.58
Baking the cloth

13. After the cloth simulation is baked, you should be able to move back and forth along the Timeline at normal speed and see the mesh at the corresponding state in the cloth simulation. The simulation frames have all been saved, so they can be quickly accessed without further computation. The simulation, however, is appropriate only for this specific animated shot. Now is where you will use the simulation to create a new static mesh model. Making sure you're in Object mode with the sleeve object selected, choose Scripts → Apply Deformation from the Object menu in the 3D viewport header, as shown in Figure 4.59. This will create a new static, unmodified mesh with the same shape as the modified, cloth simulation mesh you selected. For illustrative purposes, the new mesh is shown side by side with the old mesh in Figure 4.60. You don't need to move the new mesh, but you should put it on a separate layer so you can work with it without worrying about the old cloth sim mesh. Do that by pressing the M key and choosing a new layer for the object from the layer buttons dialog that comes up. Do the same thing for the arm object; apply the transformation and the new arm mesh to a separate layer.

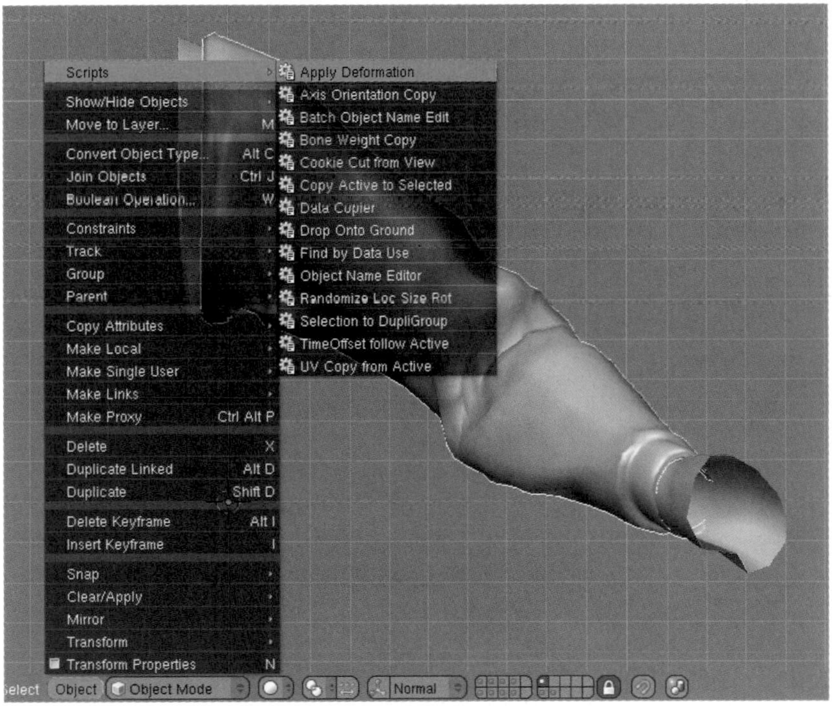

Figure 4.59

Running the Apply Deformation script

Figure 4.60

The newly
created mesh

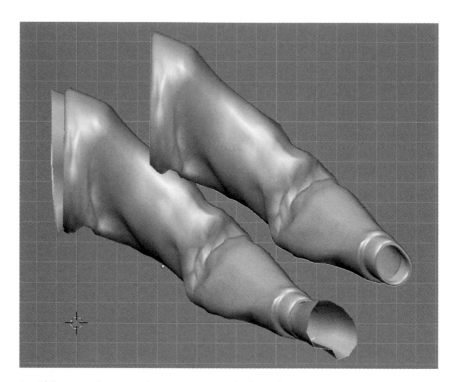

14. In Object mode, copy the armature and place the copy on a separate layer so that you can work with it and the new meshes without dealing with the old armature and meshes. The copied armature will have the same action associated with it as the original armature. Without changing frames, enter Pose mode and choose Apply Pose as Restpose from the Pose menu in the 3D viewport header, as shown in Figure 4.61. This does what you would expect, based on the name. The current bent-arm pose will become the rest pose to which the armature returns when all the transformations on it are canceled. Because you applied the deformation to the arm and sleeve meshes, the new rest pose should fit them perfectly. Rig the sleeve to the armature by parenting it, as shown in Figure 4.62, and choosing Create Vertex Groups from Bone Heat just as you've done with other meshes before. Do the same thing to the new arm mesh.

15. In a final rigged mesh for animation with no active simulations, there is no reason to have multiple layers of mesh. On the contrary, having mesh clothes over a mesh body will likely result in penetration, where the inner mesh pops through the surface of the outer mesh. Because the sleeve now has the arm shape modeled into it, there's no need for the actual arm model to extend through the sleeve. Delete the vertices of the arm that will not be seen so that you have an arm object, as shown in Figure 4.63.

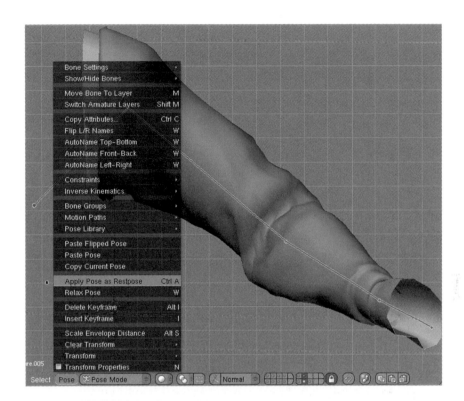

Figure 4.61

Applying the pose as the rest pose

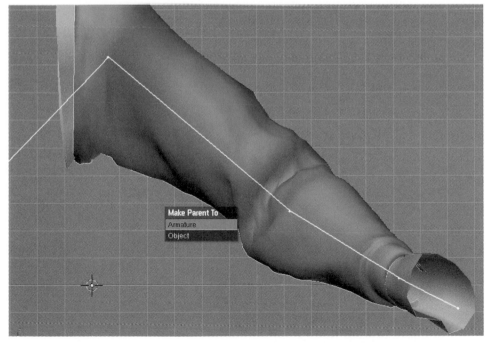

Figure 4.62

Rigging the new sleeve mesh to the new armature

Figure 4.63

The arm Mesh
object with unseen
vertices deleted

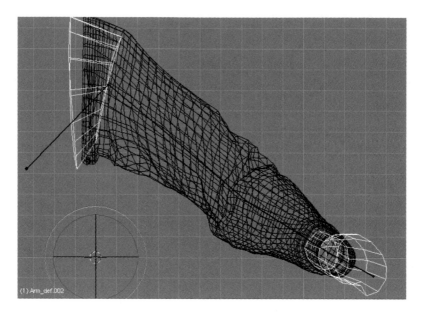

16. You're basically finished now. You can create a simple action to test the new rigged sleeve and arm meshes along the lines of the one shown in Figure 4.64. Try to get a range of positions roughly representative of what your character will be doing so you get a sense of how the sleeve will look when bent and extended in different ways. Figure 4.65 shows renders of the same process but with the subsurf level set at 3 and with self-collision activated on the cloth simulation. If your resources allow, try running a simulation with these settings as well.

Figure 4.64

A test action to
see how the mesh
deforms

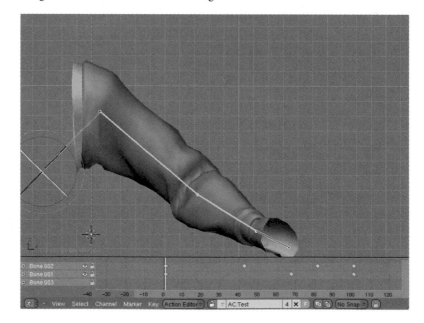

Figure 4.64
(continued)

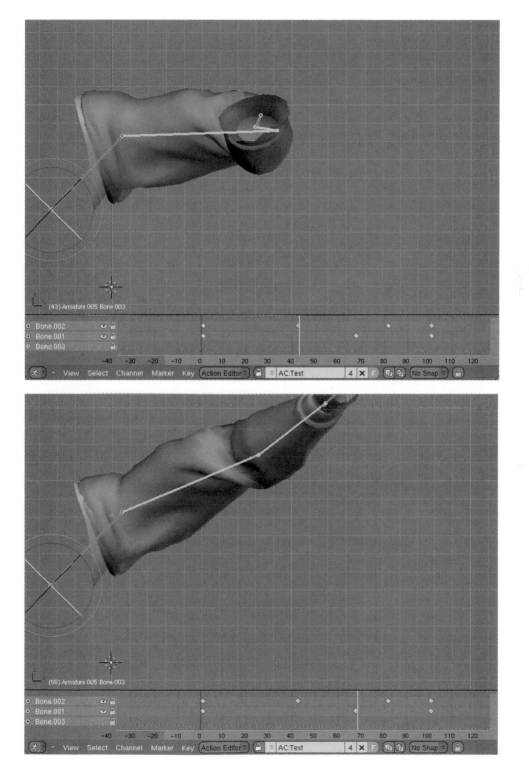

Figure 4.64

(continued)

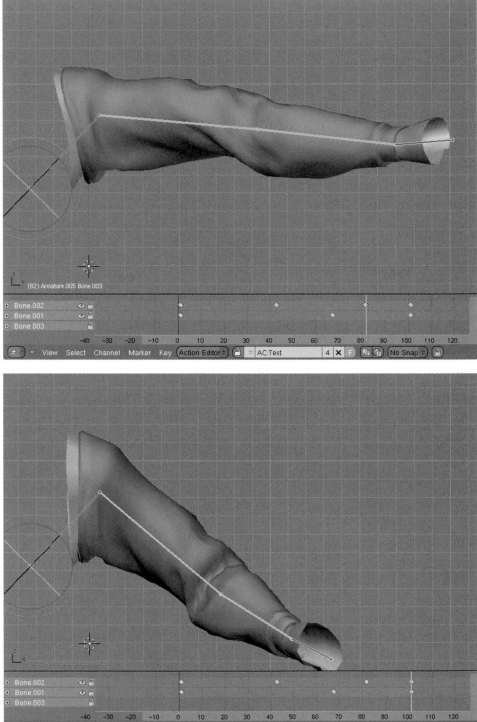

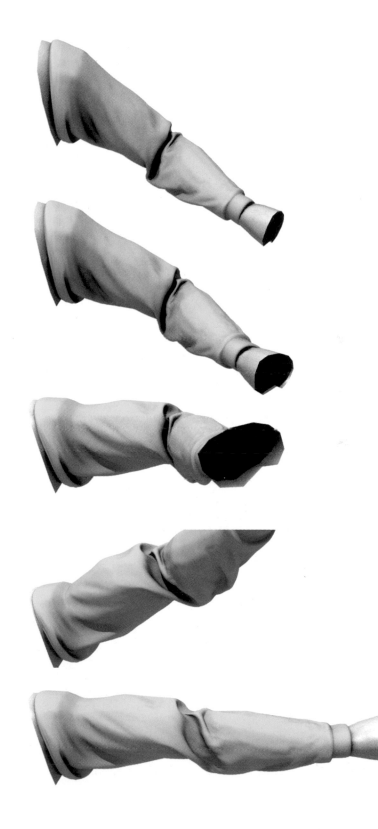

Figure 4.65
A rendered
sequence using
level 3 subsurfacing

Inorganic Modeling

In the *Mercator* project, the expedition ship *Eleanor*, shown in Figure 4.66, is central to the movie. Throughout the movie, the ship is a prop, a set, and even to some extent, a character. For this reason, the inorganic modeling of the ship is a crucial task for this movie. The *Eleanor* is a good example of the kind of modeling tasks that often come up when making a CG animated movie. The model is complex and high-poly, so working with it in the 3D viewport and rendering it must be organized to conserve resources. The model should be created so that only the parts that are needed at a particular time can be rendered. Once again, a variety of techniques were brought to bear on creating the complex ship model. In addition to traditional poly-by-poly inorganic modeling, lattices, Array modifiers, curves, and cloth simulations were employed. The last of these, cloth simulation, also found a surprising and unusual use in modeling the icy snow that covers the ship.

Figure 4.66

The *Eleanor*

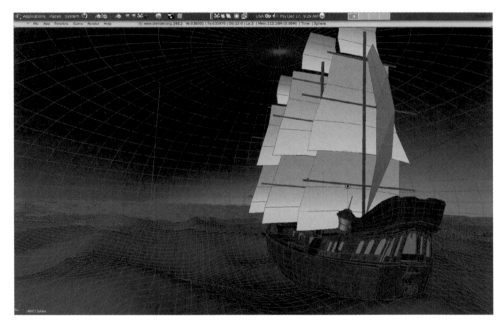

As with most complex modeling tasks, modeling the *Eleanor* begins with two-dimensional drawings. The rough outlines are done by hand either with pencil and paper or in a paint program such as GIMP or MyPaint. An example of such a sketch of the *Eleanor*'s hull is shown in Figure 4.67.

After sketching is done, the next step is to create orthogonal patterns to use as guides in the modeling process. For inorganic modeling, this is often best done in a vector graphics application such as Inkscape, which makes it easy to maintain a higher degree of control over the shapes than painting programs typically do. None of these tools are suitable for the levels of precision required for computer-aided design (CAD), but this level of precision is not necessary when creating models for animation. Guide images produced in Inkscape can be seen in Figure 4.68.

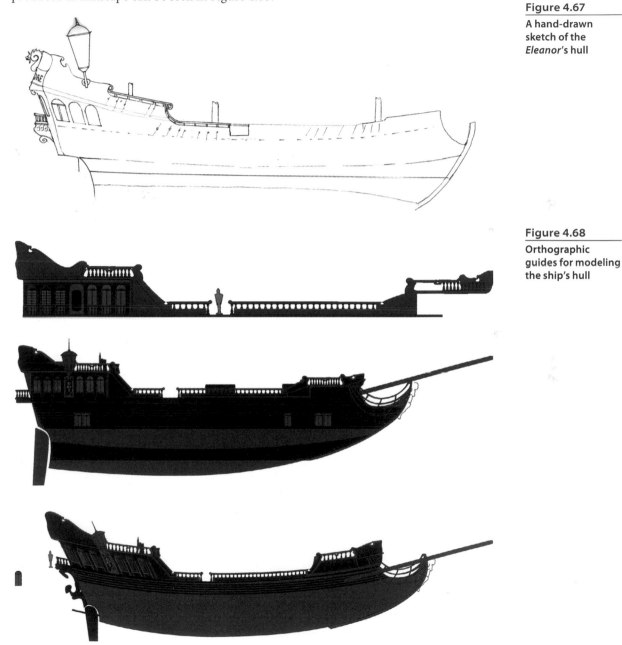

Figure 4.67

A hand-drawn sketch of the *Eleanor*'s hull

Figure 4.68

Orthographic guides for modeling the ship's hull

Blender itself is capable of modeling precision that is more than ample for most CAD purposes, and with some effort it is possible to use Blender as a basic CAD application. This is not what it is designed for, however, and it does not have a complete tool set for CAD work. This is not likely to change.

The sails of the *Eleanor* will be modeled using cloth simulation, so it is not so important to represent them entirely accurately in the Inkscape guide. The completed vector graphics guide for the ship is shown in Figure 4.69. Details such as the windows can be represented in separate vector images, as shown in Figure 4.70. These images are exported from Inkscape to PNG files by using Inkscape's File → Export menu option. Vector images can also be imported as curves in Blender by using the import script found at File → Import → Paths.

Figure 4.69

An orthogonal view of the ship done with Inkscape

The process of modeling from the Inkscape-exported guide begins as shown in Figure 4.71, with the outline of the boat's deck. Each piece progresses in order. Not all the pieces were modeled directly using traditional mesh modeling. Lattices were also used to curve the parts of the boat in a smoother manner than would be easily done with straight mesh modeling.

An area where lattices are of particular use is in the rigging (of course, before the days of meshes and armatures, this term commonly referred to the system of ropes and pulleys related to the control of a ship's sails). The mesh of ropes shown in Figure 4.72 gets its shape from the lattice shown in Figure 4.73. For deformations such as the triangular deformation of these ropes, lattices are an obvious solution.

Figure 4.70

Detailed windows in Inkscape

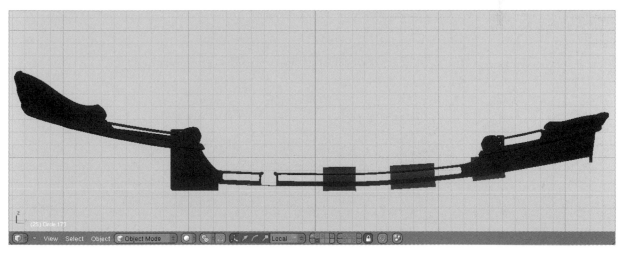

Figure 4.71

The 3D hull model in an early stage

Figure 4.72

Models of ship
rigging

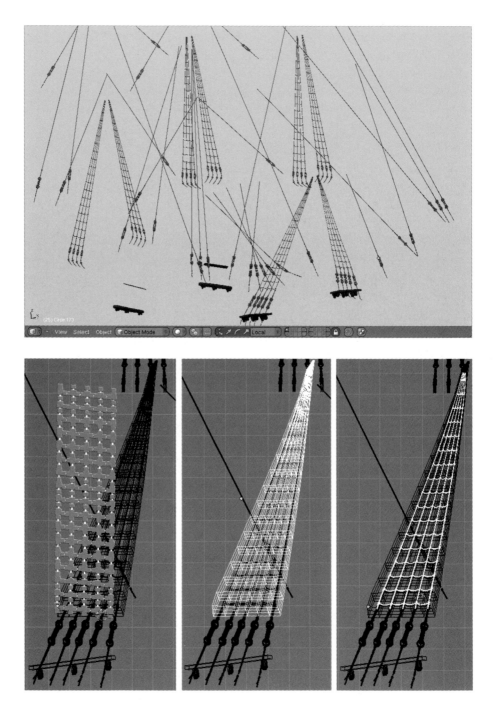

Figure 4.73

Deforming rope rig-
ging with a lattice

Once again, cloth simulation makes an appearance as a modeling tool. This use is even
more unexpected than the sleeve creation method discussed previously, because the subject
of the modeling is not even cloth. Rather, cloth simulation is used here to roughly model

snow and ice accumulation on the surface of the boat. Looking at Figure 4.74, you can see that the cloth-like qualities of this simulation are apparent. After a round of simulation, the resulting model was tweaked at a vertex level and sculpted to more closely resemble the kind of build-up of ice that might occur on a polar explorer such as the *Eleanor*.

The full model of the *Eleanor* can be seen in Figure 4.75. From above, with the background of a blue mesh as the sea, the ship appears as in Figure 4.76. A rendered view from the deck with all layers active is shown in Figure 4.77.

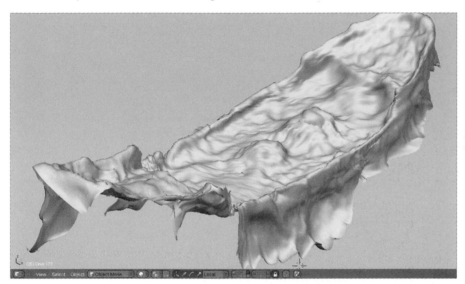

Figure 4.74

Ice from the *Eleanor's* deck modeled in part with a cloth simulation

Figure 4.75

The completed boat in Orthographic view

Figure 4.76

The ship on the sea in the 3D viewport

Figure 4.77

A rendered view from the deck

As you've seen by now, modeling covers a lot of ground and a lot of different techniques. The basic techniques and tools are covered in great detail in books and tutorials that are currently available, but many more-advanced techniques or less-obvious approaches tend to be known mainly to experienced pros. Hopefully, your own skills have benefitted from this look into the Licuadora workflow.

In the next chapter, you'll move on from mesh modeling and take the first steps toward bringing these inanimate meshes to life. You'll learn the secrets behind Licuadora's professional rigging techniques and see how a few bones, lattices, and shapes can be employed to make your characters do exactly what you want.

CHAPTER 5

Rigging Characters

Before any character animation occurs, mesh models need to be rigged with whatever armatures, deformation modifiers, and morph shapes are necessary for the animator to quickly and easily create and keyframe poses and facial expressions. Blender offers a variety of tools for rigging, and professional animators like those at Licuadora Studio typically use a combination of these tools to achieve just the right rigging solution for a given character.

CHAPTER CONTENTS

- **Using Armatures, Modifiers, and Deformation**
- **Mastering Complex PyDrivers**
- **Controlling Textures with PyDrivers**

Using Armatures, Modifiers, and Deformation

After modeling is done, the next step in an animation pipeline is to prepare those models for animation. Depending on the model and what you have in mind for it to do, it might not need much preparation. If an object just needs to move around, it may be fine to just key the animation directly on the object-level Ipos. However, in most cases, objects to be animated require more setting up than this. In a nutshell, this setting up is referred to as *rigging*.

There are two closely related objectives to rigging. The first is to make it possible for the necessary movements or deformations to be represented concisely as Ipo curves (or, in the more general Blender 2.5 terminology, *function curves*). For example, an armature enables the bending of a character's arm to be represented with a single joint angle value, whereas in reality the deformation involves a complex displacement of numerous vertices. The second object of rigging is to give the animator the controls needed to efficiently create poses and key animations. The two goals are obviously closely aligned, and they both point to the same conclusion: A good rig is a balance between simplicity and constrained control.

Character rigging is a particularly demanding area of rigging because of the complexity of the movements and deformations that need to be controlled. Unlike most machinery or other inanimate objects, living beings move and change shape in subtle ways, and rigging must control these changes of shape on the vertex level and even below. The demands of convincing character animation also mean that the controls of the rig must be as intuitive and easy to work with as possible.

Blender's armature system has a number of features that separate the parts of the rig concerned with deforming the mesh itself, from the parts of the rig that constrain or drive other parts, and from the parts of the rig intended to be used as controls by the animator at the next stage in the pipeline.

Rigging for Deformations with Mesh Deform

Deformations are caused when the vertices in a mesh are displaced because of the influence of some component of the rig. Typically, posing is done with armatures, so the direct or indirect influence of a bone on the mesh is what causes the deformation. Very simple deformation patterns can be created by using bone envelopes. When envelopes are used, vertices within a particular distance from the bone are affected by the bones' movement. This is a crude way to deform a mesh, however, and with more-recent advances in Blender's ability to automatically create weighted vertex groups for bones, there are rarely any advantages to using envelopes.

The more common way for bones to directly influence the mesh is by using weighted vertex groups whose weights are set automatically, painted on using weight painting, or input numerically by hand. You went through the process of rigging an arm and setting its bone weights in Chapter 4, "Modeling," so this process should be fresh in your mind.

Understanding Mesh Deform Basics

There are other ways to make a bone's movement influence a mesh. A very useful technique is the use of a Mesh Deform modifier. A Mesh Deform modifier uses a second mesh, the mesh deformer, to deform the main mesh. The mesh deformer is in turn deformed directly by the armature or some other modifier. Mesh Deform modifiers can give a smoother deformation than direct deformation by an armature. They are especially useful for fat or fleshy areas. In Figure 5.1, you can see the mesh deformers active on the Virginia rig.

In Figure 5.2, the arm is not being deformed directly by the armature. Rather, the arm is being modified by a mesh deformer, displayed in wireframe. This mesh deformer (which is an ordinary, closed Mesh object) is deformed by the armature using ordinary bone-weighted vertex groups, as shown in Figure 5.3.

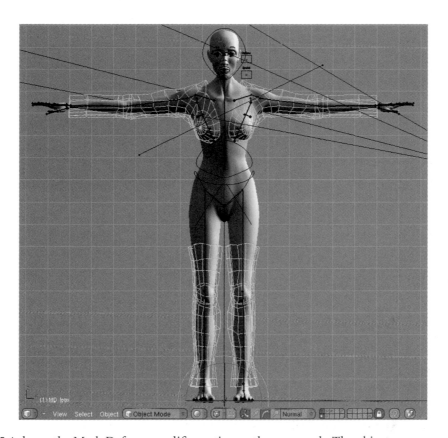

Figure 5.1

Mesh deformers for the Virginia rig selected

Figure 5.4 shows the Mesh Deform modifier active on the arm mesh. The object name of the Mesh Deform object is MD, so this is entered in the Ob field. Like most modifiers, a vertex group can be used to control the overall influence of the modifier. This is important and will be discussed shortly. The Unbind button is displayed because the modifier has already been bound. In order for a Mesh Deform modifier to influence a mesh, its influence on each vertex must be calculated once in advance. For this reason, when you first set up a Mesh Deform modifier, or any time you make changes to the mesh or the modifier in Edit mode or alter the weight painting, you must bind the modifier by clicking the Bind button. Binding depends on the number of vertices and can take a few minutes on a very dense mesh. After the modifier is bound, it will deform the mesh and must be unbound in order to bind it again if necessary.

A mesh to be used as a Mesh modifier must be a topologically manifold, closed mesh. This means that its inside should be entirely sealed off from its outside by faces and that at any edge, exactly two faces should meet. Rather than an open-ended tube, you must use a closed-ended cylinder, for example. There should be no missing faces, and the shape should not form a donut or other complex structure of rings.

Figure 5.2

An arm deformed by a Mesh Deform modifier

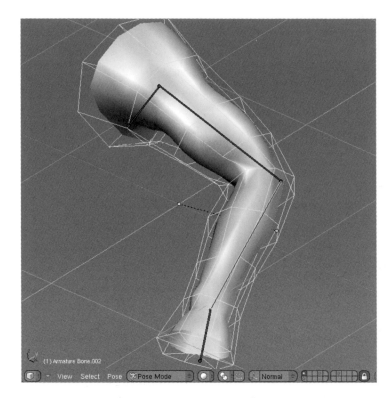

Figure 5.3

The Mesh Deform modifier in Weight Paint mode

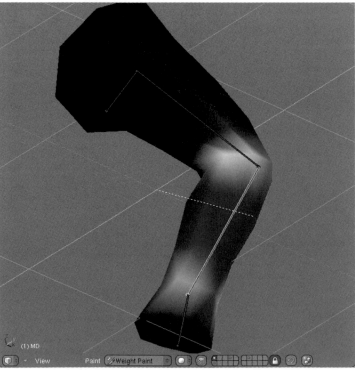

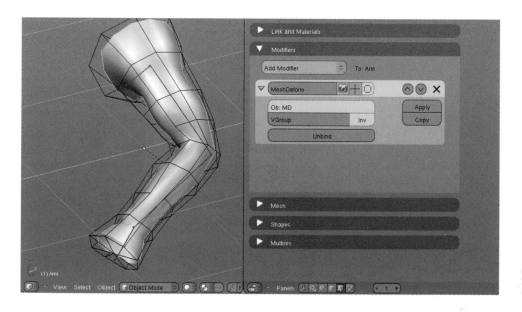

Figure 5.4
The Mesh Deform modifier active on the mesh

In Figure 5.5, you can see that this is the case for the mesh deformers on the Virginia rig. If you're not clear on the topological restrictions on Mesh Deform modifiers, a safe rule of thumb is to always start with a closed cylinder for your mesh deformer. You can subdivide it, scale, and move vertices around to your heart's content, and it will always be an acceptable topology to be used as a mesh deformer. Only parts of the deforming mesh that are inside the mesh deformer will be affected.

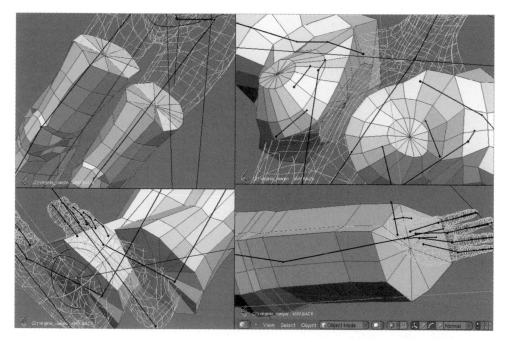

Figure 5.5
A closer look at the closed mesh structure of each of the mesh deformers

Dealing with Multiple Modifiers

The arm example shown previously in Figure 5.2 is very simple in that the entire arm mesh is contained within the MD mesh and deformed only by the Mesh Deform modifier. However, it is often the case that you will want to combine the influence of a Mesh Deform modifier, for example, with the influence of an armature. You may want both modifiers to influence the same vertex. This can cause a problem if you're not careful. If you simply add an Armature modifier to your mesh, the two modifiers' influences will add together, making your mesh deform much more than you want it to, as shown in Figure 5.6.

The solution to this problem is to normalize the influences of the Armature modifier and the Mesh Deform modifier so that they add to one on all vertices. Places where the Armature modifier has full influence should not be influenced by the Mesh Deform modifier, and places where the Mesh Deform modifier has full influence should not be influenced by the Armature modifier. In addition, in places where one modifier's influence is 0.5, the other modifier's influence should also be 0.5, so that both modifiers contribute to the deformation, rather than adding to each other's influence.

Figure 5.6
With an armature and a mesh deformer both acting on the mesh, the mesh overdeforms.

This can be accomplished with the use of a single vertex group defined over the mesh. The Armature modifier is assigned this vertex group to modulate its influence. The Mesh Deform modifier is assigned the *inverse* of the same vertex group to modulate its influence. Thus, depending on the value of that vertex group's weight, you can precisely control the degrees to which each modifier affects the mesh.

On the Virginia model, the vertex group that serves this purpose is called NO_MD. The name expresses the fact that the higher weights represent the places that the Mesh Deform modifiers are *not* influencing. The Weight Paint view of this vertex group can be seen in Figure 5.7. Note that the blue areas are the ones where the mesh deformers are set up. Figure 5.8 shows a closer view of the weights for the arm, where the elbow is weighted to the armature to give a bony effect, while the bicep is deformed by the mesh deformer, yielding a softer, fleshier deformation.

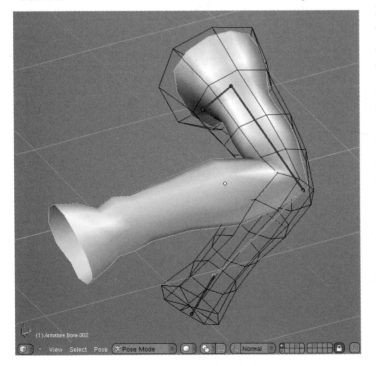

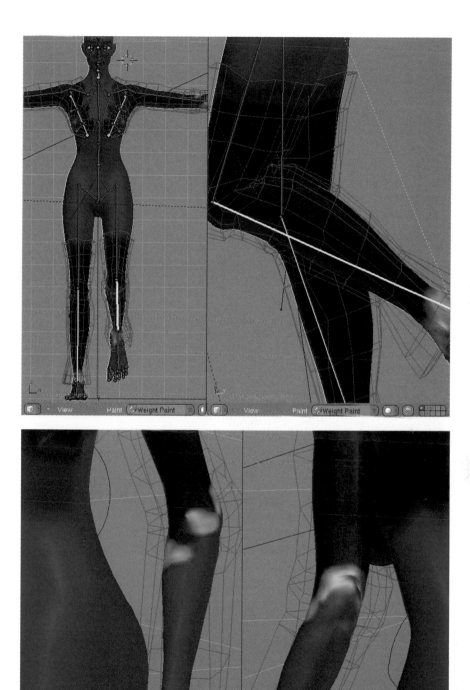

Figure 5.7

The NO_MD vertex group displayed in Weight Paint mode

Figure 5.8

A closer look at the weights for the elbow

Figure 5.9

The modifier stack

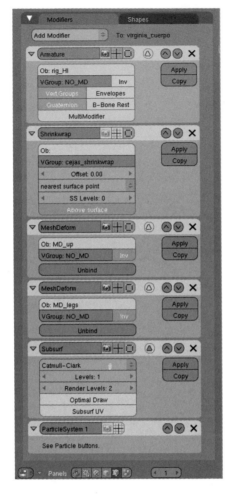

Figure 5.9 shows the modifier stack for the Virginia rig. The topmost modifier is the Armature. Notice that NO_MD is entered in the VGroup field. This makes the modifier's influence dependent on the value of that vertex group's weight for each vertex. The third and fourth modifiers down are the upper body and leg mesh deformers, respectively. Both of these modifiers also have NO_MD entered in the VGroup field, but unlike the Armature modifier, the Inv button is toggled on, inverting the weights of this vertex group. In this way, the Mesh Deform modifiers' influence is normalized with the Armature modifiers, yielding correct deformations.

Rigging for Control

The armature plays an important role as the animator's interface with the model. Custom bone shapes are an important feature that enable the technical director (TD) to create intuitive and easy-to-understand control bones, as shown in Figure 5.10.

Creating nice, unobtrusive custom controllers is simple. To do this, a handy script, align2bone.py, is included on the DVD that accompanies this book. Copy that script to a convenient place on your hard drive, and then follow these steps to see how to use it:

1. You'll need a rig to work with first. Create a simple armature-modified mesh like the one shown in Figure 5.11. The shape of the model and the rig don't matter at all, so you can use a rig you already have lying around if you like. Choose a bone that you'd like to replace with a custom bone shape. In this example, the head bone is being replaced. Its name is bone.001.

2. Enter Object mode and add a NURBS circle object to the scene by pressing Shift+A and choosing Add → Curve → NURBS Circle, as shown in Figure 5.12. Set the circle to be a 3D curve in the Curve and Surface panel of the Edit buttons, as shown in Figure 5.13.

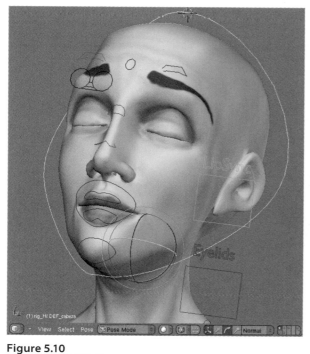

Figure 5.10
Custom bone shapes enable you to create an intuitive control interface.

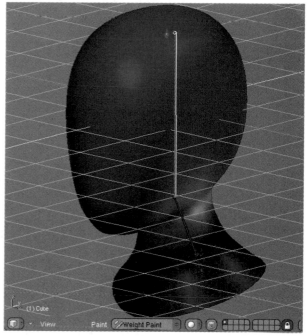

Figure 5.11
A simple rigged mesh

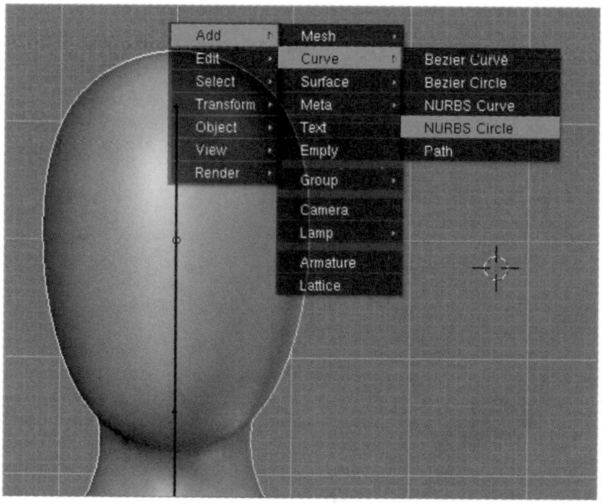

Figure 5.12
Adding a NURBS circle

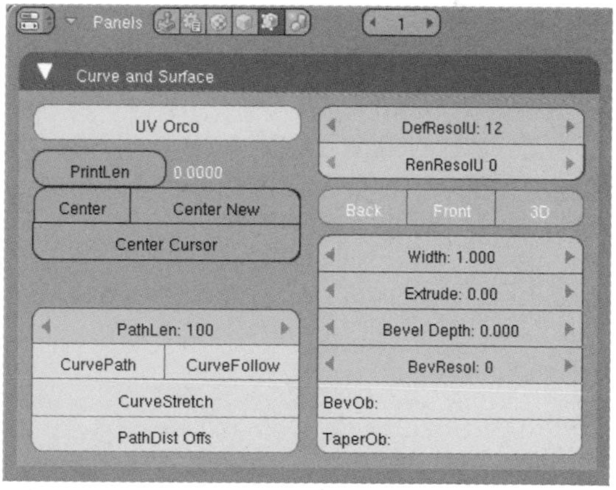

Figure 5.13
Curve settings for the NURBS circle

3. Open a Text Editor window and open new text from the drop-down menu in the header, as shown in Figure 5.14. Navigate to the align2bone.py script on your hard drive. Open the script in the Text Editor, as shown in Figure 5.15. Select the bone you want to work with in Pose mode and run the script with Alt+P. You'll see the widget shown in Figure 5.16 appear. Enter the name of the NURBS circle object (by default, this will be **CurveCircle**) in the OB field as shown, and then click Make. The object will be copied and aligned with the bone, as you can see in Figure 5.17. You can now delete the original NURBS Circle object.

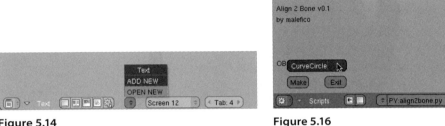

Figure 5.14

Opening new text

Figure 5.16

Running align2bone

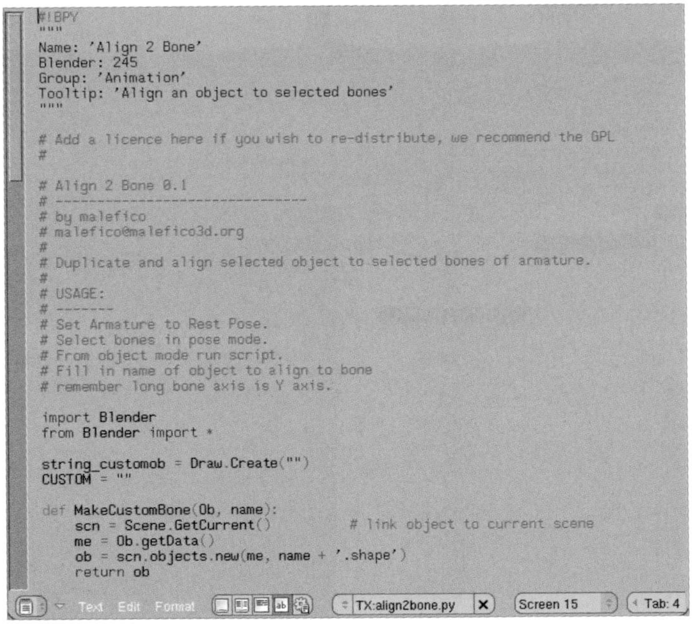

Figure 5.15

The align2bone.py **script**

4. Tab into Edit mode and edit the NURBS circle to create an intuitive, unobtrusive control for your mesh. The shape you create should be recognizable from different angles and should give a sense of its relationship to the part of the mesh it controls.

Of course, controllers for different body parts will look different. For the head, something along the lines of Figure 5.18 is appropriate. When you've done this, convert the NURBS circle to a mesh by pressing Alt+C and clicking Mesh, as shown in Figure 5.19. The resulting Mesh object is shown in Figure 5.20.

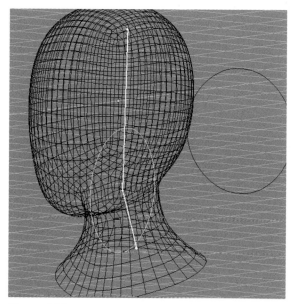

Figure 5.17

The duplicated and aligned NURBs circle

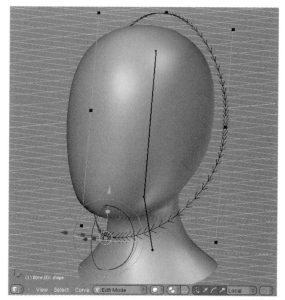

Figure 5.18

Editing the NURBS curve

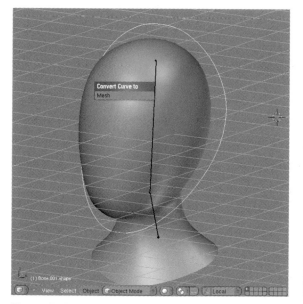

Figure 5.19

Converting to a mesh

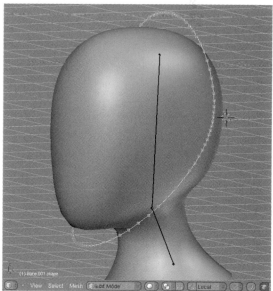

Figure 5.20

The custom object mesh

5. Select the bone and find the Armature Bones panel in the Edit buttons area. Enter the name of the custom Mesh object into the OB field, as shown in Figure 5.21. Click the W button to the right of the text field to ensure that the object is always displayed in Wireframe view; otherwise, the object will not be visible, because it has no faces. When you've done this, the object shape will replace the bone. Depending on how your armature is set up, however, the scaling will probably be off, as shown in Figure 5.22.

6. Fix the scaling by scaling the original Mesh object in Edit mode, as shown in Figure 5.23. Scale and translate the object's vertices in Edit mode until they are placed as they should be, as shown in Figure 5.24.

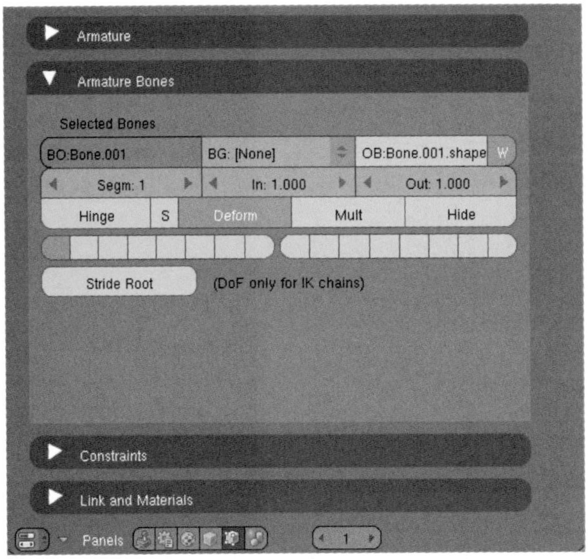

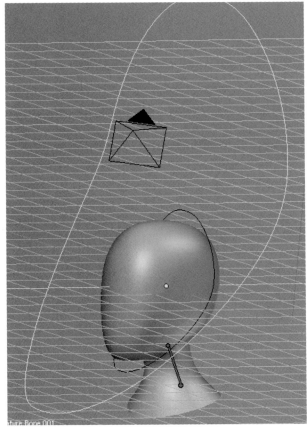

Figure 5.21
Setting the custom shape for the bone

Figure 5.22
The custom bone shape with incorrect scale

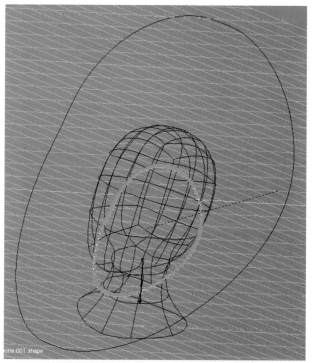

Figure 5.23

Scaling the original object in Edit mode

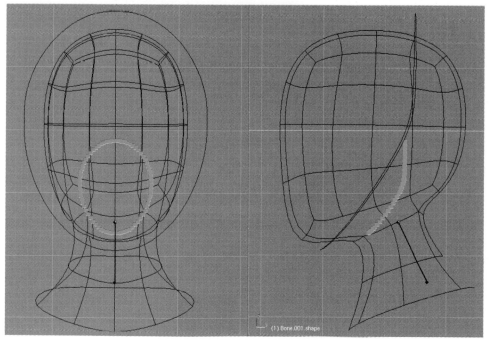

Figure 5.24

Placing the shape in Edit mode

LOOKING FORWARD TO *RIGIFY*

Much of the tedium of character rigging may be eliminated in future versions of Blender with the official release of the meta-rig templating system known as *Rigify*, which is currently under development. With that system, you'll be able to add a variety of different ready-made full armature templates such as humanoid and quadriped, or partial armatures for specific body parts. You'll just tweak the armature to fit your model, and then activate the Rigify functionality to build a complete, fully constrained rig "automagically"!

7. Tab back out of Edit mode. You can now hide the original Mesh object on a different layer, or set it to be invisible, unselectable, and unrenderable in the Outliner. Be sure X-Ray display is turned off for the armature. X-Ray display is valuable when editing the mesh, but for animation, it is better to turn it off so that your controllers can give you better visual feedback about the depth and volume of the body parts you are working with. Figure 5.25 shows the head posed. You can see in the image on the left that the controller is partially concealed by the posed head, making the depth and position of the controller more readable than if it were entirely visible.

Figure 5.25

Posing with the custom bone shape

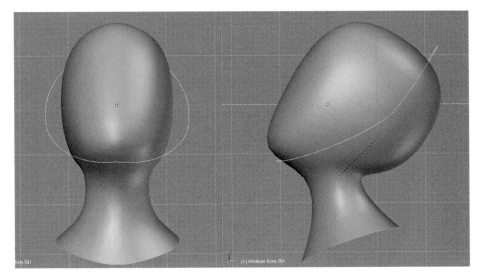

Mastering Complex PyDrivers

In addition to using bones to deform the character mesh or a Mesh Deform modifier mesh directly, Blender enables you to use a bone to make the mesh morph into a shape that has been modeled in advance. To do this, you create a shape key and set up a bone as an Ipo driver for that shape key. This is part of the basics of rigging, and you can read about how to do this in *Introducing Character Animation with Blender*. In the case of the

Virginia rig, a complex PyDriver is used, which enables multiple shapes to be combined smoothly and controlled intuitively with a single driver in such a way that the proportions and intensity of the driver's effect on the different shapes change with each location coordinate of the driver.

A simple PyDriver is composed of a single-line Python expression that defines the relationship between the driver's transformation and the value of the driven Ipo. There is a limit to how much code you can pack into a single line, so Blender enables you to define arbitrarily complex functions in a file called pydrivers.py, and then call these functions as your one-line PyDriver. In this example, you'll see how to set up a single bone to control two shape keys on the Virginia character's mouth, yielding a simple and intuitive way to control a smile.

Preparing the Rig

A rig has been prepared for you to use, to follow along with the steps of setting up the PyDriver. You'll find this on the DVD that accompanies this book, in the file virginia-mouth-driver.blend. The file virginia-mouth-driver-complete.blend includes the completed PyDrivers setup for you to check your own work against.

Before you begin, it's worthwhile to go over the contents of the virginia-mouth-driver .blend file to see what has been done. When you open the file, you'll see the objects shown in Figure 5.26 in the 3D viewport. There are three objects you'll be dealing with in this section. They are the mesh model of the Virginia character's head, a divided plane displayed in Wireframe mode with quadrants numbered from 1 to 4, and an armature called Armature. There is only one bone in the armature, and it is located at the center of

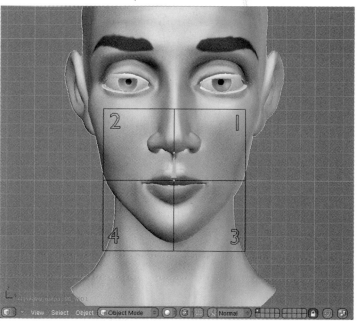

Figure 5.26
The Virginia head mesh and driver rig

the divided plane, in front of the character's mouth.

The goal of this section is to implement a PyDriver that will drive two morph shapes representing the left half of a smile and the right half of a smile. The shapes you'll be working with, including the Basis shape, are shown in Figure 5.27. The first shape key shown is the Basis shape, which is the original shape of the mesh without any shape keys active. The expression of the Basis shape should be neutral. The second shape key shown is called MT_WID.L. This is the morph shape that represents the smile applied to the left side of the face, and the last shape key shown, MT_WID.R, is the smile applied to the right side of the face.

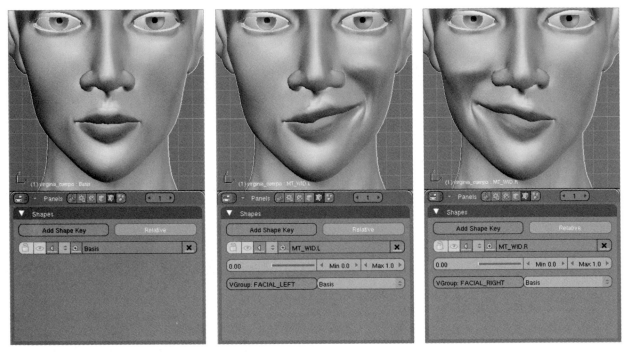

Figure 5.27

The Basis, left mouth-wide and the right mouth-wide shapes

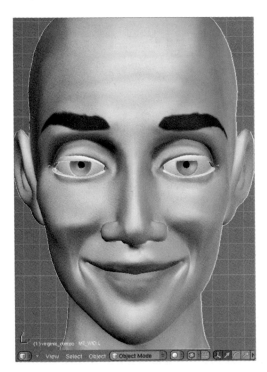

These two shape keys are actually applications of the same shape to different vertex groups, FACIAL_LEFT and FACIAL_RIGHT, which are entered in the VGroup field of their corresponding shape key panel. The original smile shape as it was modeled is shown in Figure 5.28. You can see this shape if you delete the vertex group name in the VGroup field for either of the half-smile shape keys, as shown in Figure 5.29. The FACIAL_LEFT and FACIAL_RIGHT vertex groups themselves are shown displayed in Weight Paint mode in Figure 5.30. Notice that they are not exact mirror-image copies of each other. At this point in the modeling and rigging, perfect symmetry is not especially desirable. Imperfections and asymmetries help to make a character more natural and believable.

Figure 5.28

The basis for the MOUTH_WIDE shape

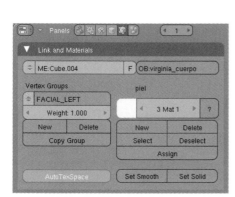

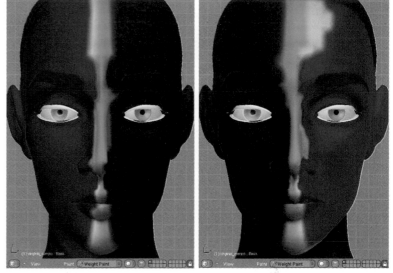

Figure 5.29

A vertex group representing the left side of the face

Figure 5.30

Left and right facial vertex groups shown in Weight Paint mode

If you try to select the divided plane or the text numerals that identify the quadrants, you'll find that they cannot be selected in the 3D viewport. If this were an actual animation rig, having elements selectable unnecessarily would make it more difficult for the animator to quickly select the controls needed to animate. For this reason, parts of the rig that do not need to be touched by the animator should be toggled unselectable in the Outliner, as shown in Figure 5.31. In the Outliner, each 3D object has three corresponding icons: an eye, an arrow, and a camera. These toggle visibility (in the 3D viewport), selectability, and renderability for the objects, respectively. Note that the Plane objects and all four Font objects (the text numbers) are toggled not to be selectable or renderable.

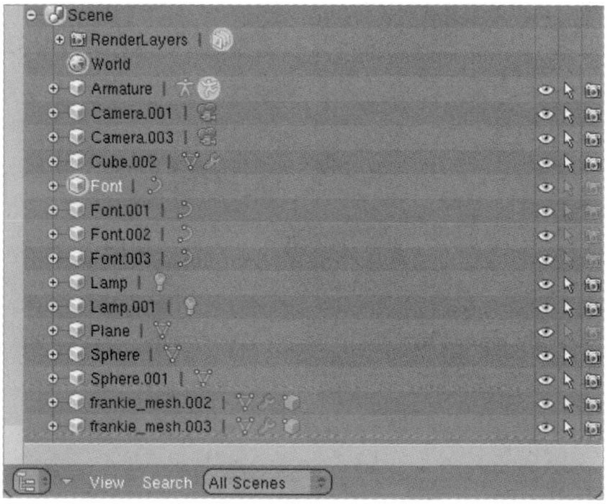

The bone's name is slider, and its possible movements are limited to those that are pertinent to the example. Again, restricted controls enable the animator to focus on doing only what he needs to do, rather than having to worry about keeping the controls organized. If a bone is effective only when moving along a single axis, for example, don't force the animator to constrain the bone's movement to the axis; do it in advance so the animator doesn't have to bother about it. In this case, only the local x and y axis movement of the bone are of interest to the shape driver, so the other transformations are all locked in the Transform Properties panel, as shown in Figure 5.32.

Figure 5.31

Render and selectability settings for the objects

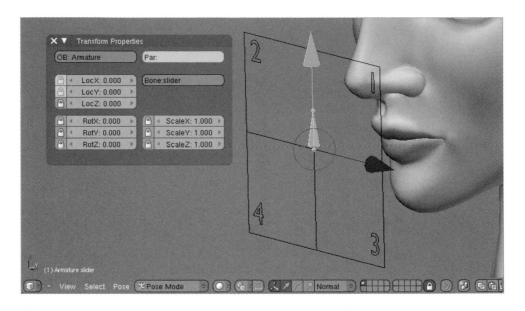

In addition to limiting the movement of the bone to the x and y axes, it can be limited even further to only the area within the quadrants of the plane, which will represent the range of influence on the shape keys. This is done by adding a Limit Location constraint, as shown in Figure 5.33. Here the minimum and maximum values for the bone's x and y locations can be set. Note that the minimum y (minY) value is set to 0. This will restrict the movement of the bone to the area within the first and second quadrants. Later, if you want to try to add further controls yourself, you can adjust this minimum y value to include all four quadrants. When the bone is constrained in this way, it can be moved only as far as the edges of the plane. Figure 5.34 shows the bone pulled as far as it can go to the corner of the first quadrant.

So far, this has been a description of only the included file. If you've been poking around the file as you've read this, you should have seen how all of these details are working. In the next section, you'll create the drivers necessary to control the smile.

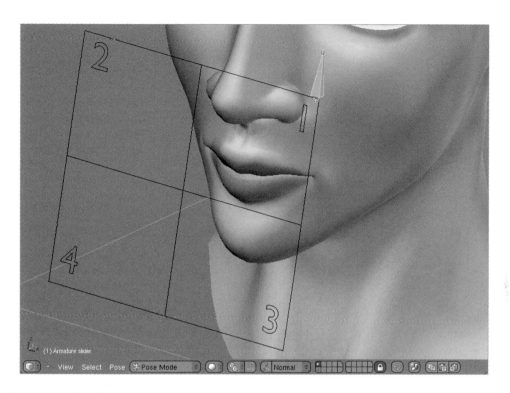

Figure 5.34
The bone constrained to the corner of the first quadrant

Creating the PyDrivers

To set up the bone to control the two shapes, you'll need to create a complex PyDriver. Do that by following these steps:

1. Open a window and select the Text Editor option from the Window Type menu. Select Add New from the menu in the header to create new text to edit. Change the name of the text by typing **pydrivers.py** into the TX field in the header, as shown in Figure 5.35. It's important that this file have exactly that name, so be sure not to mistype it. Also, click the button with the colored *ab* icon on it to toggle on color syntax highlighting.

2. Type the following code into the editor. Python is very strict with left indentations, so be sure that your indentations match those shown. A screenshot of the full script as it appears in the editor is shown in Figure 5.36. If your syntax highlighting deviates from what's shown in that screenshot, take a close look to ensure that you don't

Figure 5.35

Naming the text
pydrivers.py

have typos or indentation problems. A line-by-line breakdown of this script is given in the following section, but for now it's enough to note that it includes a definition of the function SliderJoystick(rig, bone, sector, minX, maxX, minY, maxY), which is the function that you will be calling in the PyDriver.

```
import Blender
def math(X, Y):
    value = 0
    if Y > 0:
        value = Y
        if X > 0:
            value = value * (1 - X)
    return value
def getbone(rig, bone):
    ob=Blender.Object.Get(rig)
    pbone= ob.getPose().bones[bone]
    return pbone
def SliderJoystick(rig, bone, sector, minX, maxX, minY, maxY):
    if sector == 1:
        Xval = -getbone(rig, bone).loc[0]
        Yval = getbone(rig, bone).loc[1]
    elif sector == 2:
        Xval = getbone(rig, bone).loc[0]
        Yval = getbone(rig, bone).loc[1]
    FX = 1 / (maxX - minX)
    FY = 1 / (maxY - minY)
    X = Xval * FX
    Y = Yval * FY
    return math(X, Y)
```

Figure 5.36

The full code in the Text Editor

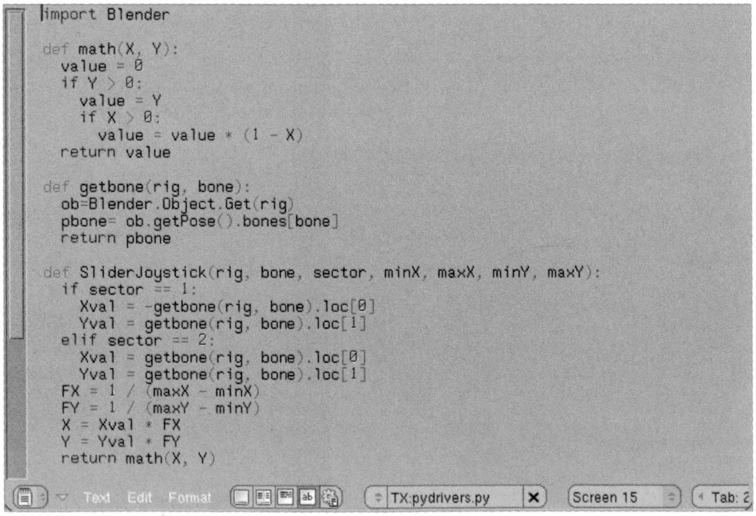

3. Open an Ipo Editor alongside the 3D viewport. Choose Shape from the drop-down menu in the header and press the N key to bring up the Transform Properties floating panel, as shown in Figure 5.37. You'll see a list of shape keys along the right edge of the window. Left-click `MT_WID.L` to select the left-side smile shape key as shown.

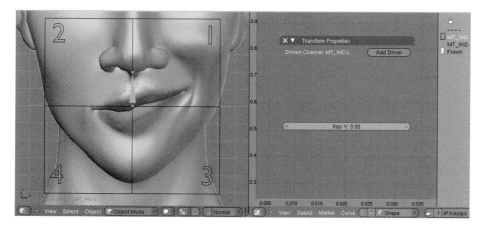

Figure 5.37

The Shape Ipo for the left shape key

4. Click Add Driver on the Transform Properties panel. This will add a driver field, as shown in Figure 5.38. To the left of the OB field is a button with a script icon. (In the figure, the icon is a small gear. Your icon may have a small snake on it, representing Python.) Click that button to make the driver a PyDriver.

5. Add an Ipo curve by holding the Ctrl key and clicking on the <0.0, 0.0> point on the graph (you don't have to get it precisely, because you'll input the point numerically shortly) and then Ctrl-click again at the <0.05, 1.0> point on the graph. From the header Curve menu, choose Interpolation Mode → Linear, as shown in Figure 5.39.

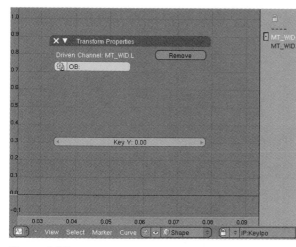

Figure 5.38

Adding a driver

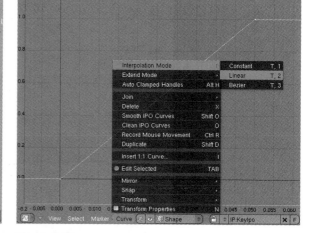

Figure 5.39

The Ipo curve that will drive the shape

6. In the PyDriver field on the Transform Properties panel, enter the following line of code and make sure the Xmin, Ymin, Xmax, and Ymax are as shown in Figure 5.40. Xmin and Ymin should be 0.0, and Xmax and Ymax should be 0.05 and 1.0, respectively. Notice that this line of code begins with p., followed by the name of the function you defined previously in your pydrivers.py file.

```
p.SliderJoystick('Armature', 'slider', 1, 0.0, 0.05, 0.0, 1.0)
```

7. Left-click MT_WID.R to select the right-side smile shape, and repeat steps 4 and 5 to create the Ipo. For the PyDriver, change the third argument to the function from 1 to 2 to change the quadrant the driver influences. The right-side shape driver is shown in Figure 5.41.

```
p.SliderJoystick('Armature', 'slider', 2, 0.0, 0.05, 0.0, 1.0)
```

8. You now have both shape drivers set up. Test the rig by posing the bone in various positions in the first and second quadrants. Your shapes should blend nicely to create a variety of subtle combinations, as shown in Figure 5.42.

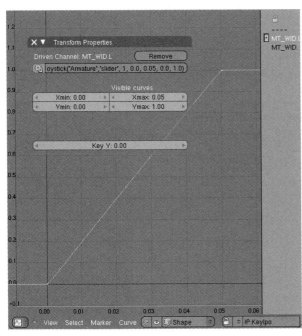

Figure 5.40
The Ipo driver for the left side

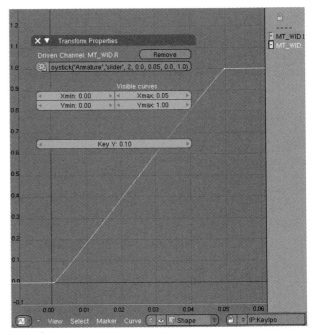

Figure 5.41
The Ipo driver for the right side

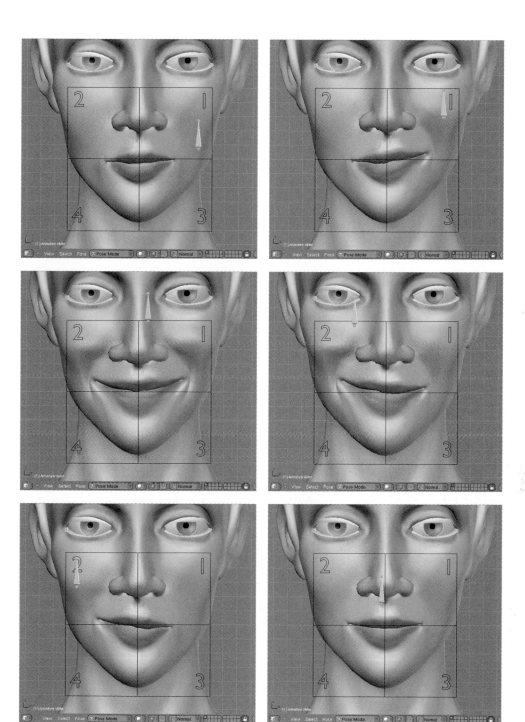

Figure 5.42
The smoothly blended shapes

A Closer Look at *pydrivers.py*

The way that the `pydrivers.py` script is called, using the `p.` prefix to automatically identify PyDriver functions defined in the script, is an example of Blender's script links functionality. Script links are enabled by default and can be controlled in the Script Links panel of the Scripts button area, shown in Figure 5.43. You don't need to touch this panel, but it's worthwhile to be aware that if script links are disabled here, the driver will cease to work.

The content of `pydrivers.py` is as follows. The first line, as in all Blender Python scripts previous to Blender version 2.5, imports the Blender module, accessing Blender-related functions.

Figure 5.43
Script links enabled by default

```
import Blender
```

The next few lines define a function called `math`, which takes two normalized values (between 0 and 1). The Y value corresponds to the up and down movement of the bone within the four quadrants. If the X value is 0 or less, the Y on its own will determine the degree to which the shape is applied. If the X value is greater than 0, then its inverse is used as a multiplier for the Y value, causing the influence of the Y value to taper as the X value approaches 1.

```
def math(X, Y):
    value = 0
    if Y > 0:
        value = Y
        if X > 0:
            value = value * (1 - X)
    return value
```

The `getbone` function simply retrieves the posed bone information from the current scene by using `Blender.Object.Get` and then `ob.getPose`. You can learn more about how these work in *Mastering Blender* or by studying the Blender Python API for version 2.49.

```
def getbone(rig, bone):
    ob=Blender.Object.Get(rig)
    pbone= ob.getPose().bones[bone]
    return pbone
```

The `SliderJoystick` function is the one you call in the PyDriver. This takes seven arguments: the armature name, the bone name, the quadrant of the divided plane that you want associated with the shape, the minimum x value of the driver curve, the maximum x value of the driver curve, the minimum y value of the driver curve, and the maximum y value of the driver curve. The x value will be related to the output of the script, and the y value will correspond to the degree to which the shape is activated.

```
def SliderJoystick(rig, bone, sector, minX, maxX, minY, maxY):
```

The only difference between driving the left side and driving the right side (or, for example, driving a left or right frown using the third and fourth quadrants) is the quadrant you're working in. For this reason, you need to create consistent x and y values from movement of the bone within the quadrant. The Xval and Yval variables need to range from 0 to 1. The Yval value will represent the contribution of the bone's vertical position to the application of the shape key. In sectors 1 and 2, therefore, a positive y value should increase the application of the shape key in both cases. The Xval value will represent the degree that the bone's x position *diminishes* the shape. In the case of quadrant 1, then, when applying the left-side smile shape, the shape is diminished as the bone moves away from zero in the negative direction (into the second quadrant area). Therefore, Xval is the negation of the x value of the bone.

```
if sector == 1:
    Xval = -getbone(rig, bone).loc[0]
    Yval = getbone(rig, bone).loc[1]
```

The case of the second quadrant is the same as the first insofar as the y axis is concerned, but is reversed along the x axis. The shape will diminish as the bone moves in the positive direction on the x axis.

```
elif sector == 2:
    Xval = getbone(rig, bone).loc[0]
    Yval = getbone(rig, bone).loc[1]
```

The next section simply normalizes the values over the span of the x and y ranges and sends them to math to convert them to a final value for the shape key.

```
FX = 1 / (maxX - minX)
FY = 1 / (maxY - minY)
X = Xval * FX
Y = Yval * FY

return math(X, Y)
```

When you've completed the steps described in this chapter for creating blended PyDriven shape keys, you should be ready to try the whole process on your own. For practice, consider implementing two more shape keys that the bone can drive in the third and fourth quadrants. A Frown shape has already been modeled for you to try this with. Use the Frown shape and the existing vertex groups to create two half-frown shape keys, and then drive them by adding code to pydrivers.py to cover the third- and fourth-quadrant cases.

Controlling Textures with PyDrivers

Figure 5.44

Sculpted forehead wrinkles

In addition to modifier deformation and driven shapes, there is another commonly used method of controlling the appearance of the mesh: the use of driver-controlled normal maps. *Normal maps* are textures that change the values of virtual normals for each point on the surface of a mesh. Normal mapping works similarly to bump mapping, but enables more control over the direction of the virtual normals. Highly detailed surface characteristics such as those created by sculpting a high-resolution mesh can be baked to a normal map texture and then applied to a lower-poly mesh to mimic the appearance of the more detailed mesh's surface. The workflow for doing this is shown in detail in *Mastering Blender,* so if you aren't sure about the role of normal maps in creating surface detail, please refer to that book.

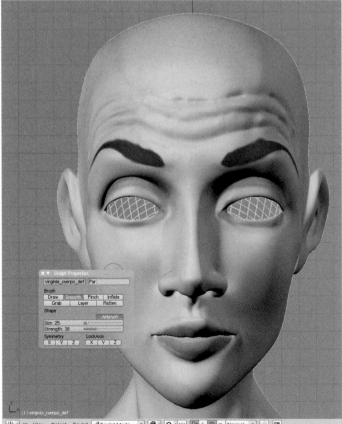

The key insight in terms of rigging and animation is that the influence of normal maps on the surface of a mesh is variable and can be animated and driven by Ipo drivers or PyDrivers. In the Virginia rig, wrinkles in the forehead are controlled in this way.

The first step in creating this effect was to sculpt the wrinkles on a subdivided multiresolution mesh, as shown in Figure 5.44. After that, the lower-poly, retopologized mesh was unwrapped and a texture was applied to the forehead, as shown in Figure 5.45.

Figure 5.45

Creating an image
texture for the fore-
head normals

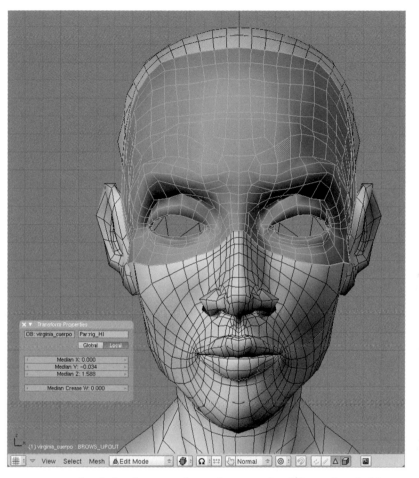

After a texture was created to bake the normals to, the normals of the sculpted object
were baked to the texture, as shown in Figure 5.46. The resulting normal map image is
shown in Figure 5.47.

Obviously, because the character can raise its eyebrows independently of each other,
it is desirable to be able to control the wrinkles of the left and right side of the forehead
independently. This is done similarly to the way the smile shape key was controlled in
the previous section. The first thing that must be done is to create a left and right texture
from the original texture. This can be done in any photo manipulation application such
as GIMP. The texture shown in Figure 5.48 represents the wrinkles of the left side of the
face only.

The wrinkles must be applied as a texture to the material on the mesh. Figure 5.49
shows the texture settings for one of the normal map textures. Figure 5.50 shows the
mapping settings for the relevant texture on the material. The texture is of course UV
mapped.

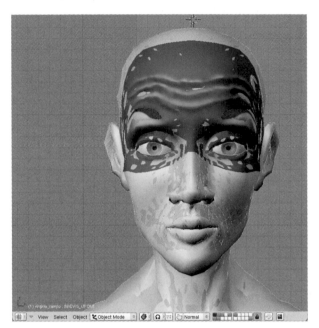

Figure 5.46
Baking forehead normals to the texture

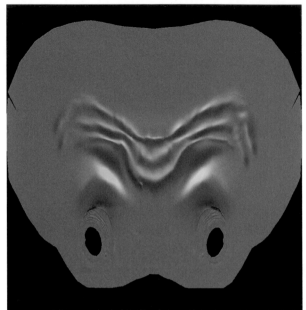

Figure 5.47
The normal-baked forehead wrinkle texture

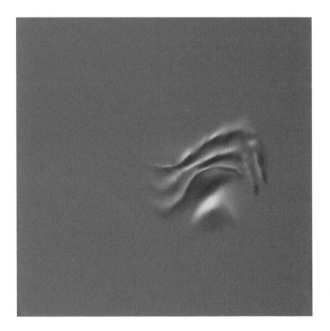

Figure 5.48
The left-side
wrinkles only

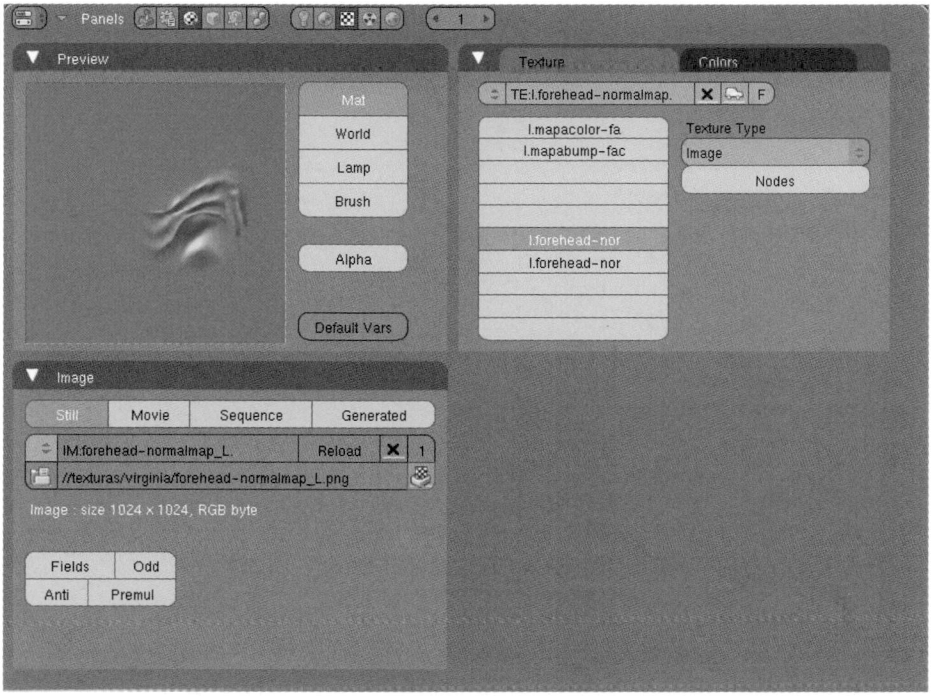

Figure 5.49

The image texture for the skin material

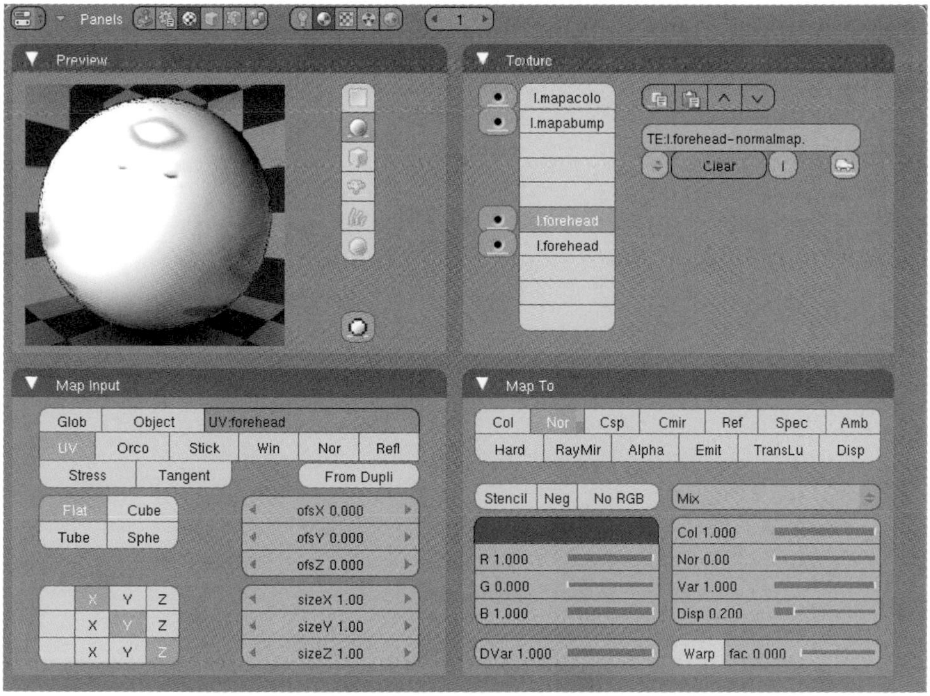

Figure 5.50

The skin material and wrinkle texture mapping values

The final step in the process is to set up a PyDriver-driven Ipo as shown in Figure 5.51. This is done in the Ipo Editor. Material Ipos can be accessed by using the drop-down menu in the header of the Ipo Editor. To the right of this drop-down is the number that represents which texture channel the Ipo controls. In this example, the left-side brow texture is being driven. This is the fifth texture channel on the material (counting downward on the Texture panel, with the topmost texture channel being 0). The Nor value is the normal map intensity, so that's the value highlighted for this curve. Creating the Ipo curve and driver is carried out exactly identically to the way you did it in the previous section on driving shape keys. The PyDriver function call is even analogous:

```
p.SliderJoystick('rig_HI', 'CA_BROWS.R', 1,0.0, 0.0125, 0.0, 0.0125)
```

As you can probably guess, this will work only if you have pydrivers.py defined with the code described previously and script links are activated. This is a good example of the general usefulness of this script.

The left-side texture is driven by the control bone CA_BROWS.R, as shown in Figure 5.52. A render of the resulting deformation can be seen in Figure 5.53.

You can look at the complete setup for the driven textures in the ***.blend file included on the DVD.

As you can see, rigging involves setting up a combination of mesh deformations, morph shapes, and driven textures to create a convincingly lifelike, easy-to-control character. Complex PyDrivers are a powerful tool that can enable you to create intuitive, flexible rigs. Any technical director working with Blender in a professional setting will benefit from having an understanding of these techniques.

Figure 5.51

The PyDriver for the Nor curve on the material Ipo

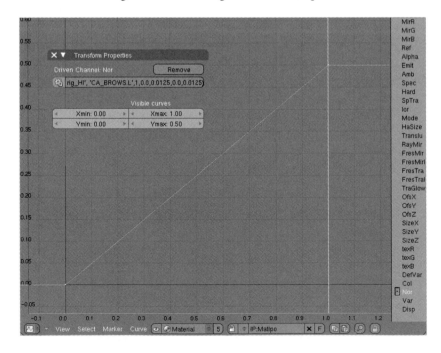

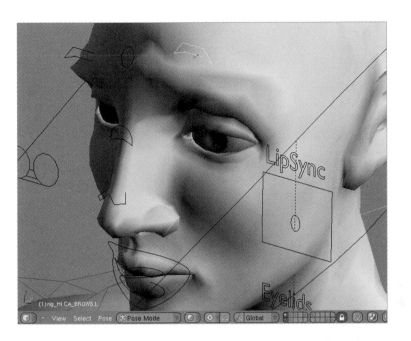

Figure 5.52
The eyebrow bone
controller

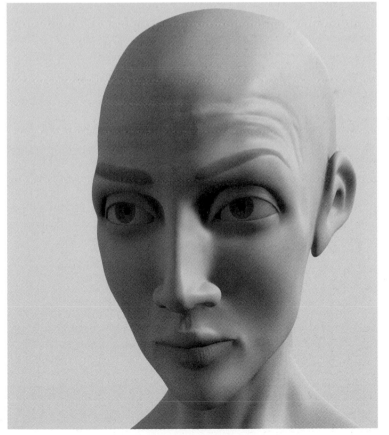

Figure 5.53
The resulting
deformation

CHAPTER 6

Animating a Character Scene

In this chapter, you'll see how a scene incorporating character animation is dealt with in Blender. You'll look at how to prepare the scene to be animated, and how to progress incrementally through the process of character animation to achieve the best results. You'll also find some helpful tips about how to incorporate cloth and hair simulations in your character animation scene.

CHAPTER CONTENTS

- **Preparing to Animate**
- **Implementing the Stages of Character Animation**
- **Creating Facial Animation**
- **Adding Cloth and Hair**

Preparing to Animate

Character animation is one of the most demanding stages of the movie production pipeline. Just as in effects shots such as the one you will look at in Chapter 7, "Descent into the Maelstrom," there are numerous technical points that need to be adjusted and corrected during the process. A full character animation shot will most likely involve interaction between multiple objects and modifiers and may involve cloth or hair simulation or other complicating factors. Furthermore, convincing posing and good mesh deformation is a must. Viewers are highly sensitive to the shapes, poses, and expressions of characters, so the threshold of believability is especially high with these forms of animation. Good deformation of a character mesh requires that the correct choices be made at all stages of character creation and animation; model topology, armature or modifier object structure, weighting, shape key creation, and posing must all be done correctly to achieve an acceptable result.

There is a great deal to know about character animation that is entirely software independent. In fact, the most important principles in character animation don't require any software at all to put into practice; they were fully developed in the era of hand-drawn 2D animation long before anybody had even thought of 3D CG animation. Most of this technique is beyond the scope of this chapter. For an excellent learning resource on the fundamentals of character animation, I highly recommend William Reynish's Blender Open Movie Workshop tutorial DVD, *Learning Character Animation Using Blender,* available from the Blender Foundation's online e-shop. Although created in Blender and geared to an audience of Blender users, the DVD focuses on the principles of character animation. You will learn how to create believable character movement that expresses force, weight, and emotion. For a more software-oriented introduction to character creation and animation tools in Blender, refer to *Introducing Character Animation with Blender* (Sybex, 2007).

Setting the Scene

This chapter breaks down a single shot from *Mercator.* In this shot, the character Virginia wakes suddenly from uneasy sleep. As discussed in Chapter 3, "Creating a 3D Animatic," a 3D animatic has already been created for this shot. The 3D animatic will be used as the basis of the final animation. A few frames from the 3D animatic for this shot can be seen in Figure 6.1.

Figure 6.1

Frames from the
3D animatic

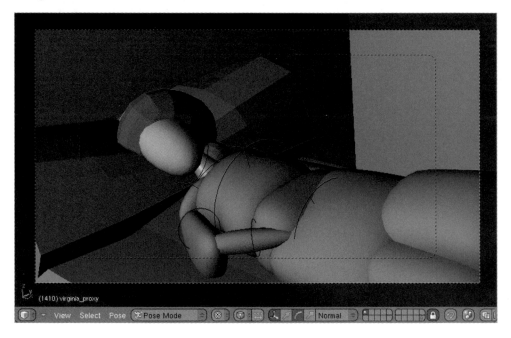

Figure 6.1

(continued)

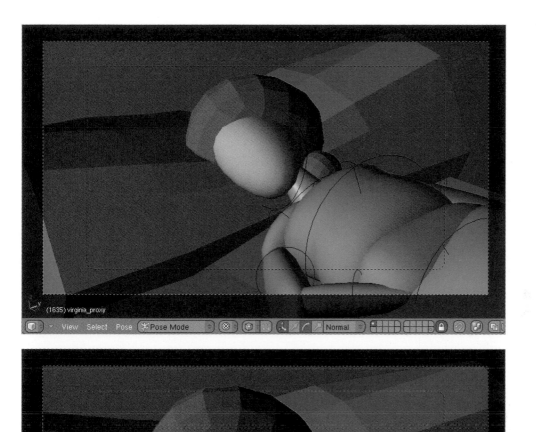

Figure 6.1
(continued)

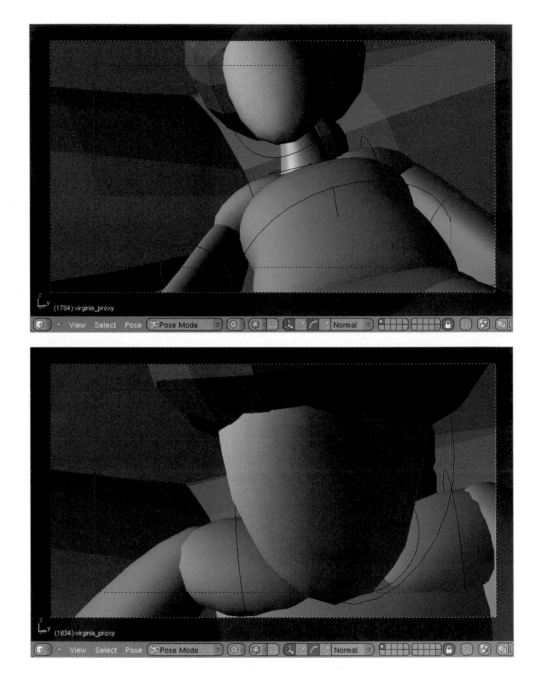

Initially, proxy versions of the props such as the bed and walls are appended directly from the 3D animatic for use as references for camera framing. The camera from the 3D animatic is shown with its animation curves in Figure 6.2. The camera and its Ipos are also imported into the new animation scene. From that point, they will be adjusted in a variety of ways. Some lead time in the animation is also necessary because cloth simulation is used for the character's clothing. The cloth will require a few frames to settle into its natural position from the original shape of the mesh model. The Camera object in the final animation and its Ipos are shown in Figure 6.3.

Figure 6.2

Camera Ipos in the 3D animatic

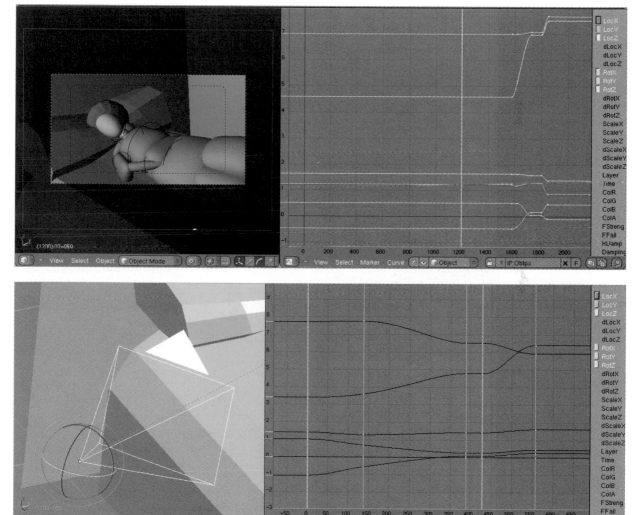

Figure 6.3

Appending the camera

After the camera and the props are in place, the character rig is linked from the character library by using a proxy rig setup as described in Chapter 3. This enables the character mesh and armature to continue to be updated even as the animators work with the rig in the animated scene. The character's clothes cannot be linked in the same way, because their vertex data must be available for the cloth simulation. For this reason, the clothing will be appended separately, and the character animation will be carried out first on the unclothed rig. Because the rig uses PyDrivers, the pydriver.py file also needs to be imported into the shot file.

The character is lying down in bed for this shot. It would be possible to pose the lying character entirely in Pose mode, leaving the Armature object at its original rotation and position. However, it's simpler to put the entire rig into a reclining position in Object mode, as shown in Figure 6.4, and from there to adjust the details of the pose in Pose mode.

Figure 6.4

Placement of the
Virginia rig in
Object mode

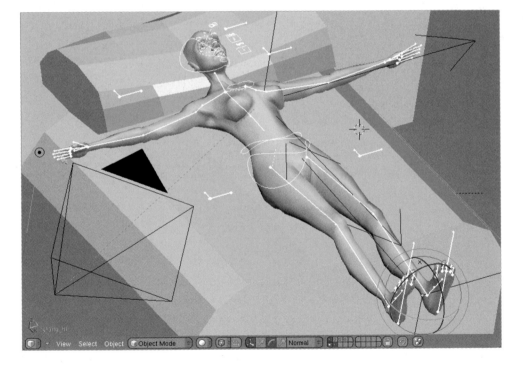

Referring to the 3D Animatic

The timing of the shot has already been planned in the 3D animatic. The final animation should stick close to a visual reference of the 3D animatic. For this, the background image is set to the rendered animatic sequence, as shown in Figure 6.5. This is done in exactly the same way as setting the 2D animatic as the background image for the 3D animatic, as described in Chapter 3.

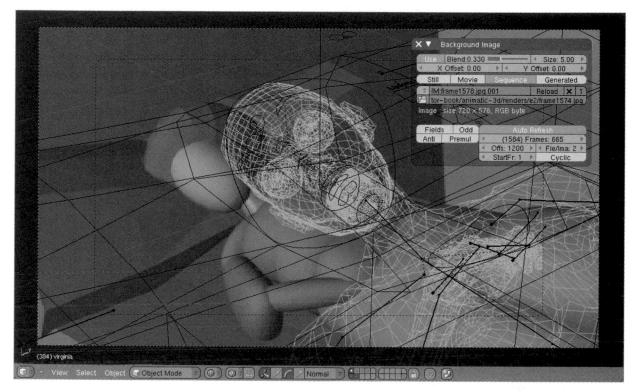

Figure 6.5

Setting the 3D animatic render as the background image

After the temporary props, the camera, and the character are in place and the 3D animatic render has been set as a reference for timing, you can begin posing and animation.

Implementing the Stages of Character Animation

There are several ways to approach character animation. Typically, they are separated into the straight-ahead method and the pose-to-pose method.

The straight-ahead approach to character animation involves keyframing poses in essentially a chronological order along the Timeline. Refinements may be added later, of course, but the general idea is to pose and key as you go. This is an intuitive approach, and an inexperienced animator might take this approach without a second thought. It also has the advantage of giving the animator a lot of freedom to be creative and to let the action take its own course. On the other hand, using the straight-ahead method can make it difficult to time the animation and make sure that extreme poses occur when and where they need to.

The *pose-to-pose* approach requires going through the animation in several passes, beginning with setting the most extreme or representative poses first at the appropriate points along the Timeline, and then going back and adding detail in subsequent passes. When you have a clear idea of the overall character movement you want in the shot, some variant of pose-to-pose is the best approach. In the shot discussed here, the animation is carried out using the pose-to-pose approach.

Regardless of how you plan to progress in posing the character, posing must start somewhere, and typically it starts at the beginning. In Figure 6.6, you can see the initial pose of the character in Pose mode.

You'll notice something new here about the bones: They are organized into color-coded groups. There are several reasons for this. For one thing, color-coding the armature can be a great help in distinguishing left and right sides of the armature, particularly if it is necessary to work in Wireframe view or from certain orthogonal views where left and right can be easily confused. Furthermore, organizing bones into bone groups enables keys to be organized in the Action and NLA Editors, giving you much more control over which frames you key and when.

Figure 6.6

Posing the character

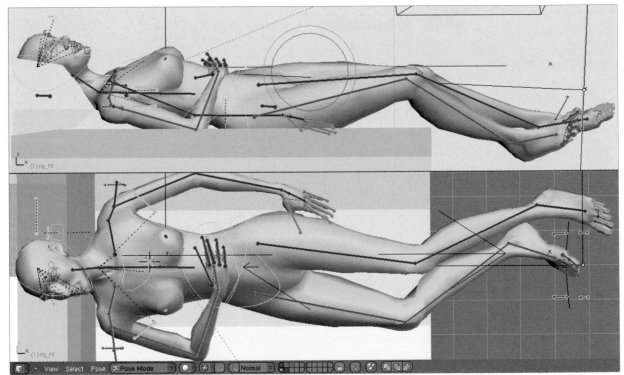

Bone groups are created by clicking Add Group in the Link and Materials panel with the armature selected, as shown in Figure 6.7. The Theme Color Set drop-down menu lets you select from a variety of bone-group color-theme presets representing colors for unselected, selected, and active Pose-mode states. Individual bones are assigned to specific bone groups in the Armature Bones panel, by selecting the desired bone group from the BG drop-down menu for the bone, as shown in Figure 6.8.

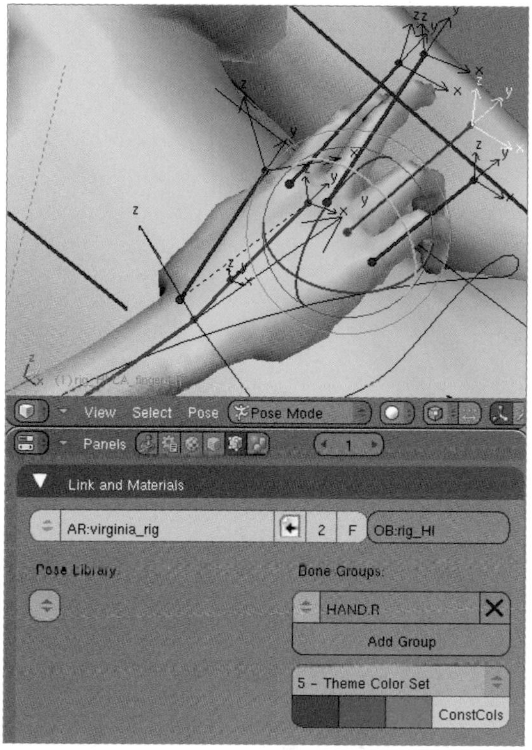

Figure 6.7
Color-coded bone groups

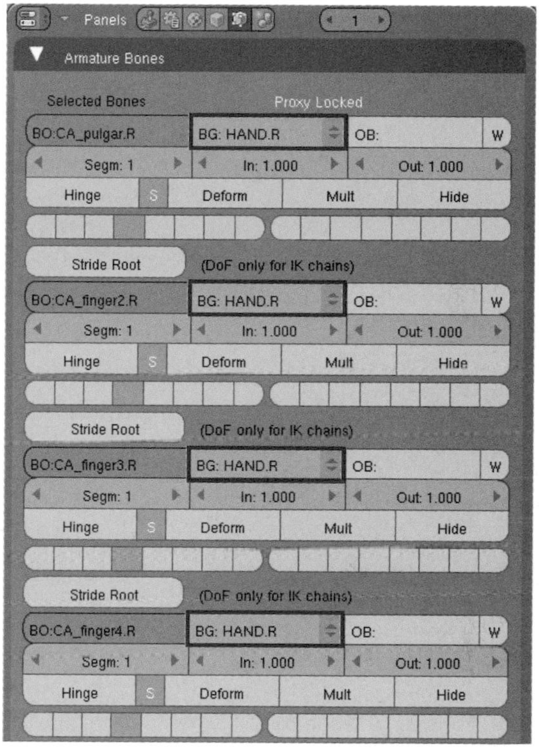

Figure 6.8
A selection of bones with their bone group entry highlighted

The big advantage of these bone groups becomes more apparent after the pose has been keyed. In frame 1 on the Timeline, with only the necessary pose bones visible in the viewport (the others should be out of view on hidden armature layers), the bones are selected with the A key and keyed with the I key. Location, rotation, and scale Ipos should be keyed with the LocRotScale menu item, as shown in Figure 6.9.

After the pose has been keyed, you can see the keys organized by bone group in the Action Editor, as shown in Figure 6.10. Each bone group channel can be locked by click-

Figure 6.9
Keying the pose

ing the lock icon, which prevents its keys from being deleted and further keys from being added to it. The bone group channels can also be expanded by clicking the small plus symbol to the left of the channel label. When the bone group channel is expanded, its constituent bone channels are shown. These can be further expanded into their constituent keyed Ipos, as shown in Figure 6.11. The colors used to highlight these channels correspond to the colors used for the bone group in the 3D viewport. The keys of each Ipo, or all keys for a given bone, can also be toggled as visible or not visible, using the eye icon to the right of the channel label. If toggled as not visible, the motion represented by the channel will be suppressed in the animation.

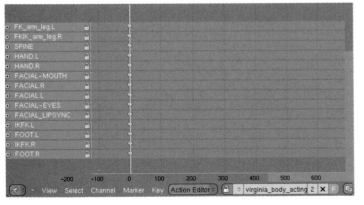

Figure 6.10
Keys in the Action Editor

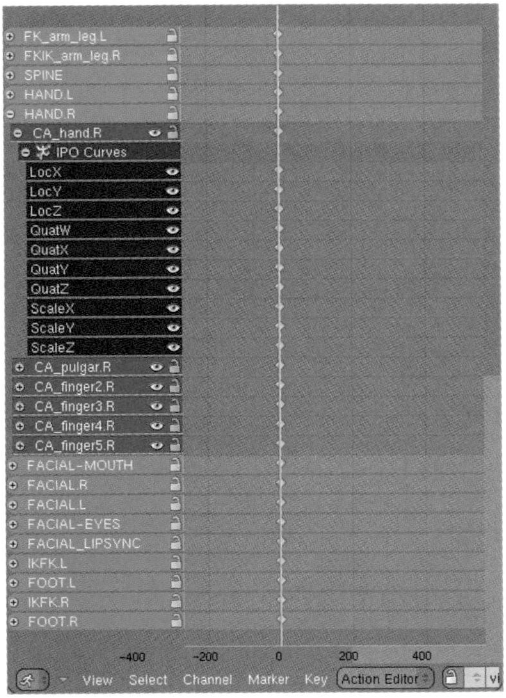

Figure 6.11
A closer look at the right-hand bone group

Using Pose-to-Pose Animation

Blender's Ipo curve system supports the pose-to-pose approach to animation by enabling you to select from three kinds of curve interpolation: Constant, Linear, and Bezier. The interpolation type determines how Blender draws a curve between the values keyframed by the animator. *Constant interpolation* holds the keyed value the same until the next keyframe is reached, at which time the curve jumps to the new value immediately. *Linear interpolation* fills in the values between keyframes as straight lines from one keyframe to the next. By default, *Bezier interpolation* fills in the values with a smooth curve that runs from one keyframe to the next in a manner mathematically calculated to be as smooth as possible. Bezier interpolation also enables the curves to be modified by hand to be arbitrarily smooth or jagged.

Using Constant interpolation, poses are held perfectly still until the next keyframe, and the armature takes the new pose instantly, in the space of one frame. Rather than motion, the effect is a sequence of still poses. This is conceptually in line with what's needed for the first pass of pose-to-pose animation. A sequence of extreme poses can be arranged, one after another, with no consideration given to the movement between them. For this pass, Constant interpolation is set in the Ipo Editor, as shown in Figure 6.12. The interpolation mode can also be set in the Action Editor, where it will be applied to all the Ipos in the action.

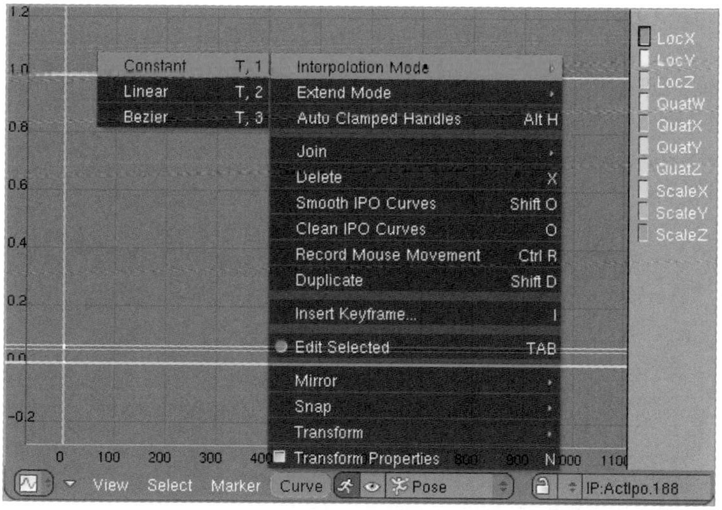

Figure 6.12

Constant interpolation

Some examples of the first-pass key poses in the Virginia waking animation are shown in Figure 6.13. At this point, there is no motion between the poses, simply a jump from one to the next.

The keyframes for the head bone are shown in the Action Editor in Figure 6.14. You can see what the Constant-interpolated curves look like for the same bone in Figure 6.15. As you can see, the shape of these curves is not *curvy*. Rather, they are a series of abrupt steps from one value to the next.

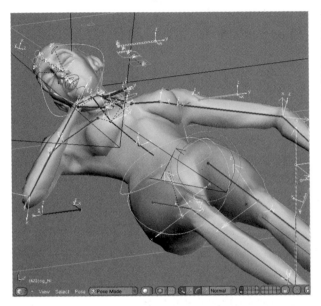

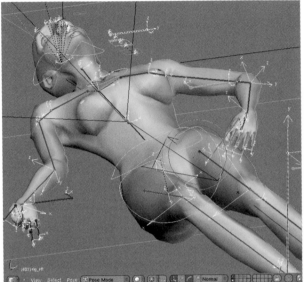

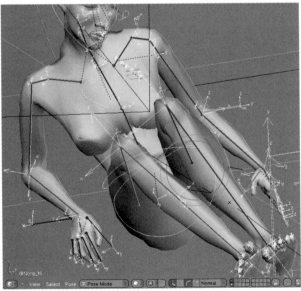

Figure 6.13

Some key poses

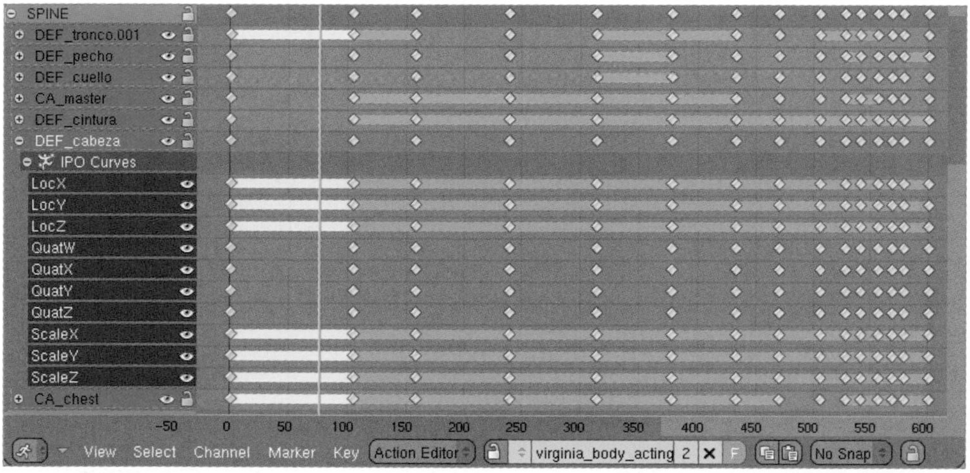

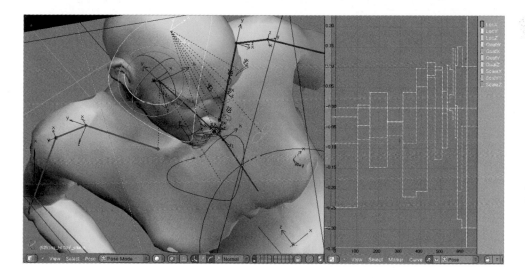

Figure 6.14

Keyframes for the head bone

Figure 6.15

Ipo curves for the head bone

Refining the Curves

After the first pass of animation, where the extreme poses are set, the interpolation type is changed to Linear, as shown in Figure 6.16. Rather than abrupt steps, the curves become a series of diagonal straight lines from one point to the next. This makes it possible to see a range of positions between each keyframed position, as shown in Figure 6.17, and gives the animator a better sense of the timing and speed of the motion between the poses. At this point, new keyframes might be added, or existing keyframes might be adjusted along the Timeline with respect to each other.

Figure 6.16

Setting Linear-
interpolated Ipo
curves

Linear interpolation gives a sense of the motion between poses, but it does not result in natural, organic-looking movement. The speed of the movement is constant from one pose to the next, and the changes in direction or speed of the movement are abrupt, giving a mechanical impression.

Bezier curves create smoother transitions that fade to a gentle change at the keyframed points. Setting Bezier interpolation is shown in Figure 6.18, and the resulting curves are shown in Figure 6.19.

Bezier curves yield smooth transitions, and furthermore can be adjusted precisely by tabbing into Edit mode and adjusting the control points on the Bezier handles, as shown in Figure 6.20. This gives the animator total control over the fine details of the animated movement. In this stage, the slope of each Ipo is edited directly, wherever a moving hold pose is needed. A *moving hold pose* is a pose in which the character holds still overall, but moves slightly to create a more lifelike effect. Including moving holds at this point gives the animator a better idea of how the movement should be timed and how natural it looks.

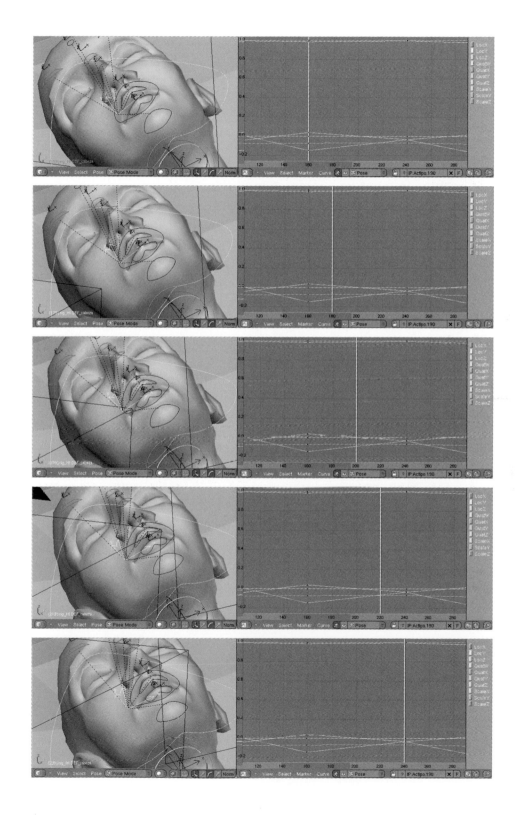

Figure 6.17

**Gradual motion
with linear curves**

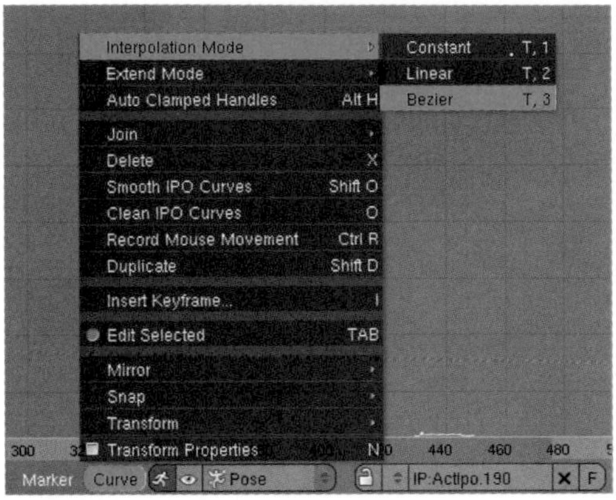

Figure 6.18

Setting Bezier interpretation

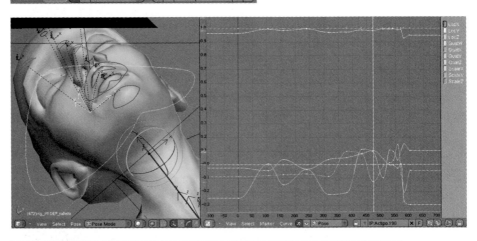

Figure 6.19

Smooth transitions with Bezier curves

Figure 6.20

Using control point handles to adjust the curve shapes

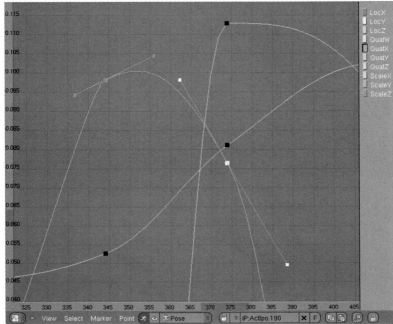

Creating Facial Animation

This particular shot doesn't involve a great deal of facial animation; there's no lip sync or expressive facial interaction with other characters. However, the minimal facial animation that exists, primarily the movement of the eyes, is quite important to the shot. The control for the direction of the eyes is the selected yellow custom-shaped bone shown in Figure 6.21. Note that not only does the gaze of the eyes follow the movement of the bone, but the upper and lower eyelids also move accordingly, as they do naturally when a person looks up or down. With what you've learned in Chapter 5, "Rigging Characters," you should be able to understand how the rigging for this works by studying the Virginia character .blend file included in the characters directory of the production tree included on the DVD.

Figure 6.21

Eye direction control

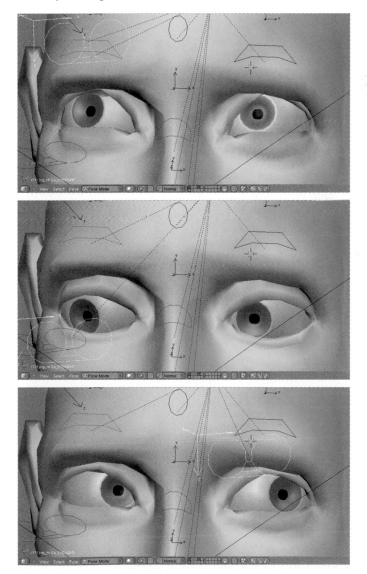

The facial animation is carried out similarly to how the body animation is done, beginning with Constant-interpolated poses (some of them are shown in Figure 6.22), and then refined through multiple passes of Linear- and finally Bezier-interpolated curves.

Another notable aspect of this shot is that body animation, specifically the animation of the quickening breathing, is synchronized to the facial expressions to represent the character's troubled sleep. For this, being able to group channels is a great help, because it enables the animator to hide all the channels that do not need to be synchronized, and concentrate on synchronizing the bones that control the facial expressions and the breathing movement.

Figure 6.22
Eye poses through-out the shot

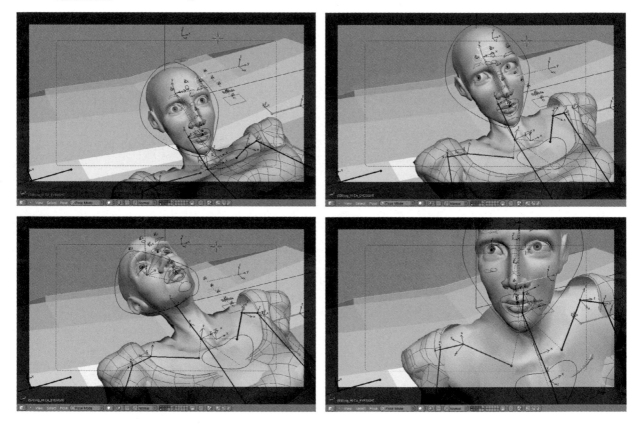

Notable Changes in Blender 2.5+

Like many aspects of Blender, the animation system has changed considerably from Blender 2.49 to Blender 2.5, currently in its first alpha release. As you can see from the unaltered face of the Virginia character as she looks in this scene when opened in the current development version of Blender 2.5 (Figure 6.23), the transition is not guaranteed to be painless!

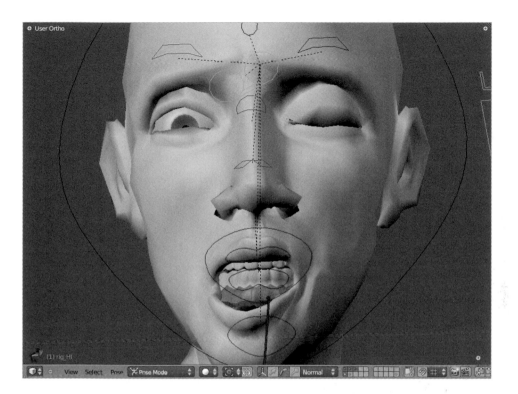

Figure 6.23

The Blender 2.49 scene unceremoniously opened in Blender 2.5 Alpha 0

This isn't too surprising. A lot of rigging details have changed, and even in places where functionality is similar, the underlying representation has changed considerably, particularly in regard to the Python API. Another important change is the disappearance of the beloved Ipo. From 2.5, the word *Ipo* will most likely drop out of the English language altogether, because animation function curves in Blender will henceforth be known by the unsurprising moniker of *animation function curves*, or *F-Curves* for short.

The name change really is more than just terminology, and it reflects under-the-hood changes in the animation system to make it more flexible and general, in keeping with the longtime goal of making everything in Blender capable of being animated. The window type where you'll work with F-Curves directly is called the *Graph Editor* and is shown in Figure 6.24. As you can see, it's not all that different looking from the current Ipo Editor. The drop-down menu in the header that reads *F-Curve Editor* enables you to select the Drivers display window, where you can work with driver function curves.

Figure 6.24

The Graph Editor in Blender 2.5

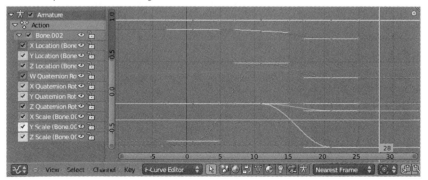

The Action Editor also has added functionality. In the header menu of the Action Editor, you can select the Shape Key Editor, the Grease Pencil viewer, and the Dope Sheet in addition to the familiar Action Editor. The Dope Sheet gives an overview of all animated objects and actions in the scene. You can see both the Dope Sheet window and the Action Editor in Figure 6.25.

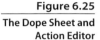

Figure 6.25

The Dope Sheet and Action Editor

Adding Cloth and Hair

Flowing clothing requires cloth simulation to animate correctly. This makes the process of posing and animation more complicated than when working with meshes deformed only with modifiers, lattices, or other rigging tools. For this reason, clothing and hair simulations are usually dealt with separately from the main character animation.

Working with Cloth Simulation

When working with simulations, it's important not to do more work than necessary—or to make your computer do more than is necessary! Because the character is in bed, covered by a blanket, only the portion of her nightgown that will be shown in the shot is used for the cloth simulation. In Figure 6.26, you can see the cloth objects. The blanket is shown in wireframe so that you can see the character model beneath it.

In Chapter 4, "Modeling," you saw how to use weights to pin cloth so that the weighted portions of the cloth did not move freely during the baking process. Although that chapter was discussing cloth simulation as a modeling tool, the technique of pinning cloth is identical when animating. Figure 6.27 shows the pinning weights on the portion of the nightgown that is used here. Weights are also used on the Cloth objects to do bone deformations, as you can see in Figure 6.28, which shows some of the bone weightings for the upper-body clothing objects.

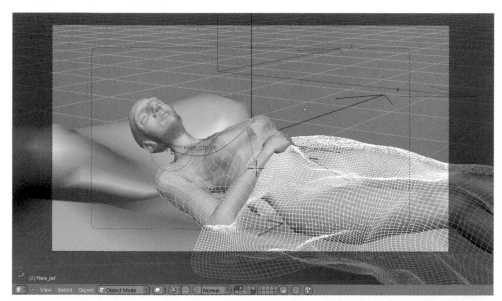

Figure 6.26

The cloth objects in the scene

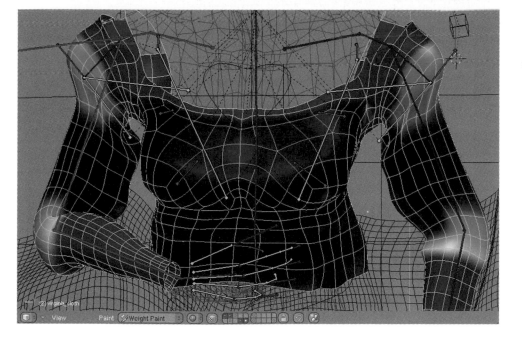

Figure 6.27

Pinning weight for the nightgown

Figure 6.28

Weights for upper-body clothing

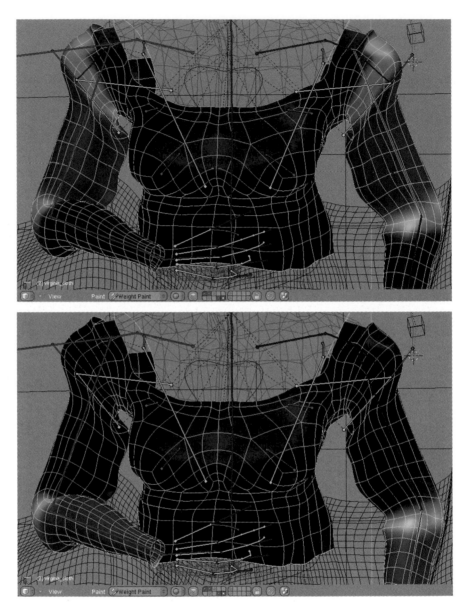

Working with Particle Hair

Convincing hair can be created in Blender by using strand particles. The basics of working with Blender hair, including generating the particle systems and working with the hair-styling tools, can be found in *Bounce, Tumble, and Splash! Simulating the Physical World with Blender* (Sybex, 2008). Working with hair is very similar to working with other particle systems in Blender. However, even when you know the basics of working with Blender hair, it still can be difficult to know exactly how to integrate the effect into a complete animation.

In order to work with the parts of the hairstyle independently, they are each implemented as separate particle systems. The main hair for the head comprises four separate particle systems, shown in Figure 6.29. The braid hair is made up of yet another particle system, shown in Figure 6.30. The shape of the braid is controlled by a curve, as shown in Figure 6.31. The mesh emitter for the hair must be set to be a Collision object in order for the hair to collide with it.

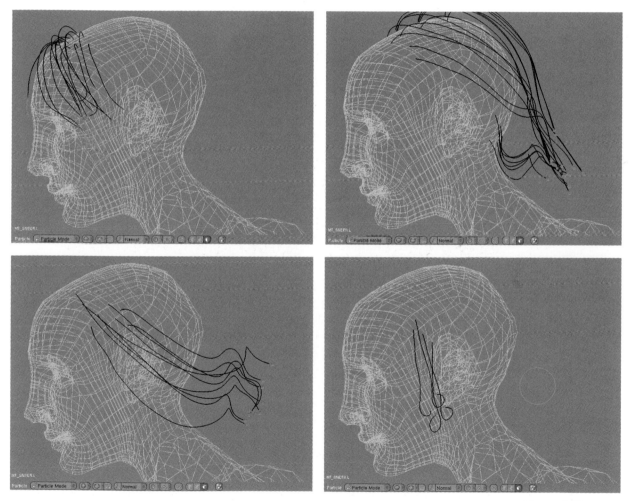

Figure 6.29

Hair is organized into separate particle systems.

Figure 6.30

A hair system for the
long braid

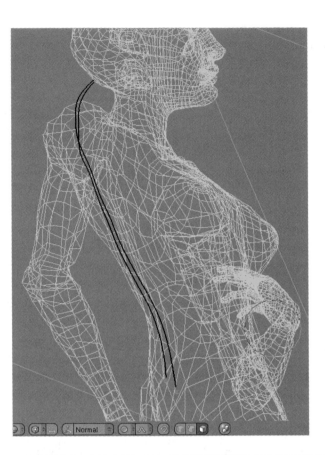

Figure 6.31

A curve guide for
the hair braid

Figure 6.32

The vertex group for the braid

Setting Up the Braid Rig

It's worthwhile to look a bit closer at the details of setting up the hair braid and its control rig. As with each of the other particle systems that make up the hair, the hair braid particles are emitted from a vertex group defined on the character mesh. The vertex group for the hair braid is shown in Figure 6.32.

The step-by-step details of setting up and initially styling the hair itself are beyond the scope of this book, but Figures 6.33 and 6.34 show the main settings for the particle system and the Children and Extras settings, respectively. You can also check the character .blend file in the production directory on the companion DVD to see all the details. The resulting braid, styled but not yet modified by a curve, is shown in Figure 6.35.

The curve guide should be placed exactly at the spot at which the hair emits from the mesh. This is done by selecting the vertex group on the mesh in Edit mode and snapping the cursor to that spot with Shift+S and then choosing Cursor to Selected. Then, in Object mode, without moving the cursor, a Curve object is added by pressing Shift+A and choosing Bezier Curve from the menu, as shown in Figure 6.36. This will result in the addition of a Bezier curve to the scene, as shown in Figure 6.37.

Figure 6.33

Settings for the braid particle system

Figure 6.34

Children and Extras particle settings

Figure 6.35

The unmodified
styled braid

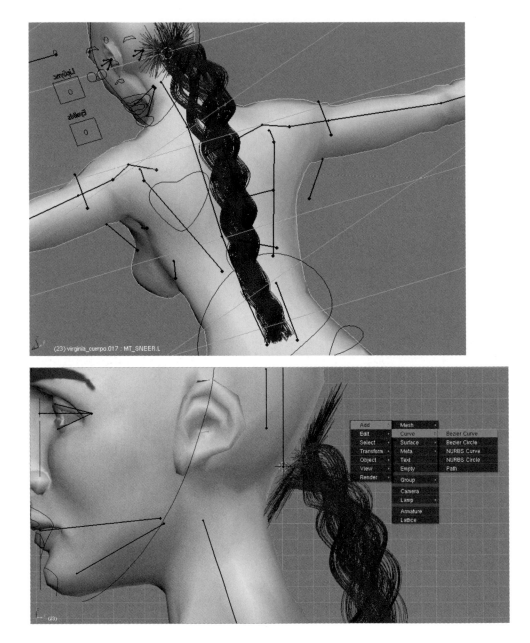

Figure 6.36

Adding a curve at
the base of the hair

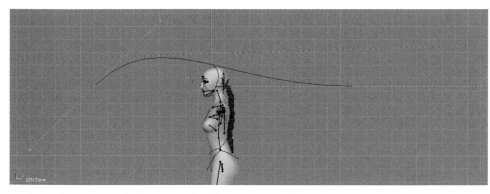

Figure 6.37
Adding a Bezier curve

The curve is extruded once so that there are a total of three control points, and they are then edited to follow the shape of the hair braid. The resulting curve is shown with its properties in Figure 6.38. Note that the 3D button is toggled on the Curve and Surface panel, making it possible for the Bezier curve to be modeled freely in three dimensions. For the curve to behave as a force on the particles, it must be made into a Curve Guide effector, which is done in the Fields panel of the Physics buttons area, as shown in Figure 6.39.

Figure 6.38
Curve properties and control points

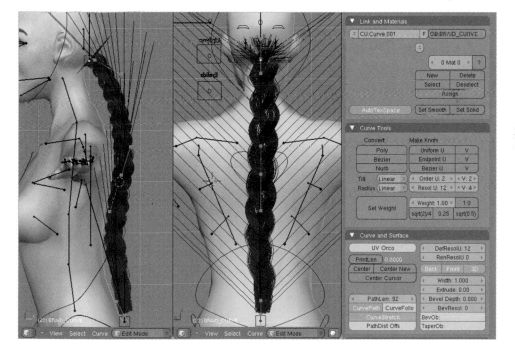

Figure 6.39

Force field settings

To rig the curve and enable it to be posed and animated, hooks are added to each control point. Hooks are added by selecting a control point and pressing Ctrl+H, and then selecting Add New Empty. Each time you do this, a Hook modifier is added to the Curve object, as shown in Figure 6.40. Note that in the figure, the empties are set to Cube Display mode, so they show up as cubes rather than the default axis arrow display. This can be selected in the Link and Materials panel of the Edit buttons area.

To control the movement of the empty hooks, a new bone is added to the armature for each hook, as shown in Figure 6.41. Of course, this is done with the armature in Edit mode. The cursor-snapping method is used to ensure that each bone is added to the exact spot where the corresponding empty is located.

After these new bones have been added, the empties are bone-parented to their respective control bone. This is done by selecting the empty, and then selecting the corresponding bone of the Armature in Pose mode and parenting with Ctrl+P, and finally choosing Parent to Bone.

After the curve guide is activated, it will affect all particles on the same layer as it is by default. This is not appropriate here, as you can see in Figure 6.42, which shows the particle system representing the ringlets on the character's temples. As you can see, these particles are also being swept back to follow the shape of the curve guide.

Figure 6.40

Three empty hook modifiers

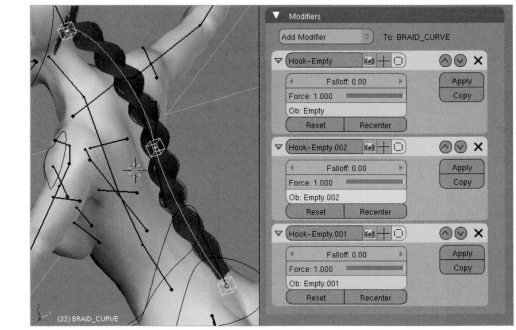

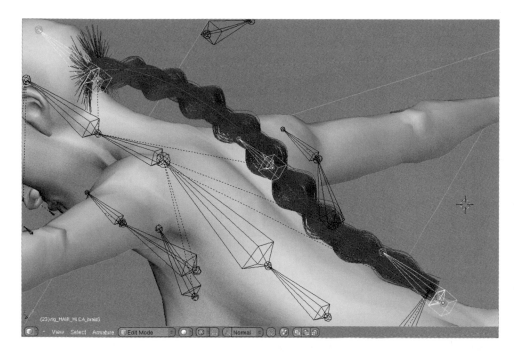

Figure 6.41

Adding bones for each hook

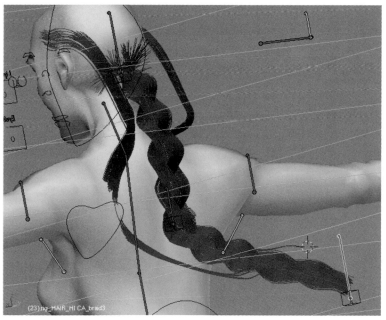

Figure 6.42

The temple ringlets influenced by the curve guide

To eliminate this problem, it is possible to create Effector groups and associate them with specific particle systems. The idea here is simple. Objects with force fields are grouped by using the ordinary Blender grouping functionality. The name of the group is then entered in the Effectors group field on the Extras panel for the particle system. A particle system with an Effectors group will not be affected by any other force fields.

The first thing to do is to create a group for the Curve Guide effector, as shown in Figure 6.43. The curve is the only object that will belong to this group, and the braid particle system will be affected by it. The group is called BRAID_CURVE. If you refer back to Figure 6.34, you can see that this is entered into the GR field under Effectors on the Extras buttons tab.

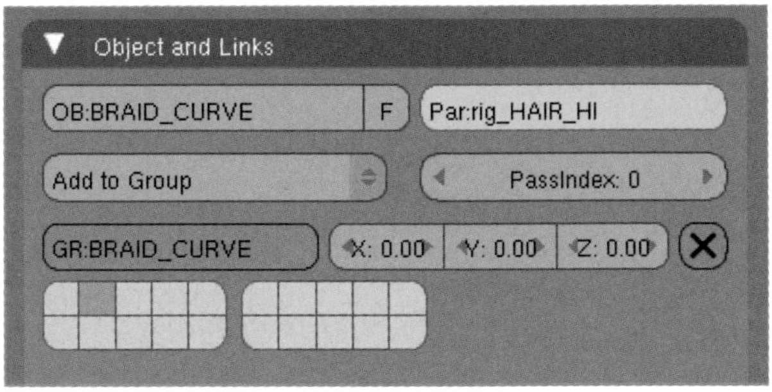

Figure 6.43

Creating a group for the curve effector

This is fine for the braid, but it still does not help with the ringlets on the temple. The reason for this is that the ringlets' particle system does not have an Effector group associated with it. Particle systems with no Effector group are affected by all force fields that share a layer with them. There's a simple solution to this. What must be done is to create an empty group, which will be called NONE. This empty group will be used as an Effector group on all particle systems that should not be affected by force fields.

In Blender, a new group can be created only by selecting Add New from the Add to Group menu in the Object buttons. But to get to the Object buttons, an object must be selected. It is not possible to create a group with no members. It *is* possible, however, to create a group with only one member, and then delete that member. To do this, a dummy empty object is added to the scene (it doesn't matter where, because it will be deleted momentarily), and a new group is created for that object in the ordinary way, as shown in Figure 6.44. This group is named NONE. Immediately upon creating the NONE group, the dummy empty can be deleted, as shown in Figure 6.45. Now there is a group called NONE with no objects in it. This group's name is entered into the Effector GR field for the temple ringlets' particle system, as shown in Figure 6.46. As you can see in that figure, the ringlets return to their correct shape, no longer influenced by the curve guide.

Figure 6.44
Creating the NONE effector group with a dummy empty

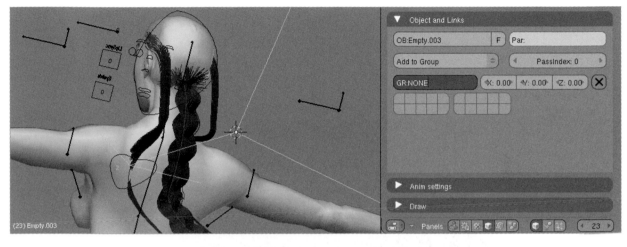

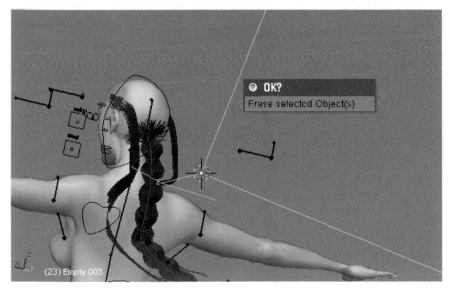

Figure 6.45
Deleting the dummy empty

Figure 6.46

Setting the temple ringlets to be influenced by the NONE group

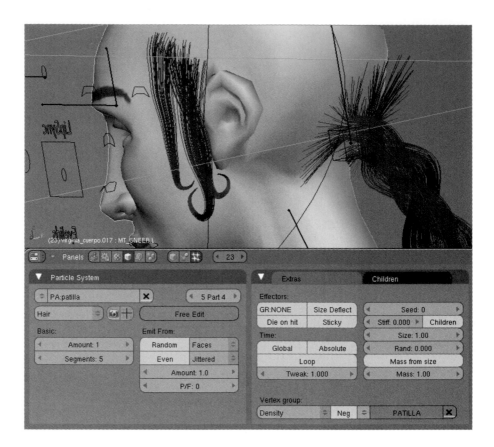

In order to have convincing hair behavior in this scene, the hair particles need to interact with physical objects in the scene. For this reason, it's best to animate the hair last. After completing the animation with the linked armature and mesh, the particle system object and its controlling armature (which is identical to the linked armature) should be appended to the file, and the actions that were created with the linked armature should be associated with the appended armature as well. This will result in having two identical armatures in the scene, one linked and one appended, but the difference will be essentially invisible, because they will both be associated with the same animated actions.

The full hairstyle with children displayed in the 3D viewport appears as shown in Figure 6.47. In this shot, a blanket has been added and replaces the lower portion of the nightdress, once again using the same techniques for cloth simulation.

In the next chapter, you'll see how a combination of many of the topics you've read about so far, plus a few new ones, can be used to create a complete scene, with animation, effects, and compositing.

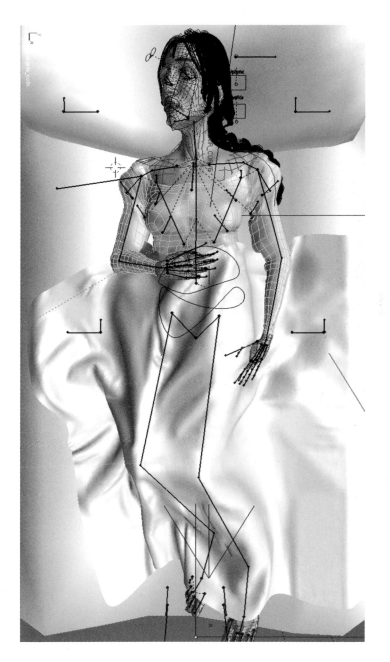

Figure 6.47

Hair with children displayed in the 3D viewport

CHAPTER 7

Descent into the Maelstrom

In this chapter, you'll take an in-depth look at a central effects shot from the *Mercator* project. In the shot, the *Eleanor* becomes trapped in a giant ocean whirlpool. In order to create the effect of the violent stormy seas tossing the ship, a variety of techniques are used in combination.

CHAPTER CONTENTS

- **Setting the Scene**
- **Using Textures, Modifiers, and Simulation**
- **Creating Finishing Touches with Node-Based Compositing**

Setting the Scene

In the maelstrom scene in *Mercator,* the ship *Eleanor* is overpowered by stormy seas and sucked into a gigantic ocean whirlpool. Such an effect requires a combination of techniques to achieve. Before discussing exactly how each component of the shot works, it's worthwhile to take a wider view and see how the shot is composed of separate .blend files and their contents to get a sense of the overall logic of how the effect is animated.

In order to split work among the team members, three separate .blend files were used to create the maelstrom shot. You can find all three in the production directory on the DVD that accompanies this book. The main .blend file, which will be the focus of most of this chapter, is the ani.blend file. This file includes all the main objects and animations except for the camera animation. The cam.blend file includes the camera animation, so that it can be adjusted in parallel with work on the main scene. Finally, light_append_blender249.blend is where mist, fog, and some depth effects are added to the shot and the final composite is created. You'll take a brief look at how this works in the final section of the chapter.

Most of the action in this shot takes place in ani.blend. In Figure 7.1, you can see the complete scene in ani.blend. At this scale, the ship is not clearly visible. You can see the sky dome and the mesh representing the ocean vortex. You can also see several empties and the outlines of armature bones. These are part of the rig that controls the ocean storm and the ship's motion in it. The biggest object in the scene is the lattice used to add large-scale undulations to the ocean surface.

Zooming in a bit closer, Figure 7.2 shows the vortex mesh and the armature. The bone shown selected in the image controls the motion of the highlighted empty. This empty, in turn, drives the rotation of a texture to create a rotating displacement map. You'll see more about how this works in the next section of this chapter.

Figure 7.1

The complete scene with the lattice selected

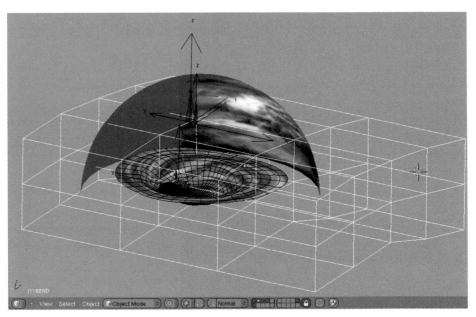

Figure 7.2

A closer look at the vortex control armature

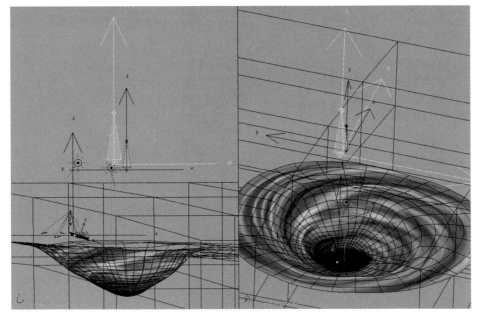

In Figure 7.3, the ocean rig is shown more closely. The bones that control the large-scale movement of the ship are part of the same armature that controls the rotation of the vortex texture. This armature also acts upon a subdivided plane representing the waves beneath the boat itself. As you can see in Figure 7.4, the boat does not rest directly on the ocean vortex mesh, but rather on this separate wave plane. This is done in order to get more-convincing close-up waves, which requires more-detailed geometry. The camera angle of the final shot will be such that the distinction between these two surfaces will be concealed.

The centerpiece of the shot is of course the ship itself. The ship is linked from an external library, as described in Chapter 3, "Creating a 3D Animatic." Because it is not necessary to edit or to modify the ship in any way in the shot, linking is the most efficient and straightforward way to work with the ship. With the ship linked, the original library file can be edited, textured, or modified in any way, and the changes will be automatically incorporated into this scene and any other scenes linking the ship. This makes it possible for animators, modelers, and other creators to carry out multiple tasks at the same time. The linked ship is shown in Figure 7.5. Later, after the animation is complete, a high-poly, fully textured version of the ship will be swapped in to replace the proxy version shown.

Figure 7.3

The ship, the wave plane, and the wave control bones

Figure 7.4

The wave plane situated over the vortex

Figure 7.5

The linked ship

As touched on in Chapter 3, linking is not always appropriate, and the example of the ship's sail rig in this shot provides an excellent case in point. In the shot, the sails are animated with full cloth simulation. Because of the way that cloth simulation frames are cached on the hard disk, completed cloth simulations cannot be linked to. It wouldn't be desirable to link to a centralized library with a fixed simulation anyway, because the deformations of the cloth simulation should reflect the movements and forces of the current scene. There's no way around having to bake the simulation specifically for a given scene. For this reason, the sail rig, including the cloth sails and an armature built to hold them in place, is appended to the scene rather than linked. Figure 7.6 shows the appended sail rig.

Figure 7.6

The appended sail rig

Using Textures, Modifiers, and Simulation

Textures play a significant role in many 3D visual effects. It might be surprising that an effect such as the one described in this chapter, a ship being consumed by an ocean whirlpool, would depend so heavily on simple 2D textures. Nevertheless, textures play an important role in creating the atmosphere, controlling displacement deformations, and creating convincing natural movement with procedural noise patterns.

The Sky Dome

Probably the most traditional use of a texture in this scene is the UV-mapped image for the sky dome. This is a very conventional use of textures, and it's done here in a straightforward way. In Figure 7.7, you can see several views of the sky dome mesh. The mesh is a simple UV sphere cut in half and scaled appropriately. Note that the normals of the object have been flipped inward. The mapped image is shown in Figure 7.8. The painted sky does not cover the whole mesh. There's no need to paint more than is necessary. Only the portion of the mesh that will be in the shot is painted. This is initially done directly in Blender, using Texture Paint mode straight from the Camera view, and then the texture is refined in GIMP. Figure 7.9 shows an orthogonal view of the sky dome with the texture applied. For rendering, the texture is associated with a shadeless material.

Figure 7.7

Several views of the sky dome mesh

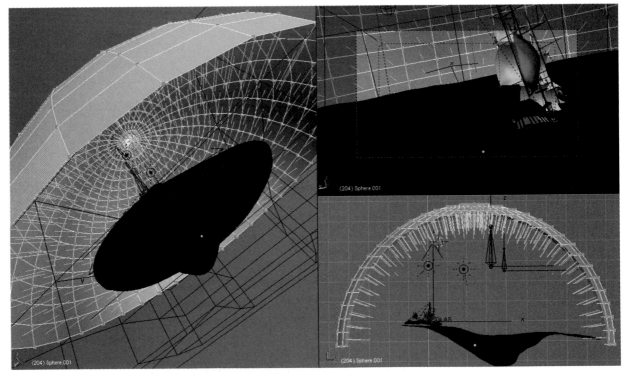

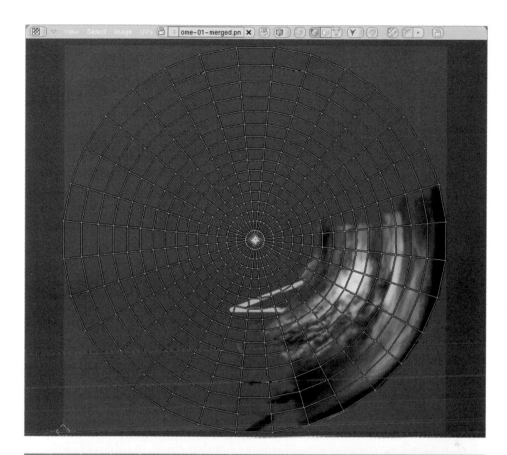

Figure 7.8

The sky texture
mapped to
the dome

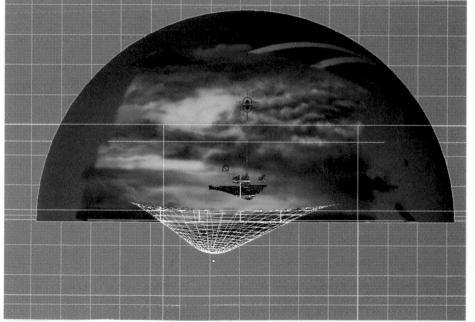

Figure 7.9

The textured
sky dome

The Vortex

Compared to the simple static color image of the sky dome, the textures of the ocean whirlpool play a more complex role, being used for bump mapping, specularity mapping, and displacement, as well as being animated. The mesh is shown in Figure 7.10, with the UV-mapped espiral-bump.tif image texture displayed. The UV mapping is shown in Figure 7.11. The bump map image itself is shown in Figure 7.12. The image was created in GIMP, using several built-in GIMP filters. First a Clouds filter was used to create a noise pattern, and then a Whirlpool filter was applied to spin the middle of the image. The method was quick and simple but very effective.

The material has several channels of textures active on it. There are some channels on the material that have textures associated with them but that are not selected as active. In some of these cases, the textures are used to control modifiers, not as standard material textures. Blender 2.49 and previous versions require that all textures be associated with a material, so for this reason textures intended to be used elsewhere can be simply disabled as material textures. This is a little bit inelegant, and it has been rectified in Blender 2.5, which enables you to create textures independently of materials. The active textures control reflection, specularity, color, and light emission. The reflection texture mapping and the corresponding texture are shown in Figure 7.13. The values of this texture affect the Col and Cmir settings by using the Value mix mode in order to add more specularity when the camera is close to the surface. The texture is mapped using the Refl coordinates. The specularity of the surface is controlled by the Spec channel. The mapping values and the texture for this channel are shown in Figure 7.14.

Figure 7.10

The textured vortex mesh

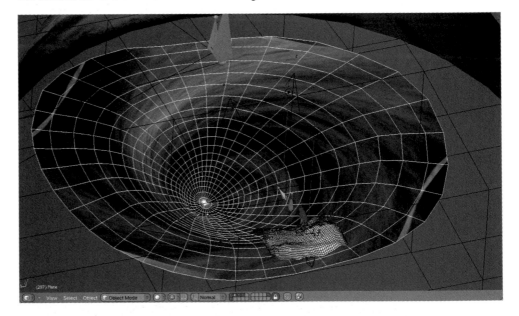

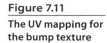

Figure 7.11
The UV mapping for the bump texture

Figure 7.12
The espiral-bump
.tif **texture image**

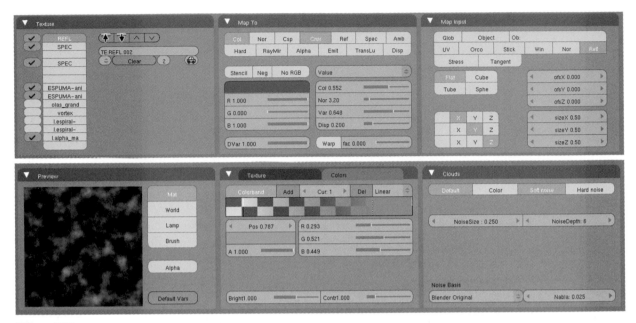

Figure 7.13

The reflection texture channel and corresponding texture

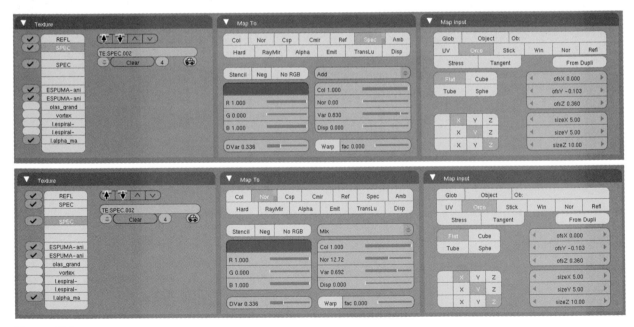

Figure 7.14

The specularity channel and corresponding texture

The image texture in Figure 7.15 is used in a different way. Instead of being actively used on the material, it is used on a modifier, as you will see shortly. Blender 2.49 requires that all textures be associated with a material, a requirement that has been lifted in Blender 2.5.

Figure 7.15

The spiral texture channel and corresponding texture

In Figure 7.16, you can see how the armature controls the rotation of the texture. The empty shown in the figure is bone-parented to the bone. The texture is object-mapped to the empty's coordinates. When the bone rotates, the texture also rotates. In Figure 7.17, you can see the Ipo curve for the rotation of the vortex Mesh object itself.

Figure 7.18 shows the modifier stack for the vortex Mesh object. The main work here is being done by the two Displace modifiers. These represent the two different methods of rotating the texture. The two modifiers are combined by means of vertex groups. The vortex and NO_vortex vertex group weights are shown in Figure 7.19.

The Lattice modifier uses the Bend lattice shown at the beginning of the chapter to adjust large-scale warping of the entire vortex mesh. This is used to quickly and easily adjust how the horizon looks from the perspective of the camera.

Figure 7.16

The animated bone that drives the vortex texture rotation

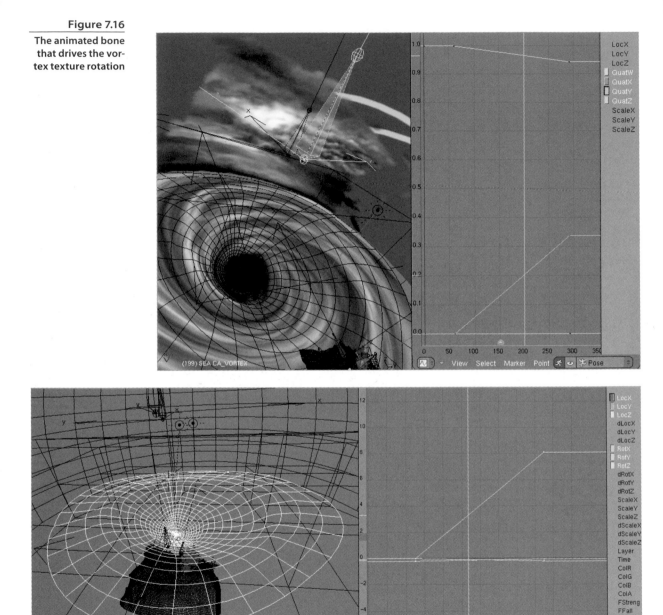

Figure 7.17

The rotation of the vortex object

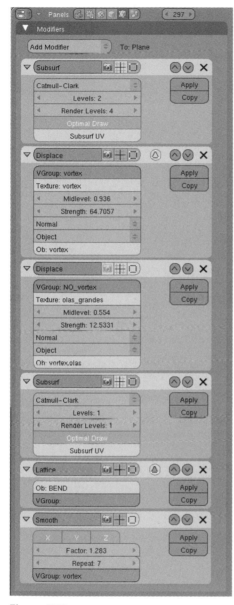

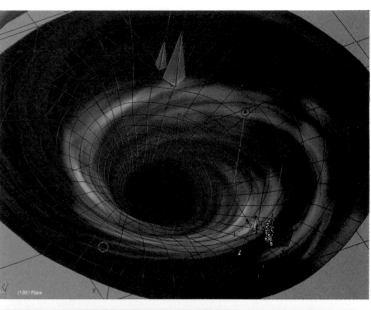

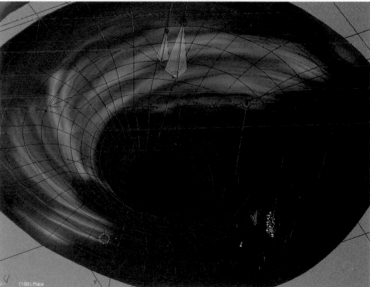

Figure 7.18
The modifier stack on the vortex mesh

Figure 7.19
The vortex and NO_vortex weight groups

The Wave Plane

A separate object is used for the choppy sea surface directly under the ship. With the camera angle of the final shot, it is not apparent that this is a separate surface, but setting up the shot in this way makes it possible to deal with the nearby wavy sea movement separately from the more distant rotating of the vortex. The relevant material options for the wave plane object are shown in Figure 7.20.

All of the textures on this object are procedural. Procedural noise textures are ideal for creating water and natural wave effects. The three texture channels active on this material are the REFL texture channel, whose texture is shown in Figure 7.21, which is mapped to Col and Cmir values on the material; the SPEC texture channel (Figure 7.22), which is mapped to Nor and Spec values; and the olas chicas (small waves) channel (Figure 7.23), whose values are mapped to Nor.

Figure 7.20

The wave plane material

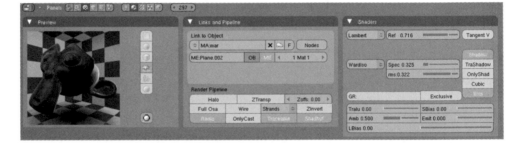

Figure 7.21

REFL texture channel

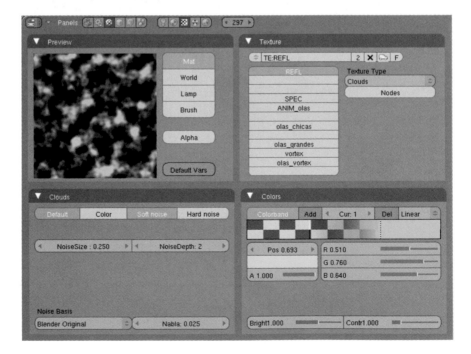

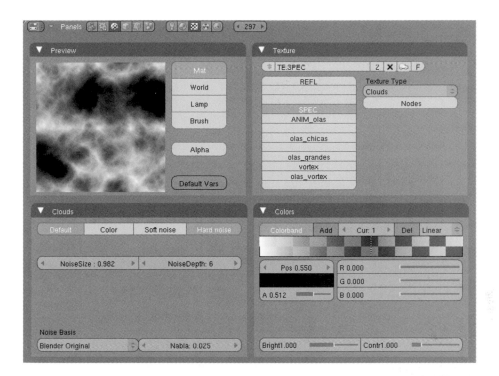

Figure 7.22

Figure 7.22

The SPEC texture channel

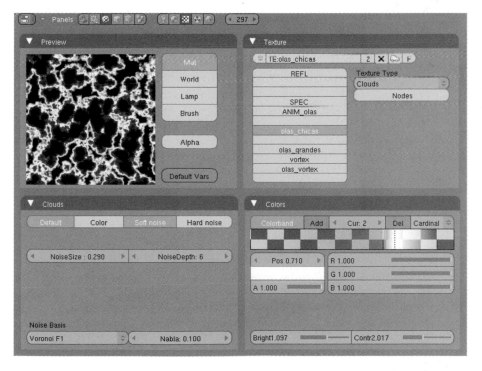

Figure 7.23

The olas chicas texture channel

The combination of these textures on the material, along with subsurface scattering and adjusted Spec and Mir color values, create a sense of depth for the water. The sense of motion is achieved in part by animating the texture coordinates with the material Ipo curves shown in Figure 7.24.

Figure 7.24

Material Ipo curves

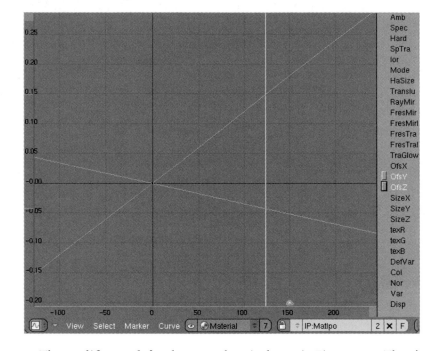

The modifier stack for the wave plane is shown in Figure 7.25. There's a fair amount going on here. In addition to two Displace modifiers, there is also a Wave modifier that adds yet another level of undulation and interference. There's also an Armature modifier that enables the animator to have a considerable amount of control for hand-tweaking of the ocean's movement. In this way, the naturalistic effects of procedural textures are balanced by manual control. Figure 7.26 shows the bones that control the ocean surface.

Weighted vertex groups are crucial to getting a nice and controlled effect from modifiers. In Figure 7.27, the Olas vertex group weights that control the displacement modifiers are shown. In Figure 7.28, the vertex group for the armature is shown.

The armature is also used to control the motion of the ship on the sea, by bone parenting. The bone that controls the ship's motion is shown selected in Figure 7.29.

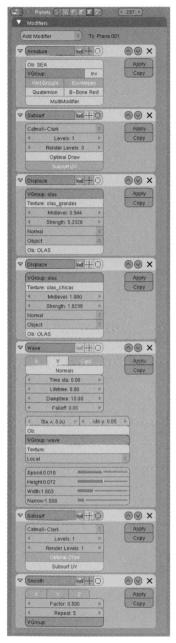

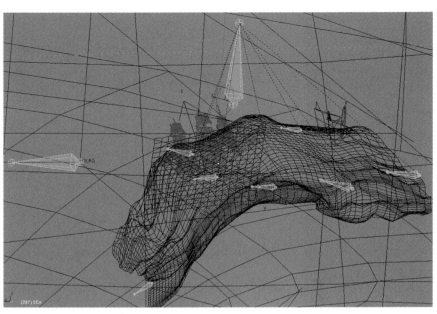

Figure 7.26
The armature controlling the wave plane

Figure 7.25
The modifier stack on the wave mesh

Figure 7.27
The Olas weight group

Figure 7.28

The armature influence on the wave plane in Weight Paint view mode

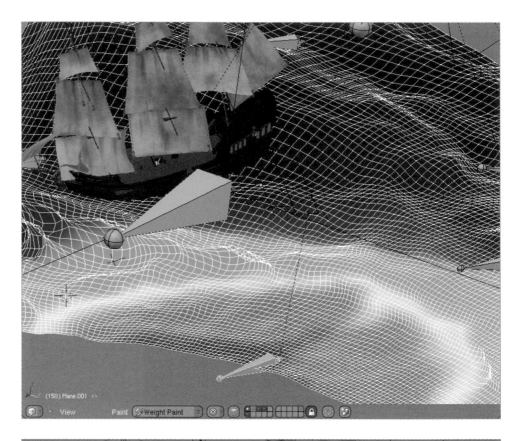

Figure 7.29

The ship's motion controlled by a bone

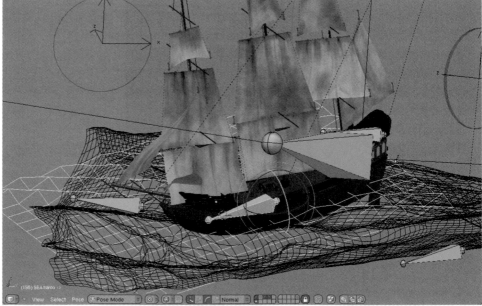

The Ship's Sails

The sails are all part of a single object composed of 11 subdivided mesh planes, as shown in Figure 7.30. The texture for the sails is a hand-painted image. The UV mapping is shown in Figure 7.31.

The sails are rigged to an armature and weighted as shown in Figure 7.32. This vertex group is called CLOTH_PIN1 and is used to pin the cloth for the cloth simulation, as you can see in the cloth simulation settings shown in Figure 7.33.

Figure 7.30

The sails in Edit mode

Figure 7.31

Hand-painted tex-
ture for the sails

Figure 7.32

The sails in Weight
Paint mode

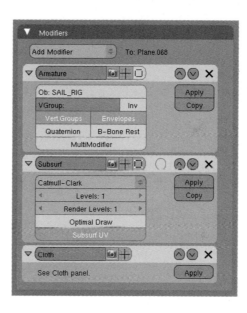

Figure 7.33
Cloth sim settings

The modifier stack for the sails is shown in Figure 7.34. The Armature, Subsurf, and Cloth modifiers are as you would expect. Two things are important here: The modifiers must be in the order shown to achieve the correct effect, and the Levels and Render Levels on the Subsurf modifier must be *the same* when you bake the Cloth. The armature is necessary so that the sails can move along with the ship. Without this, the geometry of the sails would be left behind.

Figure 7.34
The modifier stack for the sails

Sails in a stormy sea are buffeted violently, and the cloth simulation should reflect this. Force fields are used to create dynamic cloth-simulation effects. In this shot, two force fields are used, associated with empties. Their locations and force field settings are shown in Figure 7.35.

A quirk of Blender 2.49 is that the Subsurf Levels and Render Levels values must be equal to each other in order for subsurfed Cloth simulations to bake and render correctly. If the Subsurf Levels and Render Levels values do not match each other, the Cloth simulation will appear to bake correctly in the viewport, but when you render, the base meshes will be rendered without cloth simulation.

Figure 7.36 shows some stills from the 3D viewport. A rendered still from this stage of the production can be seen in Figure 7.37.

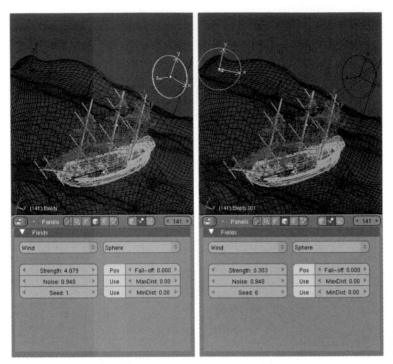

Figure 7.35

Forces acting on the cloth simulation

Figure 7.36

Viewport stills from the animation

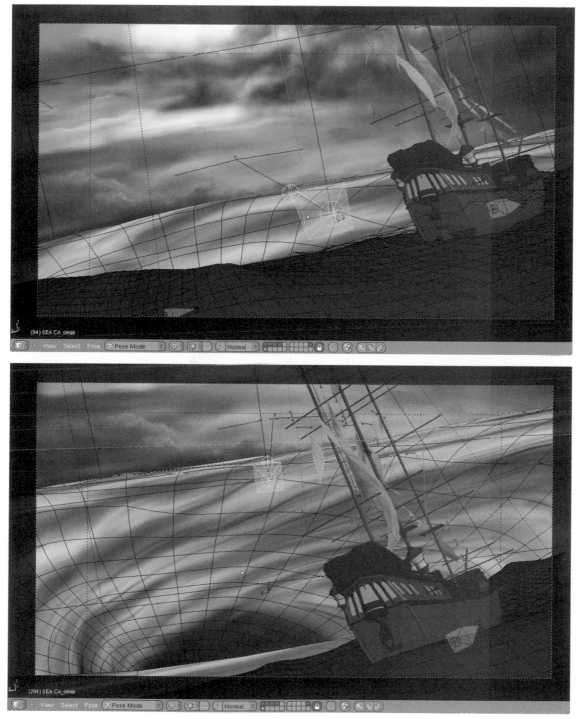

Figure 7.36

(continued)

Figure 7.37

A rendered still

Touching Up the Shot with Node-Based Compositing

The shot is almost finished but still needs some work to really look good. These final steps are taken in the `light_append_blender249.blend` file. This file contains a scene called `e05_t070_light`, in which lights are set up and some alpha-textured planes are arranged to create mist and other effects for use in compositing. The objects of this scene are shown in Figure 7.38. The scene in `light_append_blender249.blend` is then composited with nodes. We won't describe the light and texture plane setup here in detail. You can check the `.blend` file on the CD to see all the details of that.

Appending a Set Scene

The interesting thing to look at here is how exactly the lighting/atmosphere scene in `light_append_blender249.blend` is used to render the animated shot from `ani.blend` described in the previous section. The way this is done is by appending the scene from `ani.blend` and using it as a Set Scene. Blender's Set Scene functionality enables you to use one scene as the backdrop when rendering another. First, it's necessary to append the animated scene from `ani.blend`. Appending a scene is done exactly the same as appending other assets from `.blend` files. Choose Append or Link from the File menu, as shown in Figure 7.39. From `ani.blend/Scene`, the `ani-E05-070` scene is the name of the scene containing the animation, as shown in Figure 7.40.

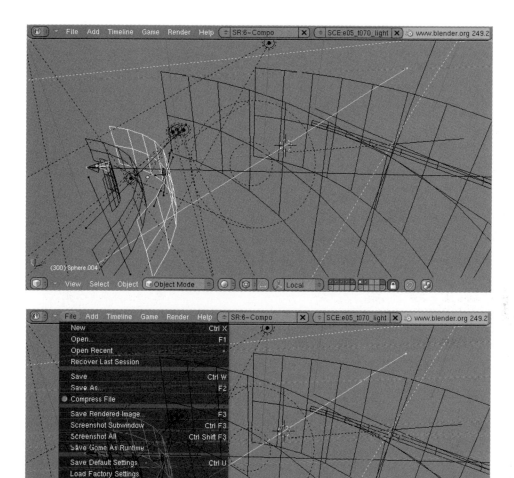

Figure 7.38

Lights and mist-textured planes in the lighting scene

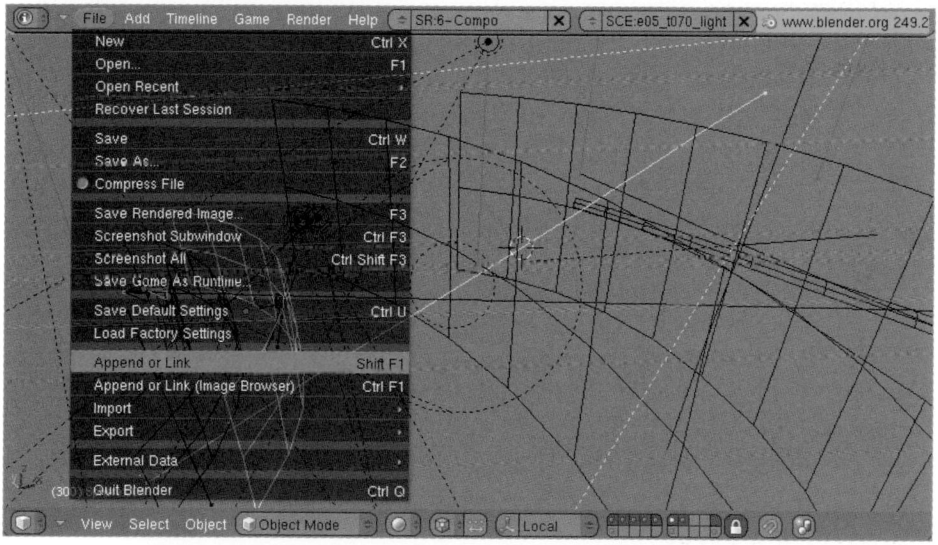

Figure 7.39

The Append or Link menu entry

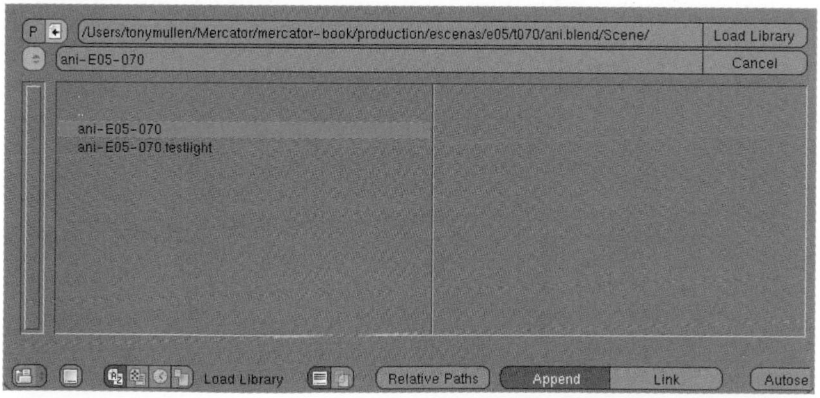

Figure 7.40

Appending the ani-E05-070 scene

When this has been done, `light_append_blender249.blend` contains two scenes: the lighting scene and the animation scene. But these scenes are separate and must be accessed one at a time with the Scene menu in the Info window header, just like any other time you have multiple scenes in Blender. In order to set one of the scenes as the Set scene

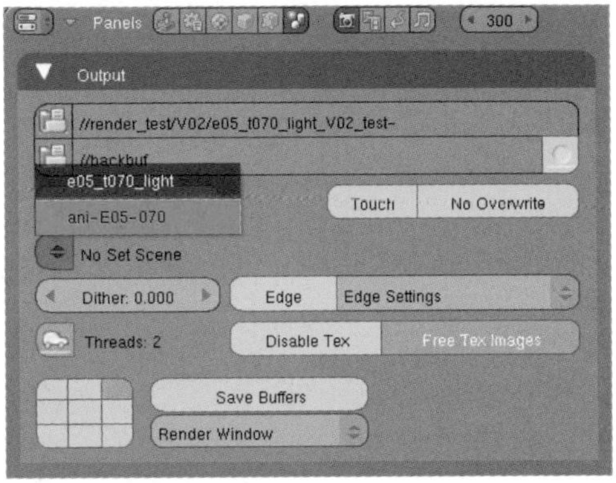

Figure 7.41

Choosing the Set scene

and render them both together, go to the Output panel in the Render buttons area and choose the scene you want as the Set scene from the menu, as shown in Figure 7.41. You will see the ship and the rest of ani-E05-070 appear in the 3D viewport, but they will be grayed out and unselectable, as shown in Figure 7.42. Any edits you make to this scene have to be made directly in the scene itself.

Figure 7.42

The Set scene in the 3D viewport

Using Render Layers for Compositing

Blender's node-based compositing functionality enables you to combine multiple input images together in various ways to create a final composited output image. The input images can be generated in numerous ways, but typically at least some of the input images you will use are themselves outputs from the 3D renderer. Splitting the scene up into *render layers* that can then be dealt with as individual image inputs by the compositor is the first step of compositing 3D scenes with Blender.

Again, the gritty details of how the scene is divided up into render layers are best left for curious readers to check in the .blend file itself. You'll find this information in the Render Layers panel of the Render buttons area. The drop-down list of render layers from that panel is shown in Figure 7.43. These seven render layers organize all the content of the scene in a way that it can be mixed together in the compositor.

Figure 7.44 shows an overview of the node graph for the scene. Don't worry about not being able to see the details here. Check the .blend file on the CD to see it all up close. The figure shows how the render layers connect to the larger node graph.

Figure 7.43

The seven render layers for the scene

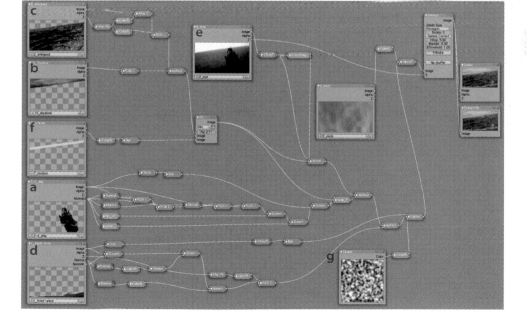

Figure 7.44

An overview of the node graph

Each individual render layer labeled in Figure 7.44 is shown in Figure 7.45. Layer *a* is the ship and sails, layer *b* is the sky dome, *c* is the whirlpool, *d* is the foreground wave, *e* is a strip used to blur the horizon in compositing (as described later in this section), *f* is a mask used to add depth to the scene, and *g* is a layer of mist.

Figure 7.45

(a) Render layers featuring the ship, (b) the sky dome, (c) the whirlpool, (d) the foreground wave, (e) a strip for compositing the horizon, (f) a mask to add depth, and (g) a layer of mist

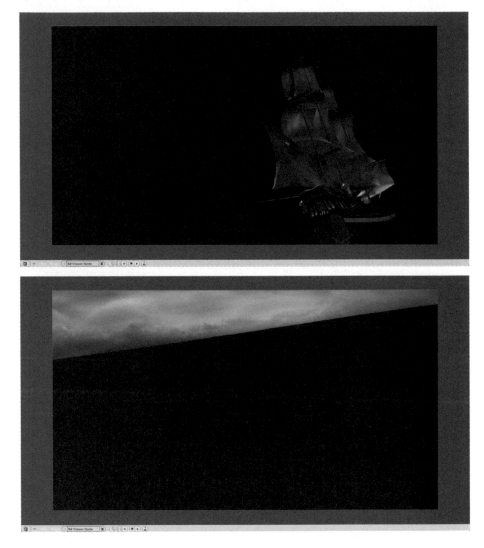

Figure 7.45

(continued)

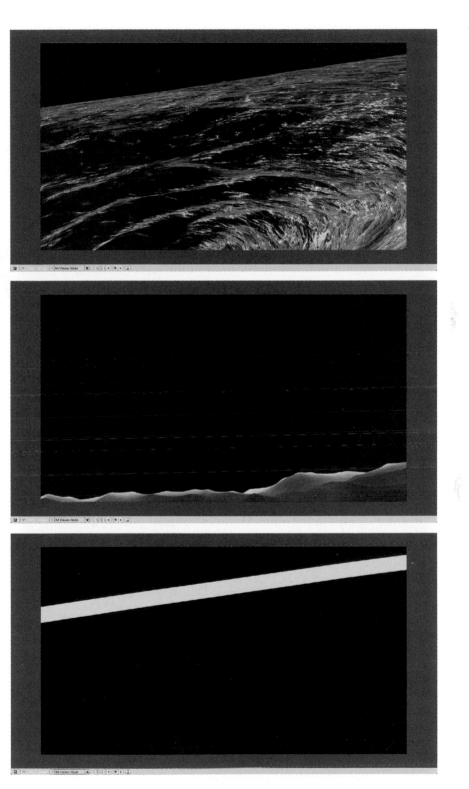

Figure 7.45

(continued)

Creating Atmosphere with Nodes

Node-based compositing is crucial to bringing the scene together and creating an evocative atmosphere. In this shot, several techniques are used to fade the horizon and to create mist rising from the caps of the waves.

Fading the Horizon

The white strip on the black background in the render layer labeled *e* in the previous figures is used to blur the horizon. Without some kind of processing, the line that should be a distant, hazy horizon appears as what it is: the abrupt end of a mesh object. To fix this, the white strip is rendered to a render layer and used as input for a sequence of nodes. The node sequence is shown over the next few figures. Each figure shows the same sequence with the Viewer node attached at a different point in the sequence. The backdrop of the node window shows the output of the Viewer node. Figure 7.46 shows the unmodified render layer. The Alpha output of the render layer is then sent through a ColorRamp node, and the output of this is shown in Figure 7.47. This output then goes through a Blur node, resulting in the output shown in Figure 7.48. Finally, the output of this node is sent through a Mix node to be combined with output of other nodes, as shown in Figure 7.49.

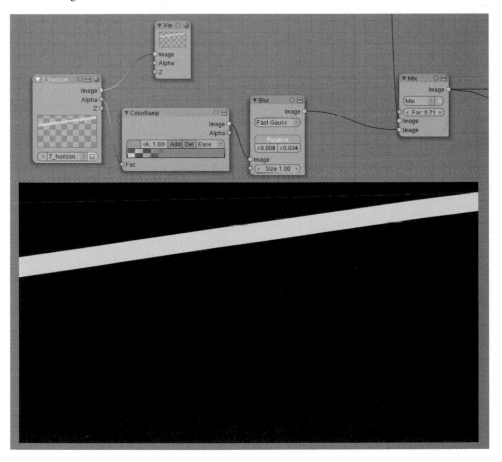

Figure 7.46

The unmodified render layer featuring a white strip on black

Figure 7.47

The output of the
ColorRamp node

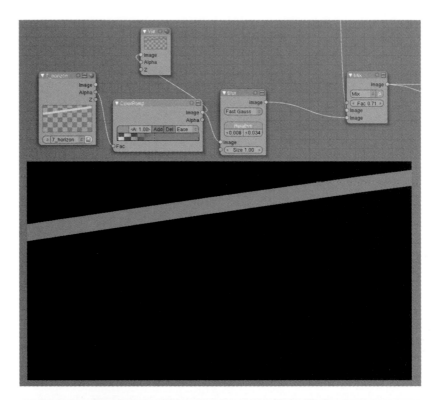

Figure 7.48

The output of the
Blur node

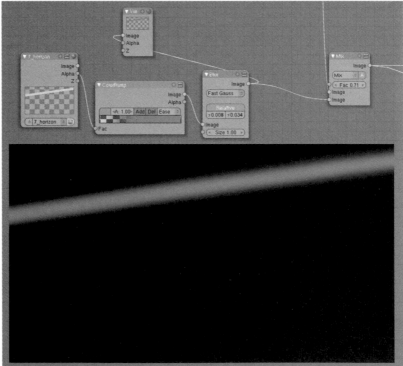

Figure 7.49
The composited scene so far

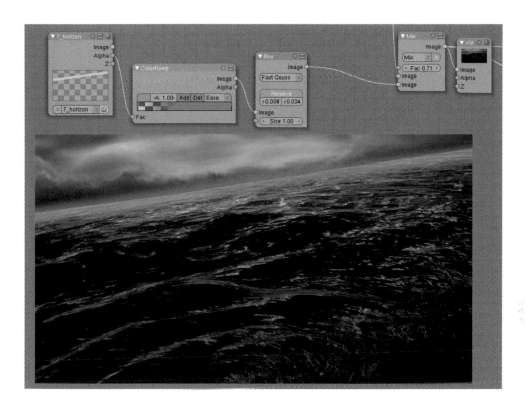

Creating Misty Waves

In stormy seas, wind carries foam and mist off the surface of the water. This mist is not uniform over the surface, but is concentrated at the tips of waves. The following figures show a node sequence for creating an effect that focuses mist around the tips of the waves.

In Figure 7.50, the output of the foreground wave render layer is shown. The image output is fed into a Sobel filter, which creates a high-contrast glow effect around the contours of the shape, as shown in Figure 7.51. The output of the Sobel node is fed into a Dilate/Erode node and dilated (expanded) by 5 pixels. An important thing to take into consideration is that, unlike Blur nodes, the Dilate/Erode node doesn't work in relative amounts, but in absolute pixels. This means that if you are working with a 5-pixel dilate for a render that is 50 percent of the size of the full render, when you go full scale, you'll need to adjust the amount of dilate by hand; in this case, 10 pixels. The output of the Dilate node is shown in Figure 7.52. This output is in turn sent to a Blur node to result in the blurred highlight shown in Figure 7.53. The resulting highlight is used as a factor on a Lighten node, which takes a green cloud texture as input, creating a cloudy mist that is limited to the blurred highlight strip along the contours of the wave, as shown in Figure 7.54.

Figure 7.50

The foreground
wave render layer

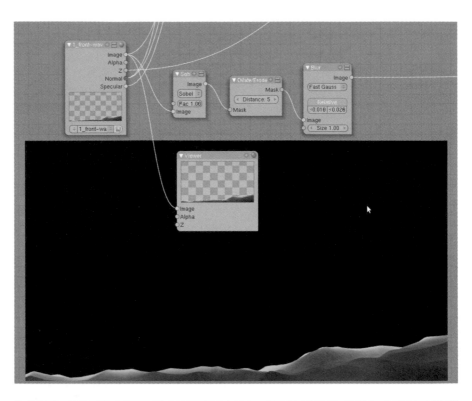

Figure 7.51

The output of the
Sobel node

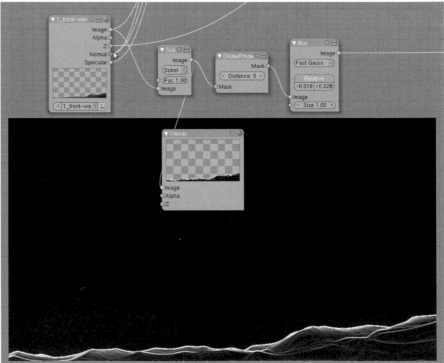

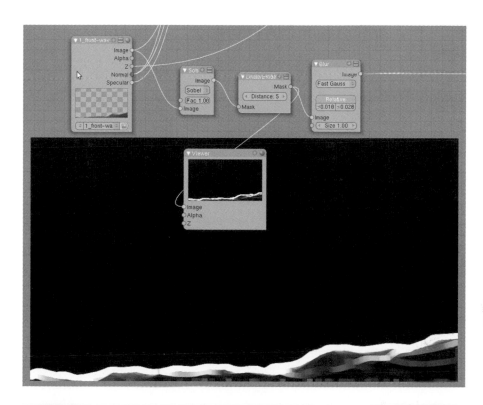

Figure 7.52

The output of the
Dilate node

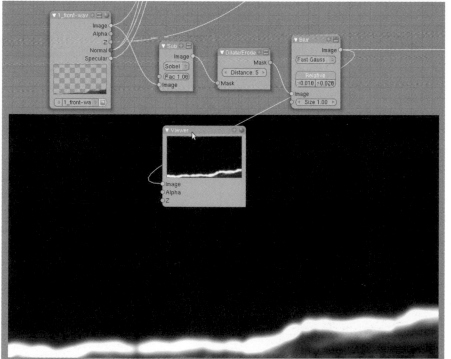

Figure 7.53

The blurred
highlight

Figure 7.54

The composited
mist

Combining these various techniques, and a few others that you can study in the
.blend itself, yields the (near) final render shown in Figure 7.55. For the final render, the
Save Buffers and Full Sample options are active. With the Full Sample option active,
Blender applies the composite to each OSA pass individually as an aliased render and
combines the passes at the end of the pipeline. This results in better compositing, better
antialiasing, and finer details.

Even after rendering, a lot of work has to be done to refine the look, fix errors, and
make sure it all animates well, and then finally to render and edit the animated sequences
together and to carry out postproduction. By now, you should have a very good idea of
how Blender fulfills its various roles in the professional animation pipeline at Licuadora
Studio. We hope you've picked up some techniques and tips along the way that you
wouldn't have picked up elsewhere and we wish you the best in putting these techniques
to work for you in your own studio or individual projects.

Figure 7.55
A rendered still

About the Companion DVD

What You'll Find on the DVD

The following sections are arranged by category and provide a summary of the items you'll find on the DVD. If you need help installing the items provided on the DVD, refer to the installation instructions in the "Using the DVD" section of this appendix.

Chapter Files

All the files provided in this book for completing the tutorials and understanding concepts are located in the Chapter Files directory, and further divided into directories corresponding to each chapter. In order to open .blend files, you will need to have an up-to-date installation of Blender on your computer. For the purposes of this book, you should use Blender version 2.49, which you can install from this DVD or download at www.blender.org.

The Mercator Production Tree

The full production tree for the portions of the *Mercator* project discussed in this book is included on the disc so that you can directly explore all the assets mentioned. Some of the book chapters refer to files that can be found in the production tree.

Blender 2.49 Software

Executable installation files for the current, stable Blender 2.49 are provided for Windows and Mac OS X, both Intel and PPC architectures. The source code is provided in an archive for users of Linux and other Unix-like systems. Users of these systems who would like an executable build specific to their system and architecture can find many available in the Download section at `www.blender.org`.

Blender 2.5 Alpha 1 Software

The Blender foundation has released an alpha version of the Blender 2.5 software as part of its development roadmap. Installations are included for Windows and Mac OS X, both Intel and PPC architectures, and a source code archive is included for users of Linux and other systems. This software is not stable and should be used for preview purposes only. Do not use this software for critical work without carefully backing up all files with a stable release before opening them with Blender 2.5 Alpha 1. Do not assume that `.blend` files created or edited with a nonstable version will always be readable by a stable release.

You can find out more about this alpha release and the overall roadmap plans for Blender's near-future development at `www.blender.org/development/release-logs/blender-250`.

LicuaBlender Software

A source tarball of Licuadora Studio's own in-house Blender branch is included. If you want to experiment with this, you will need to build it from the source, which requires a suitable environment for compiling and linking C code. You can read about how to build a Blender executable at `http://wiki.blender.org/index.php/Dev:Doc/Building_Blender`. Because LicuaBlender is not an official release, its special features are not supported by the Blender Foundation and you should not use it for any critical work. Be sure to always back up any files before opening them with LicuaBlender.

GIMP Software

Executable installation files for GIMP are provided for Windows and Mac OS X, both Intel and PPC architectures. A source code archive is included for users of Linux and other systems.

Celtx Software

Executable installation files for Celtx are provided for Windows and Mac OS X. A source code archive is included for users of Linux and other systems.

System Requirements

Make sure that your computer meets the minimum system requirements shown in the following list. If your computer doesn't match up to most of these requirements, you may have problems using the software and files on the companion DVD.

- A PC running Microsoft Windows 98, Windows 2000, Windows NT4 (with SP4 or later), Windows Me, Windows XP, or Windows Vista
- A Macintosh running Mac OS X or later
- A PC running a version of Linux with kernel 2.4 or greater
- An Internet connection
- A DVD-ROM drive

For the latest information on system requirements for Blender, go to www.blender.org.

Using the DVD

To install the items from the DVD to your hard drive, follow these steps:

1. Insert the DVD into your computer's DVD-ROM drive. The license agreement appears.

Windows users: The interface won't launch if autorun is disabled. In that case, click Start → Run (for Windows Vista, Start → All Programs → Accessories → Run). In the dialog box that appears, type D:\Start.exe. (Replace D with the proper letter if your DVD drive uses a different letter. If you don't know the letter, see how your DVD drive is listed under My Computer.) Click OK.

Mac users: The DVD icon appears on your desktop; double-click the icon to open the DVD and navigate to the files you want to copy to your hard drive.

2. Read through the license agreement, and then click the Accept button if you want to use the DVD.

The DVD interface appears. The interface allows you to access the content with just one or two clicks.

Troubleshooting

Wiley has attempted to provide programs that work on most computers with the minimum system requirements. Alas, your computer may differ, and some programs may not work properly for some reason.

The two likeliest problems are that you don't have enough memory (RAM) for the programs you want to use or you have other programs running that are affecting installation or running of a program. If you get an error message such as "Not enough memory" or "Setup cannot continue," try one or more of the following suggestions, and then try using the software again:

Turn off any antivirus software running on your computer. Installation programs sometimes mimic virus activity and may make your computer incorrectly believe that it's being infected by a virus.

Close all running programs. The more programs you have running, the less memory is available to other programs. Installation programs typically update files and programs, so if you keep other programs running, installation may not work properly.

Have your local computer store add more RAM to your computer. This is, admittedly, a drastic and somewhat expensive step. However, adding more memory can really help the speed of your computer and allow more programs to run at the same time.

Customer Care

If you have trouble with the book's companion DVD-ROM, please call the Wiley Product Technical Support phone number at (800) 762-2974. Outside the United States, call +1(317) 572-3994. You can also contact Wiley Product Technical Support at `http://sybex.custhelp.com`. John Wiley & Sons will provide technical support only for installation and other general quality-control items. For technical support on the applications themselves, consult the program's vendor or author.

To place additional orders or to request information about other Wiley products, please call (877) 762-2974.

Should the need arise for an errata or replacement files, we will post them at `www.sybex.com/go/bspmovie`.

Index

Note to the Reader: Throughout this index **boldfaced** page numbers indicate primary discussions of a topic. *Italicized* page numbers indicate illustrations.